The Americanization of West Virginia

Winner of the 1995
Appalachian Studies Award

The Americanization of West Virginia

Creating a Modern Industrial State
1916–1925

John C. Hennen

THE UNIVERSITY PRESS OF KENTUCKY

Editorial and Sales Offices: The University Press of Kentucky
663 South Limestone Street, Lexington, Kentucky 40508-4008

Library of Congress Catalog-in-Publication Data

Hennen, John C., 1951-
   The americanization of West Virginia : creating a modern
industrial state, 1916-1925 / John Hennen.
       p.   cm.
   Includes bibliographical references (p.   ) and index.
   ISBN 0-8131-1960-X (cloth : alk. paper)
   1. West Virginia—History—To 1950.   2. World War, 1914-1918—West
Virginia.   3. Americanization.   I. Title.
F241.H54   1996
975.4'042—dc20   95-32714

To my mother and father

Contents

Illustrations follow page 112

Acknowledgments

Although writing is in many ways a singular and lonely endeavor, it is also a cooperative exercise. I would like to acknowledge my family and friends for their constant support and encouragement not only while I worked on this book, but always. I am indebted to Christelle Venham and the staff at the West Virginia and Regional History Collection in Morgantown. The staffs at the Morrow Library at Marshall University in Huntington, the Alderman Library at the University of Virginia in Charlottesville, and the West Virginia State Archives in Charleston were unfailingly conscientious and gracious. Fred Armstrong and Debra Basham at the West Virginia archives were especially helpful in guiding me through the archives' photograph files. I am happy to be part of the growing list of Appalachian Studies scholars who have been well served by the professionalism of the people and the richness of the collections at these facilities. The Eberly College of Arts and Sciences at West Virginia University provided generous financial support through a teaching assistantship and a Swiger Teaching Fellowship. The Appalachian College Association lent assistance in the final stages of rewriting. The staff of the University Press of Kentucky made the editing and publication process more trouble-free than I could have imagined.

My students at West Virginia University, Lindsey Wilson College, and the University of Kentucky have always renewed me when my spirits or energy have waned. I appreciate their unknowing contributions to this work and their consistently fresh, challenging, and humane perspectives on regional and American history. I could not have completed this project without the goodwill, friendship, and positive criticism of many colleagues. Sandra Barney, Jim Cook, Jeff Drobney, Elizabeth Fones-Wolf, Greg Good, Jerra Jenrette, Maureen McCormick, Barbara Rasmussen, Tom Robertson, Paul Salstrom, George Simpson, Mike Slaven, and Carol Wilson offered particularly valuable insights regarding this study, and, just as importantly, cheerful companionship.

Thanks to colleagues who have read this work at many stages of the process. The recommendations of Dwight Billings, Ken Fones-Wolf, Jack Hammersmith, John Inscoe, Mary Lou Lustig, Gordon McKinney, John

Remington, and John Super have made this a better work than it would otherwise have been. Any errors or inconsistencies are mine alone.

Ronald L. Lewis at West Virginia University embodies the spirit of collegiality and fellowship with which countless individuals in Appalachian Studies have sustained me. Dr. Lewis's high academic standards are enhanced by his kind compassion for his students and devotion to the people of West Virginia. I cannot imagine a better mentor.

Finally, my thanks to Barbara L. Laishley, whose love and support have enriched my life beyond measure.

Abbreviations

AC	*The American Citizen*
ACA	American Constitutional Association
ACLU	American Civil Liberties Union
AFL	American Federation of Labor
AL	American Legion
CA	*Coal Age*
CCC	*Consolidation Coal Company Mutual Monthly Magazine*
CPI	Committee on Public Information
DA	*Daily Athenaeum*
DAR	Daughters of the American Revolution
HTM	*History Teacher's Magazine*
IWW	Industrial Workers of the World
JJC	John Jacob Cornwell papers
JMC	James Morton Callahan papers
MVHR	*Mississippi Valley Historical Review*
NAM	National Association of Manufacturers
NBHS	National Board for Historical Service
NEA	National Education Association
NSL	National Security League
NYT	*New York Times*
PT	*Pocahontas Times*
UMWA	United Mine Workers of America
UMWJ	*United Mine Workers Journal*
WV [Hand Book]	*WV Hand Book* (the *Blue Book*)
WVCD	West Virginia Council of Defense
WVEA	West Virginia Education Association
WVFWC	West Virginia Federation of Women's Clubs
WVH	*West Virginia History*
WVMA	West Virginia Manufacturer's Association
WVR	*West Virginia Review*
WVRHC	West Virginia and Regional History Collection
WVSJ	*West Virginia School Journal*
WVU	West Virginia University
WVWCTU	West Virginia Woman's Christian Temperance Union

Preface

Not long after I decided on a title for this work, I realized that it came not from my cleverness but was unconsciously derived from "Economic Modernization and the Americanization of Appalachia," a chapter in Henry Shapiro's *Appalachia on our Mind*.[1] This debt is appropriate, since Shapiro's analysis of the creation and sustenance of an ideology of Appalachian "otherness" is important to any inquiry into the region's relationship to the nation. And just as Shapiro states in the opening passage of his work that it is not a history of Appalachia but of the idea of Appalachia, I should tell readers that *The Americanization of West Virginia* is not a study of Appalachian identity. Rather it is a study of the efforts of a minority of state elites to instill in the people of West Virginia an authoritarian ideology of American identity, to secure popular devotion to a universal value system that equated the interests of business to that of the nation.

Many scholars have pointed out the need to address Appalachian issues in a national as well as regional context, and to reassess the idea that Appalachian problems are exceptional in character. They point to national institutional forces that have shaped the contours of regional development and suggest that the history of Appalachia is best understood in the broad context of industrial capitalist development. It is becoming more apparent that the study of recent regional history must also transcend national boundaries, taking into account the roots of modern economic globalization. Most recently Stephen L. Fisher has suggested the connection of local events to global forces. Nearly two decades ago, David Walls and Dwight Billings noted that Appalachian historians must be prepared to expand their horizons to encompass world economic structures. In 1980 Helen Lewis and Myles Horton foresaw the internationalization of Latin American and Appalachian resistance struggles in confronting transnational corporations. John Gaventa succinctly sketched the outline for the global focus in a 1987 essay in which he introduced the memorable phrase, "the Appalachianization of America."[2]

The Americanization of West Virginia investigates, through the case study of an industrial state in a time of rapid change, rudiments of a nationalistic

developmental ideology geared toward insuring long-range American dominance of world markets. Disciples of that ideology zealously pursued legitimation of probusiness values and beliefs, impelled by a mission to control
the production and distribution of goods and the allocation of power. Although purposefully using terminology contemporary to the era 1916–25
(i.e., "molding of opinion," and "manufacture of consent"), the analysis
herein is consistent with recent observations on cultural hegemony and the
emergence of an American corporate state. T.J. Jackson Lears notes that the
closest precise definition of hegemony is Antonio Gramsci's identification of
the consent by the masses to the general direction of social life by dominant
groups. A recent study emphasizes that the notion of hegemony is a complex
process, a struggle in which class "fractions" merge, forming, in Gramscian
terms, "historical blocs."

Elites comprising a bloc build a system of dominance, assuming moral
and intellectual leadership of cultural institutions. A central task of ruling
groups is to define the permissible range of disagreement about institutional
forms and processes and to ingrain consent in subordinates. Under the challenge of cultural resistance, which could give rise to "counterhegemonic alternatives," legitimation rests on the selective accommodation of the desires and
demands of subordinate groups in such a way as to delegitimize direct challenges to the hegemonic culture. Dominance therefore implies negotiation,
usually between unequal forces, and recognition by elites that control re-
quires shaping laws, policies, and the assumptions people have about their
daily lives.[3] The management strategy of welfare capitalism in the 1920s is a
case in point. Employers exercised selective accommodation to their workers'
discontent, with the intent of influencing the direction of employees' work
and social lives.

Many historians of Appalachia have brilliantly analyzed the impact of
industrialization on the region and processes of conflict and control accom-
panying its integration into the national economy. The work of Ronald D
Eller, John Gaventa, Altina Waller, and Ronald L. Lewis stands out in illuminating the social and cultural dissonance inherent in the transformation of
autonomous individuals and communities into components of industrial
capitalism, dependent on the vicissitudes of technical and market forces
that were national and international in scope.[4] John A. Williams, Ronald L.
Lewis, Joe William Trotter, and David A. Corbin have written widely on the
commoditization of labor in industrializing West Virginia, as has Alan Banks
for Kentucky. Their contributions have done much to enrich our awareness
of the cultural heterogeneity of coal regions during the era coterminous
with this study, and of resistance to the dominance of industrial interests.
Corbin notes that the counterhegemonic movement of southern West Virginia miners in the early 1920s was attributed by federal investigators to

"the nature and racial characteristics of the people." A bloc of the dominant system of institutional power thereby bestowed the "otherness" imprimatur on the region.[5] These and other works therefore reflect Herbert Reid's call for Appalachian studies to focus on "the mainstream theatres of our emerging corporate state," in part to learn how the dominant system's "cultural ethos" relied on perpetuating the image of Appalachians as a people apart and needful of controlling influences.[6]

In some ways this book is a cautionary tale. The management state's current breathless infatuation with artificial intelligence, high-tech warfare, privatization of futuristic classrooms, and workplace re-engineering is at many tangents strikingly similar to the elite social agenda venerated by the industrial Americanizers of 1916–25. Much of the sloganeering that permeates the litany of today's "win-win," "total quality" corporate culture differs little in substance from the banalities of the early 1920s. The terminology of that time played a central role in instilling compliance, elevating corporate dominance of the nation's social and cultural life to the plane of "civic religion," "cooperation," and "mutual interests." Similarly, today's pedagogical emphasis on productivity and international competitiveness often caters to free-market demagogues who view children primarily as "human resources." That emphasis threatens to overshadow the public imperative of education to nurture imaginative and independent citizens, who can navigate the social and ethical conundrum of the continuing industrial revolution.[7]

Industrial Americanizers of 1916–25, employing the vocabulary of democracy, embraced a social model in which order and efficiency superseded social and economic justice and sought to legitimate their claim to rule by narrowing the field of tolerable discourse, dissent, and alternatives to industrial capitalism. The alleged democratic promise of post–cold war America in the Information Age will melt away unless we reject the resurgent hierarchical vision promulgated by modern industrial Americanizers and work to "democratize the structures of political economy and everyday life."[8] It should be our task to make information a tool for social liberation rather than social control, and to reverse the nation's current replication of the concentration of wealth and power that marked the period of this study.

Introduction

The Americanization of West Virginia examines complementary attempts by political, educational, and industrial leaders in the state to insure mass acceptance of state and corporate authority during and after the First World War. These leaders were convinced that a well-regulated citizenry was imperative in order to capitalize on the anticipated war legacy of expanded international market opportunities. Employing modern organizational and public relations tactics that were refined during the war crisis, state and national elites sought to connect free-market business principles to national loyalty, incorporating a business ideology into a universal form of Americanism that would guarantee a literate, loyal, and obedient producing class. As outlined here, the First World War consolidated the dominant position of professionals, business people, and political capitalists as arbiters of national values, and served to catalyze the reorganization of American society in service to these values. American business, educational, and political leaders emerged from the war devoted to the application of scientific management to all arenas of American life. They pledged to efficiently arrange society to maximize social welfare and the nation's economic expansion.

The wartime mobilization of industrial, agricultural, and human resources demanded utmost loyalty to the aims of the national government. The emotional commitment necessary to achieve the productive demands of the war was realized largely through the pervasive propaganda mechanism established by the Wilson administration, the Committee on Public Information (CPI). Determined to carry the urgency and mission of the war into every community and home, the CPI organized with remarkable swiftness to reach not only urban areas but the most remote rural settlements, one-room schools, small-town theaters, daily and weekly newspapers, and churches. Acknowledging the principle that an open society must permit its people to have access to information, the committee proceeded to manage the production and distribution of that information, calling on tens of thousands of volunteers to deliver officially approved war news from Washington. National and local CPI volunteers sought, with a great degree of success, to insure unity of thought and action through processes called the "engineering of consent" by the architects of the molding of public opinion.[1] As explained in chapters 1 and 2, the propaganda mechanism was well-organized in West Virginia. The mobilization of public opinion in the state depended largely on West Virginia's nearly two hundred newspapers, with a combined circulation of more than four hundred thousand, and on the published and spoken exhortations of influential individuals from the business, religious, civic, and educational communities.[2]

The engineering of wartime consent occurred in the context of the organization of national, state, and corporate bureaucracies to fulfill wartime production demands. A major task of the Wilson administration was to reconcile longstanding labor-management hostility, exacerbated by the rapid late nineteenth and early twentieth-century transformation of American social and work relations during the growth of industrial capitalism. To effect this temporary reconciliation, the national government created a maze of regulatory bodies, merging business and labor sectors, to arbitrate disputes, rationalize production and distribution, and eliminate radical influences among American workers. These regulatory bodies reflected the dominant position of corporate capitalism in American culture and created wartime opportunities for business leaders and conservative unionists to marginalize alternative ideologies. The functions of these regulatory bureaucracies, especially the national Council of Defense and its West Virginia counterparts, are addressed in chapter 3, with particular emphasis on labor-management relations.

When the war ended, business, political, and educational leaders across the country applied the tactics of the engineering of consent to the "labor problem." Alarmed by widespread industrial conflict and fearful of the destabilizing of the American business culture by radical activism, industrialists led the national movement to organize private patriotic bodies to resist the potential power of industrial unionism. The result, prompted by the 1919 national steel strike, was the "open-shop" drive, which was led in West Virginia by a coalition of business leaders under the banner of the American Constitutional Association (ACA). The ACA, one of dozens of similar organizations nationwide, articulated a body of principles designed to create a productive, content working class that would identify the well-being of business with the well-being of the country. An analysis of these ideals, which were promoted under the rubric of "industrial Americanization," forms the basis of chapter 4. This chapter studies the convergence of the social purpose of scientific management with the successful mobilization tactics of the war years and lays the groundwork for analysis in chapter 5 of the political culture of the immediate postwar period in West Virginia.

Chapter 6 addresses the course of the open-shop drive in West Virginia in the context of the industrial strategy of "welfare capitalism," which was essentially the recognition by modern industrialists that company flexibility and benevolence would maximize production and expedite employer social control over workers. Open-shop and welfare-capitalism objectives were incorporated into the concept of the "American Plan," a manifesto for anti-union activists that promoted a preindustrial ideal of individually negotiated contracts for the age of mass industrial capitalism. The purity of individual bargaining, however, applied only to workers; the proponents of the American Plan saw no inconsistency in their own collective association to protect their corporate and class interests, which they equated with the public welfare. Assisted by access to teacher training and classroom programs, by 1923 anti-union forces in West Virginia had rolled back wartime gains of the United Mine Workers of America, the state's largest industrial union. As a corollary to the growing power of industrial leaders to influence national law and domestic policy, many union leaders, notably John L. Lewis of the United Mine Workers of America, cultivated complex working relations with industrial leaders. Lewis and other conservative unionists, modernizing and strengthening the diverse tenets of traditional "business unionism," capitalized on general fears of domestic radicalism to push industrialists toward the bargaining table and neutralize radical internal union opposition.

Just as the CPI and private patriotic organizations, such as the ultranationalist National Security League, had depended on public schools to transmit their particular brand of Americanism, the middle-class voluntary associations, which permeated American society in the early 1920s, sought to reach the people, in a common phrase, "through the medium of the children." Campaigns to "inculcate" industrial Americanization typically donned the vestments of the late war as educators sought to train "our army of young workers" for work "that needs to be done."[3] West Virginia teachers were instructed that the mobilization campaigns of the war "have trained us well in methods of getting action in any cause of general importance." They should understand that their pupils represented "the capital of civilization," to whom teachers must impart the knowledge for them "to contribute intelligently to the fundamental needs of human welfare: production, exchange, and wise consumption."[4] Led by the American Constitutional Association, the American Legion, and the West Virginia Federation of Women's Clubs (WVFWC), the industrial Americanizers gained access to public schools to organize, with authorization from the state, patriotic observations, "America First Day" celebrations, and Americanization campaigns. Chapter 7 focuses on the efforts of some of these voluntary associations, who aspired to make native and foreign-born West Virginians "think as we do, live as we do, and feel as we do, and have the same hopes that we have for our country."[5] Chapter 8 studies the widespread application of the Americanizers' campaigns in West Virginia and the institutionalization of the goals of industrial Americanization, symbolized by legislation mandating loyalty and state-defined patriotism.

Essentially, this work demonstrates how proponents of an ideology, in this case industrial capitalism, seek to implant their principles into the consciousness of a culture and thereby transform ideas into commonly held values that are immune to debate in the political arena. It is less a study of the power or force of ideas than of the importance of access to the knowledge and means to transmit ideas. It examines how a relatively small sector of the public sought to manipulate that access to direct public attitudes in an industrial state during a period of national crisis and rapid change. This study places West Virginia in the mainstream of the nation's social, economic, and political currents of the era, in which the values of business achieved almost religious status and alternative visions of the social, industrial, and political organization of the country were virtually expelled from the national discourse. Far from being isolated during America's transformation into an international industrial and imperial power, West Virginia's people and natural resources served crucial functions as producers and fuel for the post–World War political economy. Linked to the centers of power by transportation, communication, and professional networks, West Virginia's educational, political, and industrial leaders helped insure the state's designated role as a resource zone for the perceived greater good of national expansion and strength.

It is in this broad sense that I use the expressions *Americanization* and *industrial Americanization,* rather than in the prewar and relatively benign sense of assimilating immigrants into the national mainstream. *Americanization* in this study implies the struggle by a class-conscious minority of socially, politically, and professionally well-positioned leaders to insure that their hierarchical vision of community and nation, which they defined as the national interest, was accepted as valid and incontrovertible by the mass of Americans. While the Americanization of immigrant populations presented unique obstacles to the objectives of industrial Americanizers, industrial Americanization implies far more sweeping objectives than, for example, universal hygiene, thrift, and English training. Industrial Americanization sought to achieve these, of course, but only as contributors to the greater task, made tangible by the World War, of instilling national "habits of industry," obedience to authority, and worship of law and order. To industrial Americanizers, true independent thought and action were unproductive and disruptive, and, ultimately, un-American. Their task, therefore, was to establish loyalty to the state and nation as interchangeable with obedience to one's employer, teacher, or leader. "Obedience," said one corporate journal, "helps make men truly great."[6]

1

War Propaganda and the Mobilization of Public Opinion in West Virginia, 1916–1918

On Sunday, April 29, 1917, an estimated four thousand McDowell County, West Virginia, citizens assembled in Gary, a company town owned by the United States Steel Corporation. Only a few weeks earlier, the United States had entered the World War against the Central Powers, and the object of the Gary demonstration was to show the community and the world that the people of McDowell were "heart and soul, tooth and nail behind the government of the United States and the President in the present national crisis."[1]

Although native-born whites and blacks predominated in the crowd—Matthew Whittico, editor of the *McDowell Times*, a black newspaper, announced that the "colored people" were loyal to the nation in the emergency—a "generous intermixture" of foreign-born also participated in the day's events. *Coal Age* noted that the "foreign element" in the crowds, including Hungarians, Poles, Slavs, Italians, and Greeks, lacked "nothing of the patriotic spirit shown by their neighbors and co-laborers." The parade, which preceded a flag-raising ceremony and a program of patriotic speeches, passed by company housing with neat gardens lining Gary's tidy main street. America's German enemies were "remarkably proficient in the matter of food production," and the gardens bore witness that "the people of McDowell would do well to imitate them." The war would be waged not only by the men at the front but by Americans helping to feed the Allies, and practically every house in Gary sported a small garden for this purpose. Efficiency was the keynote of the day, with Circuit Court Judge Isaiah C. Herndon of Welch explaining that it was efficiency that had made United States Steel a mighty industrial organization, and it was efficiency that made effective fighting machines of the German and English armies. In war and peace, "it is efficiency that counts for most."[2]

The Gary demonstration was one of many anticipated in the valley of the upper Tug River to arouse public sentiment. Similar expressions of national unity were organized in communities throughout West Virginia as America went to war. A patriotic meeting was held in St. Mary's, in Pleasants County, on the heels of President Woodrow Wilson's April 2 war message to Congress. On the same day Congress declared war, "patriotic and zealous" citizens gathered for a loyalty meeting in the town auditorium to affirm that St. Mary's did not lag behind other communities in declaring loyalty to Wilson and the government. In Marshall County, Moundsville Mayor Evan G. Roberts urged his neighbors to "unite in a fervent and stir-ring patriotic demonstration." Crowds jammed a Moundsville movie theater and spilled into the street, cheering the patriotic speeches and eliminating any doubts "as to the Americanism of the people of Marshall county." In the wake of the meeting, industries, churches, and schools in the county con-ducted flag-raising ceremonies, and within a week "Marshall county was burning with patriotic fervor, which was to continue, until the defeat of the German Imperial government." Fairmont staged a successful patriotic cel-ebration, with the business houses closed and the city proudly decorated with flags and bunting.[3]

College campuses also stirred with patriotic ardor. As war loomed, West Virginia University's (WVU) *Daily Athenaeum* had announced that the "Men and Spirit of the Gold and Blue Eagerly Await the Call to Arms." WVU took its place beside other American universities in its passionate enthusiasm for the country and the president, and the campus anticipated the "almost certain prospect of service to the nation." Flag raisings at university buildings were held almost daily, and a mass demonstration called for April 2 promised patriotic addresses by distinguished speakers including university president Frank Trotter, history professor James M. Callahan, economics professor E. Howard Vickers, and former governor William E. Glasscock, a Morgantown attorney. Vickers would also speak at "the next scheduled outburst of enthu-siasm" a few days later.[4]

Newspapers across West Virginia recommended ways for citizens to express their patriotic sentiments and protect their neighborhoods and country as the war crisis grew. A typical appeal admonished readers to be loyal "in thought, word and deed," and to eliminate "any sore places" in their communities. Responsible citizens were advised not to embarrass the government by criticizing "that which you do not fully understand," dis-courage seditious talk by others, and "inculcate in the hearts of the young the blessings of a free country." Suspected un-American or pro-German be-havior was quickly becoming intolerable. In Huntington, American factory workers compelled recalcitrant, unnaturalized German workers to fly the American flag in their department by turning a firehose on them. To gen-eral approbation, Wisconsin's antiwar senator Robert LaFollette, who had "opposed the will of the people," was burned in effigy in St. Albans, West Virginia.[5]

These few examples reflect broad support for the United States declar-ation of war, but policymakers at the national and state levels sought a mechanism to regulate the flow of information about the war to sustain and deepen the public's commitment to the cause. President Wilson had campaigned for reelection just a few months earlier on the slogan "He Kept Us Out of War" and had resisted until late in his first term the privately led "preparedness" movement for substantial increases in the nation's armed forces and weapons capacity. Preparedness advocates insisted that France and England were fighting a war that was also America's and that defeat for the Allies would imperil democracy everywhere. Capitalizing on growing public fears of armed invasion by Germany and increasing suspicion of German immigrants, the preparedness lobby had attracted considerable support for their contention that German military might had to be resisted. From August 1914 until April 1917, these private lobbyists had assumed a major role in education and propaganda about the war. With the United States declaration of war, the Wilson administration quickly moved to direct the molding of public opinion. The mass mobilization of the American mind was entrusted to the Committee on Public Information (CPI), established by Wilson's Executive Order 2594 on April 13, 1917.[6]

The Committee on Public Information technically was overseen by the secretaries of state, war, and the navy, but the heart of the organization was its civilian director, a muckraking journalist named George Creel. So closely linked was Creel to the CPI that it was commonly called the Creel committee.[7] Creel and his nominal superiors were aware that the American press objected to the widespread censorship imposed upon newspapers by the belligerent states in Europe. The Europeans depended on their papers for all war news, a West Virginia newspaper reported, and special efforts had been expended by the Allied and Central Powers alike to allow only such news approved by their military commanders. The article warned that "a bad touch of militarism" had accompanied preparedness and war talk in the United States, which must not devolve into government censorship. The CPI planners envisioned an official information agency that would instill in Americans a sense of partnership with the Wilson administration based on full public disclosure of the government's war actions. The committee, therefore, adopted a policy of literally choking the channels of communication with officially approved news and opinion, generated in staggering volume by the CPI. Josephus Daniels, Wilson's secretary of the navy, explained that President Wilson and his cabinet

> were very anxious that we should not fall into the stupid censorship which had marked the action of some countries in dealing with war news. Immediately upon our entrance into the war I called in all the newspapermen in Washington, and particularly the representatives of the press associations, and told them that we would have no censorship but that the President and his Cabinet wished them and all newspaper-

men in America to impose self-censorship; that we would give them
freely the information that would let them know what was going on and
request them from time to time to publish nothing which might fall into
the hands of the enemy or embarrass war operations. . . . Determined to
have no censorship and to give the public all information possible, we
decided to establish the Committee on Public Information.[8]

Based on the overwhelmingly positive reaction to Wilson's war message and the declaration of war, Creel felt certain that the American press
would cooperate with the government to mobilize and sustain public back-
ing for the war. Moreover, within hours after Wilson requested a declaration
of war, professional advertising men volunteered their talents as opinion-
makers to the government, proclaiming that "publicity men can be turned
loose at any moment, for any purpose desired." The ad men disavowed
secret propaganda for improper purposes, seeking only to effectively organize "facts . . . which the people ought to know. It is a means of turning the
nation's patriotism to practical use." President Wilson gratefully accepted
the ad men's offer, and appealed to the nation's advertising agencies, editors,
and publishers to incorporate the administration's "Ways to Serve the
Nation" into their publications and campaigns.[9]

Aware of the print media representatives' sentiments and with an
abiding faith in the power of positive media reinforcement, Creel guided the
CPI to a strategy based on aggressive publicity of the government's war aims
and ideals rather than on rigidly secretive censorship. He knew well the potential for shaping public opinion through the conscious and at times inflammatory manipulation of words, images, and sentiment, and, in words
William Pencak later used to describe the American Legion, realized that
patriotism "is a way of life inculcated through symbols and ceremonies
rather than a set of intellectual principles." The CPI propaganda model assumed that only constant exposure of America's war aims and efforts could
"arouse national enthusiasm to the proper pitch." Specific appeals were designed to reach all sectors of the population, including blacks, immigrant
groups, women, businessmen, schoolchildren, industrial and agricultural
workers, and students.[10]

The work of the CPI was filtered through a network of divisions, including the Division of News; the Official Bulletin staff, which published a
daily compendium of war news and events; the Foreign Language Newspaper Division, which monitored papers and translated committee pamphlets into foreign languages; the Foreign Press Bureau; the Bureau of War
Expositions; the Division of Civic and Educational Cooperation; the Film
Division; the Alliance for Labor and Democracy; the Work with the Foreign
Born Division; and the Bureau of Cartoons. The division with the most

direct contact with the people, which was particularly effective because of its close link to the communities, was the Four-Minute Men Division, comprised of more than seventy-five thousand volunteer speakers who pitched short speeches in schools, churches, public halls, and movie theaters across America. They spoke on topics assigned from Washington, and were admitted into the service only on the recommendation of, so said Creel, "three prominent citizens—bankers, professional or business men."[11]

The social requirements for Four-Minute speakers suggest the obligations of public service for educated classes that permeated the various domestic war campaigns. Owing to their educational advantages, the college-trained citizens could help create and maintain proper public sentiment among "ordinary citizen[s]." Reliable information on war-related subjects was furnished by the United States government, which, fully aware of the need for access to "correct knowledge," was issuing the War Information Series of pamphlets through the Committee on Public Information. The CPI distributed the pamphlets in the belief that the war would not be won on the basis of established doctrine or official theory, but upon "enlightened public opinion based upon truth." The *Daily Athenaeum* reported that college newspapers had established a good working relationship with the CPI, which provided accurate war information to college students throughout the country. Not only did the CPI disseminate authoritative material, but the agency secured "voluntary censorship of the press" by providing the papers with all the necessary war news. In addition to daily press dispatches to all papers, thirty thousand newspapers got weekly feature articles from the CPI, and millions of foreign-language pamphlets were distributed overseas.[12]

These and other figures indicate the volume of CPI publications. Guy Stanton Ford, director of the CPI's Civic and Educational Cooperation Division, outlined the pervasiveness of the CPI in shaping the nations's war consciousness in a 1920 retrospective. His division published and distributed numerous educational pamphlets, including the semimonthly National School Service newsletter, issued free to all teachers in the final months of the war. The division's massive *War Cyclopedia* was a widely consulted digest of historical and military references for war-aims speakers and instructors. Ford estimated that his division alone mailed fifty-six million publications and that the total of all CPI divisions—including the daily Official Bulletin, Four-Minute Men Bulletins, and foreign service pamphlets—totaled about 125 million.[13]

Ford's figures may not be definitive, but the omnipresence of the CPI in the daily life of Americans during the war is apparent, and the words and images projected by its propagandists molded the war's issues in the national consciousness.[14] Every item of war news Americans saw in county weeklies, city dailies, magazines, schoolhouses, movie theaters, churches, county fairs, and war expositions was "not merely officially approved information but precisely the same kind that millions of their fellow citizens were getting at the same moment." They had been sanitized or given an appropriate twist either at the source of information in Washington or at the newspaper offices in accordance with "voluntary" rules issued by the CPI. Harold J. Tobin and Percy W. Bidwell report in *Mobilizing Civilian America* that Creel and the CPI orchestrated the most effective war campaign in history:

> By the most intensive intellectual and emotional bombardment, they aroused Americans to a pitch of enthusiasm where a dissident voice scarcely dared to make itself heard, and where blind support was forthcoming for everything which seemed to contribute to victory.
>
> There was no escape from the bombardment. The typical American . . . found his morning paper filled with appeals for support of war activities, both in news columns and in advertisements paid for by patriotic citizens or organizations. The business man at lunch listened to volunteer speakers urging him to get behind the current government "drive." His wife at the motion-picture matinee heard an appeal to cooperate in a "save-food" campaign. At the same time his son was perhaps urging his schoolfellows to contribute their pennies to the Red Cross. Posters boosting the war effort stared from store windows and from signboards on top of buildings, and hung from the walls of factories and offices. Theaters mixed patriotic appeals with entertainment. Millions of homes displayed service flags in their windows.[15]

Throughout the war years, the CPI faithfully adhered to its line that the committee served not as a censor or source of policing thought but strictly as an information bureau. To the extent that a war avowedly being fought for democratic principles must be carried on with the consent of the masses, the CPI conceptually represented the positive action of the national state to coerce unity from the American people. But the CPI often failed, perhaps inevitably, to channel the nation's emotions into "constructive patriotism" rather than demagoguery or hysteria, relying on methods of arousing opinion rooted in hate and fear.[16]

Negative or police powers regarding acceptable opinion were supposed to be handled by other government agencies—"another department of the government looks after those who need threats," said the *Daily Athenaeum*—notably the Post Office under Postmaster General Albert Sidney Burleson and the Justice Department under Attorney General Thomas W. Gregory. Burleson was authorized by the June 1917 Espionage Act to repress and ban from the mails material the government considered treasonous or insurrectionary, and he used his powers sweepingly. Gregory implemented broad discretionary enforcement under authority of the Trading with the Enemy Act

(October 6, 1917) and Espionage/Sedition Act (May 16, 1918), which extended the original powers of the Espionage Act. The expanded Espionage Act essentially prohibited spoken or written criticism of U.S. policy, officials, institutions, or symbols and provided penalties for violations.[17]

Gregory's Justice Department worked closely with about a quarter million private grassroots patriots in the American Protective League (APL), who assumed the task of spying on and informing on alleged violators of the Espionage Act. The chief targets of the APL were tens of thousands of German espionage agents who had allegedly infiltrated American communities. These suspected agents and saboteurs reputedly conspired to subvert the American government and the morale of the people and to generate support for Germany among immigrants from the Central Powers states, American blacks, and traditional opponents of the British Empire. President Wilson and his supporters, such as progressive reformer Florence Kelley, praised the APL's service to a country riddled with "skillful intriguers and spy captains." Wilson affirmed that Germany's masters had dispatched thousands of spies and conspirators to corrupt the opinion of the American people, and he encouraged counterconspiracy by the APL and the Justice Department.[18]

Although Wilson expressed reservations about the extremism that accompanied war fever, to the president the forcible repression of real or imagined dissent represented the legitimate negative thrust of the state when faced with threats to wartime national unity. Wilson feared the potential excesses of war fever, remarking that once the American people were led into war, "they'll forget there ever was such a thing as tolerance. To fight you must be brutal and ruthless, and the spirit of ruthlessness will enter into the very fiber of our national life." The president dismissed these fears of excess, however, when he marshaled his considerable rhetorical talents to tap the emotionalism that was brewing across the nation. Public relations pioneer Edward L. Bernays, an important figure in the CPI's Foreign Press Bureau, anointed Wilson as the country's best "public relations man" during the war. With his gift to dramatize ideas, his intellectual and verbal powers, and his ability to marry political arguments to idealistic imperatives, Wilson gave the government's wartime propaganda its "essential content and immense moral drive."[19]

The dual functions of edification and repression that were woven into the fabric of America's mobilization became virtually indistinguishable as the barrage of war-related stories escalated. Local media outlets followed the lead of Wilsonian surrogates such as Kelley, who estimated that as many as three hundred thousand German agents and subalterns worked in the United States, and James A.B. Scherer, a member of Wilson's Council of National Defense, who guessed there were four-hundred thousand spies carrying out the "Emperor's nefarious program." The *Fairmont Times* doubted the loyalty of *all* unnaturalized Germans in the United States, accounting for half a million potential "enemies in our midst."[20]

Failure to actively display loyalty was considered identical to disloyalty. Disavowing tolerance for "divided sentiment," Guy D. Goff, a native of Clarksburg, West Virginia, and a member of the U.S. judge advocate general's staff, said America would not abide the "venomous German sympathizers within our borders." Natives as well as immigrants living in the United States must either defend American democracy, or "be shot as traitors." The *Clarksburg Daily Telegram* applauded an "America for Americans" campaign, declaring that foreign-born residents of the country were either true Americans or enemy aliens. A campaign spokesman stated that foreigners should either become "Americanized" or leave, as "there is no room for aliens. . . . I hope before the war ends to find an alien a curiosity or an enemy." Local ethnic groups got the message, as the paper soon reported that Clarksburg Slavs had scheduled a patriotic celebration to prove their loyalty to America in the war with their home empire.[21]

The influence of the CPI is suggested in the prevalence and uniformity of general themes, such as German war aims and war atrocities. Inflammatory atrocity stories, calculated to excite the emotions, were often presented as factual on evidence that was questionable at best. For example, University of Indiana history professor Samuel B. Harding's "Topical Outline of the War," which Harding prepared for the National Board for Historical Service in cooperation with the CPI, went well beyond a philosophical critique of the authoritarian German state to implicitly indict the German people.[22] Harding quoted Professor A.S. Hershey, his colleague at Indiana, who wrote that the German war philosophy advocated "absolute war," "ruthlessness," and "frightfulness" as legitimate tactics of warfare. Hershey affirmed that Germany employed assassination, massacre, poisoning, torture, intrigue, arson, pillage, murder, and rape under the guise of just war. Such a civilization, stated a CPI poster, was not fit to live.[23]

The *War Cyclopedia* published by Guy Stanton Ford's educational division of the CPI also contributed much to the sensationalistic tone of the "Outline." German brutality was portrayed as calculated and inherent, marked by torture and mutilation on a wide scale. German outrages against civilians, particularly in the early days of the European war, were described as systematic, uniform, and wanton.[24] The CPI's weekly National Editorial Service also featured atrocity stories, like one in the *Wheeling Intelligencer* that attributed Germany's "slaughter of the innocents" to racial backwardness. Endemic German barbarism was described as a function of hereditary arrested development of the brain, leading to "the dominance of the lower impulses" common to the world's backward peoples. The longstanding German megalomania, "or exalted conception of their own importance," supported this "obtrusive hypoplasia" diagnosis, which was "unerring in definition of all backward races." While some individual British and American citizens may have occasionally "yielded under stress of intense provocation to punishments savagely fitting savage crimes," as nations the Anglo-Saxon powers "have long since realized their responsibility to their standards of civilization in their dealings with the lower races."[25]

Given the centrifugal distribution of ideas from the centers of information in Washington, it is not surprising that local expressions of patriotic vigilance often equaled or exceeded the CPI's use of overstatement.[26] Condemning "slackers" before a federal grand jury in Elkins, U.S. District Judge Alston G. Dayton denounced Germany as "a mad-dog nation running amuck and preying upon the civilized world." Urging all Americans to stand by the president and the flag, Dayton encouraged "spirited and merciless warfare" against the spread of "German 'kultur' throughout the civilized world."[27]

The specter of German *Kultur* begat spiraling charges of terror in the daily press, including the horrific accusation that the Germans had erected plants in which the corpses of German soldiers were treated chemically to manufacture commercial products, including lubricating oils and pigs' food. Employees of the Consolidation Coal Company learned that when dealing with this type of "savages or maniacs peace can be brought about only by such methods as are appreciated by such creatures." The enemy was "mad with lust and the spilling of much blood." To defend God and American civilization, "we must crush them beyond the power of resurrection. The end justifies any means."[28] West Virginia educator Robert A. Armstrong, an avowed pacifist, suspended his pacifistic principles when it came to Germany. "When a mad dog is running amuck in the world," said Armstrong, echoing Judge Dayton, "muzzle him at any cost."[29]

The emotionalism of the war propaganda created and reinforced the image of a brutal enemy undeserving of mercy or respect and devoid of human sentiment. To such an enemy, retaliatory outrages were not inhumane but rather just. *Our Own People*, an employee magazine published by the Davis Coal and Coke Company, predicted in October 1918 that soon the Allies would force the kaiser and his "dogs" to "grovel in the dust," begging for mercy:

> But do they deserve mercy? Would it not be better that this viper and his followers, the German people, be punished for their atrocities by being tortured by liquid fire in the same manner as they have tortured, and by so doing make an example which will convince the German people that barbarism will no longer be tolerated for all time by civilized people?[30]

Driven by these sentiments, America's role in the war took on the vestments of a holy crusade. The official propaganda bureau nurtured this impulse to further mobilize public enthusiasm for the war. A CPI pamphlet, written by Secretary of the Interior Franklin K. Lane and Secretary of War Newton D. Baker, cast the war not only in terms of political principle but also as a religious war between Christianity and barbarism. To the National Education Association (NEA), Lane proclaimed "a new Americanism," assuring NEA delegates that the United States would "put every boy and every factory and every dollar and every hand at the service of Christian civilization." Linking the mission of America for world progress with the mission of Christ, Lane concluded, "Americanism must be to us a political religion."[31]

Messianic Americanism also underlay the public-speaking campaigns of the CPI's Four-Minute Men Division. The influential West Virginia University historian Oliver P. Chitwood, a specialist in European diplomatic history, was a Monongalia County Four-Minute man. He praised the speakers as "the most important single agency in spreading the Gospel of patriotism." The West Virginia state director of the Four-Minute Men, William Burdette Matthews, portrayed them as "apostles of the spoken word . . . preaching the doctrine of undiluted Americanism and educating the people on the subjects of vital interest that constantly arise in the prosecution of the triumphant struggle for decency and democracy."[32]

The mixture of religious and political zealotry spawned the intolerance predicted by Woodrow Wilson. Indeed, Wilson encouraged the volatile spiritual climate, admonishing clergymen to embrace his "Ways to Serve the Nation" as a not "unworthy or inappropriate subject of comment and homily from their pulpits." Many Christian ministers, caught in the stream of popular sentiment fomented by Wilson and the CPI, preached a gospel grounded as much in hate and fear as brotherly love. Many of these later publicly acknowledged and repented their hateful excesses of the war years.[33] A survey of the roughly one thousand West Virginia Four-Minute Men reveals that at least 113, or over 10 percent, were men of the cloth. In some counties, ministers comprised about one-half the rosters. Churches provided the forum for countless demonstrations of war enthusiasm, such as the "great patriotic meeting" at the Morgantown Methodist Episcopal Church in July 1918. An account describes the convocation as "in line with the program mapped out by the administration for a series of patriotic meetings" all over the country. The meeting would occur "at a time in the history of the world when the flag and the cross are the symbols of the coming of a new civilization. The two were never linked so closely as now."[34]

Local ministers received direct instructions to tailor their spiritual messages to war needs. On September 30, 1918, the West Virginia Council of Defense issued a bulletin to the chairmen of the county councils of defense, the state's Liberty Loan Committees, and the Four-Minute Men advising them that Sunday, October 6, had been designated "Liberty Loan Church Day in West Virginia." The state council instructed the chairmen of the three organizations in each county to advise every minister that the government wanted at least one sermon on October 6 to be devoted to the Fourth Liberty Loan. Clergy were urged to include the singing of "America" or other patriotic hymns at each service and to preach a patriotic sermon at least once a month.[35]

The West Virginia Council of Defense was deeply involved in all facets of the mobilization of resources and public opinion. State defense councils were established under the authority of the Council of National Defense, which was formed by President Wilson within guidelines of a 1916 congressional resolution, to facilitate the concentration and use of the nation's resources for war purposes. The powers and funding available to the state councils varied from state to state. Initially, three-quarters of the state councils were nonstatutory bodies, and the remainder had varying degrees of legal authority. A few had been granted very extensive statutory powers by their state legislatures shortly after the war was declared. According to William J. Breen, historian of the state councils, only Minnesota matched West Virginia in the extreme authority granted to the council.[36]

The West Virginia Council was formed in May 1917, when Governor John J. Cornwell called an emergency war session to "strengthen the arm of the State" in fulfilling national war aims. The extraordinary session met from May 14 until May 26, granting ad hoc regulatory power to the governor and the state council for the operation of railroads, mills, and mines, and for the suppression of insurrections or rebellions in the state.[37] The executive board of the state council consisted of Cornwell as chairman and Secretary of State Houston G. Young as secretary. State Auditor John S. Darst, State Superintendent of Schools Morris P. Shawkey, Attorney General E.T. England, Treasurer William S. Johnson, and Commissioner of Agriculture James H. Stewart rounded out the executive board. Practically all control of state war matters was nominally vested in the executive board.[38] The legislature also provided for a fifteen-member advisory state council of defense, appointed by the governor on May 29, 1917.[39] The advisory council organized bureaus of information, education, and publicity; manufacturing; labor; agriculture; finance; transportation; raw materials; women's defense work; and medicine, surgery, and sanitation.[40]

One month after the congressional war resolution, the Council of National Defense called governors and state representatives to Washington to coordinate state and federal strategies for the mobilization of public opinion. The National Defense Council in Washington considered systematic publicity drives to be "of first importance." The West Virginia Council of Defense agreed that its major task was to promote patriotism "in the hearts of the people of the State," especially immigrants who needed guidance in "democratic principles."[41] Accordingly, the advisory council established the Bureau of Information, Education and Publicity as one of its major divisions. C.P. Snow of Huntington, president of the West Virginia Board of Trade, was appointed by the executive board as chairman of this bureau. Superintendent Shawkey recommended that Jesse V. Sullivan, former managing editor of the *Charleston Gazette*, be appointed executive secretary and "public man" for the State Council. Sullivan refused the appointment at the offered salary of $2,000 and demanded $3,000, which was approved by the executive board. Sullivan had worked in the West Virginia coal industry since 1904, when he migrated to the state from Ohio. He later became private secretary to Governor Ephraim Morgan from 1921 to 1925.[42]

Sullivan aggressively pursued his duties and soon reported that the state council had conducted an intensive publicity campaign of education and war information among the people of the state. In addition to the work of the Four-Minute Men, this drive was greatly assisted by the state's nearly two hundred newspapers.[43] The West Virginia press was "loyal to the core," Sullivan wrote. Newspaper columns "were filled with patriotic propaganda."[44] If not for the "cordial support given them by the patriotic newspapers of the commonwealth," wrote Oliver Chitwood, the successful wartime publicity campaigns would have been impossible.[45]

West Virginia war publicists enjoyed cooperation from the CPI and such private groups as the National Security League, the Federal Council of the Churches of Christ in America, the Federation of Women's Clubs, and the National Committee on Education in Patriotism of the National Bureau of Education.[46] Parades, propaganda films, and war expositions characterized the campaigns. In 1918, for example, a government war exposition train rode the rails in West Virginia as part of the truncated Fourth Liberty Loan Drive, featuring war trophies "from the bloody fields of France. . . . Captured cannon, flame projectors, hand grenades and other weapons of warfare. Explanations of use by returned soldiers. Everything absolutely free." Should the train be delayed, speeches and "patriotic gatherings of various kinds" would fill the time "that might otherwise be lost from war work."[47]

Other means of reaching the people included lavish patriotic spectacles. On July 16, 1917, Jesse Sullivan met in Wheeling with Thomas Wood Stevens, producer of patriotic war pageants nationwide, to finalize plans to bring Stevens's "Drawing of the Sword" pageant to West Virginia.[48] Designed to "stimulate public interest and enthusiasm in the war," the pageant was performed on three nights in Wheeling, drawing crowds of less than one thousand, before traveling to Charleston, Huntington, Clarksburg, and Parkersburg. The patriotic press described the pageant as offering a "closer

realization of the reasons America joined the allies," beginning with patriotic songs before turning "to the appeal of true Americanism." The specta-
cle of pageantry, said the *Wheeling Intelligencer*, "conveyed a proper sense of
the real causes of the fight against the destroyer of civilization." The educational quality of the pageant demonstrated that the artist could do "his bit
toward awakening the true sense of duty that lies in every American's
heart." Military draftees from Wheeling and Ohio County particularly benefitted from the pageant, since it aroused in them "a little more patriotic
feeling than they had yet experienced in the great crisis."[49] Only a few days
later, the Ohio Valley Knights of Pythias staged a patriotic demonstration
dwarfing the Stevens crowds, drawing some four thousand marchers for a
parade and speeches and including a keynote address by Senator James E.
Watson of Indiana.[50]

As part of its publicity campaign, the West Virginia defense council also
authorized publication of the *West Virginia War Bulletin*, edited by Sullivan, to
disseminate "patriotic propaganda." It was at the suggestion of the state council that the Committee on Public Information in Washington appointed
William Burdette Matthews, clerk of the West Virginia Supreme Court of Appeals, as state director of the Four-Minute Men. Matthews's organization
reached into every county, carrying the "militant message of America" into
practically every movie house and school, and to stores, factories, shops, and
street corners throughout West Virginia.[51]

Speakers gave freely of their time and energies, said Matthews, and
fully appreciated "the honor of being the mouthpiece of their government."
Some of the Four-Minute campaigns, which lasted from a few days to several
weeks, were "First Liberty Loan," "Food Conservation," "Why We Are Fighting," "The Nation in Arms," "Unmasking German Propaganda," "The Meaning of America," and "Where Did You Get Your Facts?" Oliver P. Chitwood
noted that bulletins were sent from Washington with advisories on directed
campaigns, to be fashioned into four-minute speeches by each Four-Minute
man.[52] George Creel understood that in this way each speaker "delivered an
address which he thought was his own but which actually paraphrased one of
the Committee pamphlets." These "short and frequently snappy speeches,"
said Chitwood, reached millions nationwide who might never have read the
bulletins issued by the CPI. One CPI enthusiast credited the Four-Minute
Men with reaching the "vacant minds" of Americans.[53]

In a largely rural state such as West Virginia, as in most of America in
1917–18, it was essential that the official outreach of the war mobilization
extend into remote areas as well as population centers. Therefore, the program of the state council was carried into every county and many communities by the formation of subsidiary councils, which became clearinghouses
of all official county war activities. Chitwood dismissed reservations harbored

by some commentators about the expansion of state authority. The accomplishments of the state council's "elaborate organization" in furthering the government's war policy fully justified, in Chitwood's opinion, the creation of "so much machinery and the delegation to it of such large powers."[54]

The state's Third Liberty Loan drive tested the effectiveness of the propaganda mechanism. The campaign began on April 6, 1918, accompanied by colorful demonstrations and parades in the larger cities. "Never in the history of West Virginia," one observer commented, "has there been such a revival of patriotism as was displayed on that date." The *West Virginia War Bulletin* proclaimed that enthusiasm "had been excited and stimulated by the press reports of the raging battle on the fields of Picardy."[55] Matthews expanded the Four-Minute speaking network to encompass remote rural districts, in coordination with county councils, state and local Liberty Loan committees, and school teachers. In the rural districts, state Liberty Loan chairman William A. MacCorkle dispatched speakers into the farthest reaches. MacCorkle, Democratic governor of the state from 1893 to 1897, wrote of the West Virginia bond campaigns that "never once in all of these dark times did the energy, character or patriotism inherent in the people ever falter or fail."[56] The battle line was not three thousand miles away "in bleeding France," MacCorkle said. "It is here among the mountains of our beloved state."[57]

Convinced that the rural schoolhouse was the key to inducing isolated rural families to invest their saving in the government, MacCorkle called for weekly patriotic meetings in every school. He advised county Liberty Loan chairmen, county Four-Minute chairmen, and county school superintendents to arrange a far-flung speaking campaign.[58] Livia Poffenbarger, director of women's Liberty Loan efforts, appointed officers of all Daughters of the American Revolution chapters to the state executive board for Liberty Bond issues.[59] Morris P. Shawkey later outlined the mechanics of the cooperative Liberty Loan campaign. Material was distributed from the CPI in Washington to all speakers through the county chairmen and subchairmen. The local chairmen in turn prepared careful reports of each campaign for the state director, who then submitted a summary report to Creel's office in Washington. Shawkey claimed that during the Third Liberty Loan drive, more than sixteen hundred speeches were made to nearly five hundred thousand West Virginians, "or nearly half the population of the state."[60]

Plans for an even further reaching campaign were drafted at a state council–sponsored war convention in Charleston, organized by MacCorkle, Matthews, and Livia Poffenbarger. Held on September 17 and 18, 1918, conferees at the convention planned to expand the county Four-Minute outreach to include speaking tours by Allied officers and wounded American soldiers. The worldwide influenza epidemic, however, curtailed most public meetings.[61] The quota for that drive was filled only when MacCorkle appealed to clergymen throughout the state to personally solicit donations from their congregations, urged on by Cornwell's invocation that the difficulties would be the "real test of the patriotism of all of us."[62]

While the effectiveness of the varied war drives was undeniable, some critics charged that the CPI's volunteer local propagandists sometimes approached hysteria. The committee's defenders note, however, that "hysteria was generally prevalent at the time. . . . The most fantastic atrocity stories were believed."[63] This comment by Edward L. Bernays skirts the issue of whether the CPI created hysteria or simply exploited it, but as committee spokesmen often explained, "German propaganda had to be counteracted with American propaganda."[64] Bernays was just beginning his pioneering work in the new field of public relations when he joined the CPI. There he understood that words and ideas were as important to the war effort as the world's newest weapons of mass destruction, remarking that "ideas and their dissemination became weapons and words became bullets." He described the task of the CPI as the "engineering of consent," and it was practiced on a "grand scale" for the first time in the Great War. Words were organized to develop "the climate of public opinion" needed to sustain the commitment necessary for the total mobilization of American resources. From 1914 to 1918, said Bernays, the United States government mobilized every known public relations device of persuasion and suggestion, "to sell our war aims" to the American people. Along with preserving the friendship of allies and neutrals and demoralizing the enemy, a major objective of propaganda that fell within the mission of the CPI was mobilizing hatred against the enemy.[65]

The government's war experience expanded the arts of "opinion molding," leading many in business and government to recognize the organizing force of public opinion for other purposes. When they returned to civilian life, many in the CPI, including Bernays, applied wartime publicity techniques to new public and private endeavors, refining them and "broadening the scope of their operations as the expanding postwar economy and the increasing complexity of their publics demanded."[66] After the war, Bernays wrote that the necessary manipulation of the "organized habits and opinions of the masses" was an important element of a democratic society. Those who guided this "unseen mechanism," Bernays said, constituted an "invisible government which is the true ruling power of our country. . . . it is the intelligent minority which need to make use of propaganda continuously and systematically."[67]

Guy Stanton Ford wrote in 1920 that modern war demanded an entire nation in arms, guided by specialized government agencies. These agencies of war merged with the "equally multiplex" agencies of "morale building" to control food production, regulate transportation, and maximize industrial production.[68] The bureaus of the propaganda apparatus depended on a systematic scheme to control the flow of officially generated information that the CPI approved for public consumption. The cooperation of state and local agencies, media outlets, and volunteers was required by this propaganda model. No agency was more critical to reaching the masses of Americans, native and foreign-born, than the institution of public education, from remote one-room schoolhouses to seats of higher learning.

By 1918 Jesse Sullivan could report that West Virginia schools "are indeed mobilized."[69] War planners realized "the school system comes into closer relation with all the people than does any other institution." It was, therefore, self-evident that the school system should be "used extensively in linking up the people with the numerous and important war activities launched by the government." One of the many school-based war programs was the West Virginia Junior Four-Minute Men branch, credited by William B. Matthews with "working wonders" in the spread of patriotic propaganda. Oliver Chitwood wrote that teachers created a patriotic environment by gearing curricula to war issues. At the college level, courses in history and civics "were linked up closely with the war." According to Chitwood, teachers and administrators contributed "a large share" to the propaganda of patriotism:

> In West Virginia, as everywhere else in the country, the young men in the institutions of higher learning had imbibed such high ideals of patriotism that a large proportion of those of military age enlisted in the service of their country. Many of them made the supreme sacrifice on the soil of France.[70]

The war was defined as a struggle not only for national honor, but for national existence. All Americans were expected to subordinate personal matters to the victory over Germany, and educators acknowledged "every school should be the center of war work."[71] The *West Virginia School Journal*, the professional journal of the West Virginia Education Association, advised its readers that every teacher was to be a "true blue" spokesman for the state and as such must be on guard for those individuals in every community who "through ignorance or something worse, spread discord and opposition." The state "wants no teachers with yellow streaks," and, knowing their responsibility in "drilling the great army of reserves after the war," teachers were expected to integrate the war aims and ideals articulated by the CPI and other public and private information bureaus into their classroom activities and curricula.[72]

The war enhanced the role of the state in instilling common values and beliefs in native-born and immigrant Americans. Moreover, the war crisis and its attendant mobilization campaigns led Americans of diverse social and political opinion to identify nationalistic aims as the objects of ethical commitment. Many longtime critics of the abuses of industrial capitalism joined in this nationalistic impulse, tailoring their reformism to the patriotic demands of the war.[73] This transformation is evident in the pronouncements of educational leaders. A large number of West Virginia educators attended the 1918 convention of the National Education Association held at Pittsburgh, where they heard Guy Stanton Ford credit the CPI with helping "define national life." The Committee, said Ford, enlisted every modern agency of publicity and education, and would be even more intimately connected to the schools and teachers. "The teacher is enlisted in this war," he continued, "and more and more the morale of the nation and the thinking in its homes will be determined by what she knows and teaches in this supreme crisis."[74]

Ford envisioned the nation's schools unified in a struggle to "make an Americanized, nationalized American nation." Similarly, L.B. Hill, professor of education at West Virginia University, summarized the integrative role of teachers in establishing "an ideal state system." Hill declared that the country needed soldiers, physicians, Red Cross nurses, and capital to win the war, but no less vital were teachers in the universities, colleges, normal schools, high schools, and one-room schools, who must "teach patriotism and the right attitude of mind for men of military age." Regular work habits, sanitation, and thrift were as important as patriotic rituals, Hill said. Good teachers would infuse the daily routine with broad national obligations, morale building, and social efficiency. Pupils would feel that what they did for themselves, their school, and their home, they did also for glory of the country.[75]

The war expanded upon an idea that schools and colleges essentially comprised an important American industry, with *School and Society* identifying colleges as an industry no less important than coal and steel.[76] Educators spoke of children as the "material with which the school deals, as resources greater than mines, forests, and fisheries." To realize the potential of this resource, the schools must develop ideals of discipline and efficiency, which "are not only military virtues but are also requisites for industrial, commercial, and civic success."[77] Such sentiments had long been promoted by American "New Nationalists" and pro-war progressives, who interpreted the war as a source of national fulfillment. This view cast public education as a mechanism for military and industrial efficiency, as the great laboratory for American patriotism and economic strength. In the "training camps called public schools" were seventeen million children, comprising the "great army of citizens of the future." The NEA suggested using patriotic literature and songs as well as emotive demonstrations allowing elementary schoolchildren to "share the thrill of drum and flag, to feel the pride of the pomp and parade that accompany military affairs." Children would then be part of the country's patriotic force, and teachers would learn that military discipline could be transferred to "many other kinds of discipline."[78]

Patriotic programs in West Virginia schools were consistent with such recommendations by the NEA. West Virginia schoolchildren often participated in junior pageants modeled after the more grandiose affairs like Stevens's "Drawing of the Sword." Local newspapers frequently carried stories of such events, and William Burdette Matthews proudly asserted that his Junior Four-Minute Men "saturated" the whole public school system with "a proper spirit of patriotism which should prevail in all schools and colleges." West Virginia University English professor Robert A. Armstrong urged teachers to teach patriotic poetry and music, instilling "the words and the songs into the children's hearts."[79] Dramatic programs were matched by the infusion of school aims into course work, as state Superintendent Morris P. Shawkey "brought the school organization behind every patriotic movement." In the summer of 1918, Shawkey's Department of Schools published and distributed thirty-thousand song books containing many patriotic songs and patriotic readings, for use in the schools and for community singing. Shawkey estimated that nearly all of the state's fifteen hundred Parent-Teacher Association and school social center meetings in 1917 and 1918 featured "patriotic parts." Shawkey reported that the integration of war work literature, sent to the schools from Washington, into courses in agriculture, home economics, English, and civics "made a lasting impression upon the teachers and pupils, many of whom have become leaders and efficient propagandists ready and willing to take part in the moulding of public opinion."[80]

The *West Virginia School Journal* reported that in every West Virginia community, school teachers had been leaders in public thought. Teachers were well suited to "train the public mind" and had "proven the most ardent leaders in sturdy patriotism." Applicants taking standardized West Virginia teacher examinations were asked, "What have you done to help your country win the war and what more do you intend to do?"[81] Much of the time at the state's summer teacher training institutes was devoted to discussion of the schools and the war. West Virginia historian Charles H. Ambler credits the war with reinvigorating county institutes, since through them the government taught teachers thrift, food conservation, and bond selling lessons, which they "passed on to their pupils who in turn sold them to their parents." Shawkey called teacher institutes "the most valuable of all mediums in reaching the homes of the citizens of West Virginia."[82]

War patriotism in the schools included negative demonstrations of loyalty. Calling instruction in the German language "propaganda to overthrow English," many school systems across the country abolished the teaching of the German language, and some states took similar action, some at the request of their state defense councils. German was described as a "language that disseminates the ideals of autocracy, brutality and hatred," and its defenders were often persecuted or dismissed for alleged pro-German actions.[83] William S. John, a Monongalia County Four-Minute man and secretary of the Morgantown Independent District Board of Education, was instrumental in abolishing German studies in the district, to guarantee "loyal, undivided unity of language, thought, and purpose" in the public schools.[84] Calling instruction in German "un-American and un-patriotic," Robert A. Armstrong agreed with some NEA delegates that German instruction in the schools was a potential tool for the German agent. Since a language was "saturated with the standards and peculiar views of the people who made it and speak it," let American children be exposed to "aspirations that are proper for the civilization we want in America." A note of caution was sounded by Shawkey and Oliver Chitwood, who wondered if outlawing German would undermine America's political and commercial advantage after the war.[85]

In spite of such reservations, the West Virginia Board of Education, following the lead of many local districts, dropped German from the course of study. L.L. Friend, professor of secondary education at WVU, wrote President Frank Trotter that many schools had discontinued German before the state board acted; after the board's resolution, practically all state high schools suspended German. State colleges and normal schools also eliminated German, thus, "no pupil from the kindergarten to the University was studying the language of our enemy, but a greatly increased number were studying French and Spanish in preparation for the new and better times."[86]

The role of higher education in opinion molding and the mobilization of educational forces, from state and national perspectives, was central to the war effort. Largely through the agency of academics, especially in the historical profession, propaganda came to be accepted and presented by West Virginia educators as objective truth, part of the process, said Guy Stanton Ford, of "put[ting] propaganda on a level with truth telling." But as Edward L. Bernays explained, "Honest education and honest propaganda have much in common. There is this dissimilarity: Education attempts to be disinterested, while propaganda is frankly partisan."[87]

2

National and West Virginia Perspectives on Higher Education and the Delivery of War Propaganda

When the United States entered the war, institutions of higher learning unreservedly lent their intellectual and physical resources to the effort.[1] Normal schools were defined as a "potent factor" for teaching patriotism, with hopes of faculties "so imbued with the spirit of loyalty" to the institution and the state that they would not even need to speak of patriotism.[2] Teachers were to offer themselves "as one unit in the great army of those who stand ready to give all at the nation's summons. . . . let us urge the President of the Republic to use us in some unified, direct way in the present national crisis."[3]

The technological character of the war made universities, as primary research facilities with trained experts, a natural resource for the government.[4] Chemistry classes focused research on explosives and gas warfare; physics emphasized electricity, projectiles, and the principles of aerodynamics and submarine technology; biologists taught eugenics and hygiene; geologists designed trenches; historians addressed military and diplomatic issues and international law; and sociology and economics anticipated the postwar reconstruction of "industrial and social institutions."[5] Charles H. Ambler, a distinguished historian of West Virginia, reports that West Virginia University, like other colleges and schools of the country, especially land-grant colleges, put its resources at the disposal of the federal government. As noted by Oliver Chitwood earlier, hundreds of West Virginia University students, including regular students, vocational students, and members of the Student Army Training Corps, enlisted in the armed services, and hundreds of others entered the service under the draft law initiated in May 1917.[6]

College campuses were converted to "veritable training camps for soldiers."[7] Students on the WVU campus learned that the imperatives of the war dominated the contours of the academic year. West Virginia University, said English professor Waitman Barbe, would be doing everything in its power to realize victory over Germany. The entire institution, said Barbe, had been converted into "an instrument of the United States Government in the great cause to which it is devoting all its powers."[8]

Physical plant at the university reflected the transformation wrought by war demands. The executive board of the West Virginia Council of Defense met with WVU President Frank B. Trotter, and E.W. Oglebay and Joseph F. Marsh of the state Board of Regents, to consider an emergency appropriation from the council of defense war fund to equip the Physics Department in Martin Hall for the technical training of conscripted men at the request of the United States War Department. The state council authorized $8,000 for the project.[9] University resources were also used for food production and control, in scientific investigations for the War Department, and for public speaking.[10]

Training of men for the armed services was geared to the "production" of engineers, machinists, and technicians for war purposes. College of Engineering faculty conducted most of the technical training, while Oliver Chitwood directed the war aims and English courses.[11] Student Army Training Corps cadets were required by the War Department to take either a "War Aims" or "War English" course. Chitwood's *The Immediate Causes of the Great War* was used as a text in war aims classes at several universities. Originally issued before America became a belligerent, a second edition was rushed into print for 1918, reflecting United States entrance into the war, and depending in part for new information on the CPI *War Cyclopedia* and publications of the National Security League.[12]

The *Daily Athenaeum* consistently sought to inspire the student body, observing that "colleges of America have responded nobly to the call to arms" and should expand the practice of patriotic exercises and displays. "Now is the time for America's Home Army to mobilize," the *DA* intoned. "Let Germany feel that this is a popular war in America."[13] Faculty and students at West Virginia's Salem College pledged to wear old clothes, "as far as respectability will permit," and to remit savings to the government in order to "promote the coming of the New World Democracy and to aid in the struggle against Kaiserism."[14] Students and faculty were also encouraged to ferret out enemies of the government's war program, doing their part to assist, as E.L. Bernays expressed it, the "persuasive action of the agents of the Department of Justice."[15] The *West Virginia School Journal* warned against "the disloyal teacher who is poisoning the minds of children with German propaganda"; schools were not to tolerate any teacher "whose Americanism is not so warm and vigorous as to be ever uppermost and apparent."[16] The *Daily Athenaeum* noted that the National Security League encouraged presidents and governing boards of American universities and colleges to investigate their faculties and remove disloyal professors. Scrutiny of suspected anti-American or pro-German professors and their scholarship was "a wholesome symptom of an increasing national consciousness."[17]

Just as ministers were prevalent within the ranks of West Virginia's Four-Minute Men, so were college professors. Several WVU faculty members served the cause, including James M. Callahan, a distinguished diplomatic historian. In addition to his duties as history professor and dean of Arts and Sciences at WVU (appointed by Trotter in 1916), Callahan was Monongalia County's director of Four-Minute Men and a tireless speaker at teacher institutes and civic meetings.[18] Callahan's topics at teacher institutes included "What to Teach about the War," "Savings and Serving Taught by War Activities," "Food Conservation Campaigns and Demonstrations," and "A New Brand of History and Patriotism."[19] Callahan was joined as a Four-Minute man by fellow faculty members Robert A. Armstrong, Waitman Barbe, L.M. Bristol, Oliver Chitwood, E. Howard Vickers, I.C. White, A.L. Darby, J.H. Cox, C.H. Jones, and President Francis B. Trotter.[20]

Chitwood and Callahan represented the nationwide participation in war education and propaganda among historians; George Creel wrote that the universities lent "their best men" to the cause. *History Teacher's Magazine*, published by the American Historical Association mainly for public school teachers, encouraged history teachers to write newspaper articles and address public meetings, schools, women's clubs, and other organizations on the "pressing need of united vigorous action." They could use their influence to insure that commencement addresses, either by pupils or by public speakers, address the war crisis. Readers of the magazine were advised to contact the Committee on Public Information's Division of Educational Cooperation, the United States Bureau of Education's Division of Civic Education, the National Board for Historical Service, and the Committee on Patriotism through Education of the National Security League for guidance and materials for patriotic education.[21]

The *History Teacher's Magazine* sought and claimed, just as the CPI did, to strike a balance between "intelligent patriotism" and jingoism. Some historians feared their patriotic impulses and historical training might be manipulated for impure purposes.[22] Professor Herman Ames cautioned readers against displaying the "fanaticism" of some nineteenth-century European historians, whose "nationalist histories" he blamed for contributing to the outbreak of the war. Ames quoted Morse Stephens, president of the American Historical Association in 1914, who warned that in Europe, patriotism had become "the national creed, filtered through the entire educational system of modern states."[23]

Pleas for moderation revealed that the war challenged the "posture of disinterested objectivity" of the history profession.[24] Ideals of detached criticism and noninterested deliberation fell victim as American academics, especially historians, became official war propagandists. Historians' war purview ranged from "scholarly expertise to blatant propaganda," from ethical suggestions for peace plans to writing pamphlets for the "superpatriotic" National Security League. Propagandizing historians espoused their reputation for objective expertise, while they promoted an official government point of view about the war.[25] Ames, divining no violence to his cautionary views about unhealthy nationalism, believed that the entire educational system should be designed to create patriotic citizens. It was the "especial province" of history and civics teachers, said Ames, to "lay the foundation for an intelligent patriotism and an enlightened public opinion." Citing the National Security League, Ames proclaimed that patriotic education should "create a sense of obligation to others and greatest of all to God and country." Students should be inspired to ask not "What can my country do for me?" but "What can I do for my country?"[26]

To mobilize "the intelligence and skill of the historical workers of the country," seventeen eminent American historians established the National Board for Historical Service (NBHS) on April 29, 1917, the same day as the patriotic march in Gary, West Virginia.[27] In a May 1 letter, the board contacted 165 historians for voluntary contributions, the names being supplied from the mailing list of the *American Historical Review*. Frederick Jackson Turner suggested that professors tailor their classes and seminars to relevant war issues, and the board recommended that in addition to public speaking on the war, historians develop special curricula for school systems.[28]

James T. Shotwell, the first NBHS chairman, described it as a "voluntary and unofficial organization" formed to help historians meet the needs of the public and the government.[29] George Creel typically overstated the case when he contended that the NBHS placed three thousand historians at the "complete disposal" of the Committee on Public Information, but the unofficial status of the board claimed by Shotwell is a fabrication.[30] The work of the NBHS was well-coordinated with Ford's CPI committee, and much of the board's leadership, notably Dana C. Munro, Charles D. Hazen, Evarts Green, and Harding were contributors to CPI publications, including the *War Cyclopedia*.[31] The NBHS also enjoyed a quasi-official status through its connection to the American Historical Association. The AHA donated office space to the board, and managing editor J. Franklin Jameson and his assistant Waldo G. Leland gave the NBHS extensive free publicity in the pages of the *American Historical Review*.[32] The *History Teacher's Magazine*, which became the principal outlet for NBHS propaganda, was financed by the AHA; its masthead read, "Edited in Cooperation with the National Board for Historical Service and under the Supervision of a Committee of the American Historical Association."[33]

Shotwell contended that teachers and students of history should arrange and transmit data scientifically to "aid more directly in the determination of historical outlook."[34] Effective national service required that history teachers be especially careful in "the rearrangement of material" and "*presentation* of the facts" [emphasis added]. Such care would, said Shotwell, "accomplish the desired result."[35]

Historian Peter Novick observes that the principal activity of the historians was therefore the provision of serviceable propaganda, producing a "sound and wholesome public opinion."[36] Samuel B. Harding, who produced the "Outline" for the CPI, which was carried by *History Teacher's Magazine* in January 1918 (see chapter 1), denied that the historian's ideal of impartiality was compromised in war service, writing that patriotic historians had never "consciously allowed our desire to win this war to do violence to our sense of historical truth."[37] Harding denigrated the legitimacy of neutrality in the crisis. Nothing in the name of objectivity and restraint should restrict the history teacher from "uttering emphatically his conclusions as to the responsibility for this world calamity," Harding said. If the teacher could not wholeheartedly support the war, however, "he ought at least to keep silent."[38]

Historian Carol Gruber concludes that NBHS historians were eager and voluntary prosecutors of the Central Powers, engaged in a conscious, deliberate campaign to manipulate history in the pursuit of Anglo-American harmony.[39] Many educators were alarmed at the indifference toward England displayed by some Americans, usually blaming unfair textbooks for this "deplorable prejudice." Since intermediate-grade teachers were the "advance guard" in teaching American history, they must cultivate in their students a "sympathy for and relationship to the nation whose language we speak; whose customs we have imitated; whose ideas of liberty are really identical with our own."[40]

Growing sentiments of Anglo-Saxonism fostered a mainstream revision of the American Revolution, bemoaning the divisive quarrel between "race brothers" and paving the way for Anglo-American diplomatic and wartime rapprochement. West Virginia teachers learned that responsibility for the American Revolution lay primarily with George III and a small group of political minions, and that actually "Pitt, Burke, Fox, and others, were, in spirit, the allies of Franklin, Adams, and Washington."[41] George III was, after all, a "German king," who controlled Parliament by bribery and corruption and was forced to hire German mercenaries when the English people "would not volunteer to fight us."[42] Jesse Sullivan of the West Virginia Council of Defense announced that England and America had been separated by the "mad deeds of a German king, and . . . reunited by the mad deeds of a German emperor." Albert Bushnell Hart, lauding the sense of Anglo-American comradeship that had emerged since the Spanish-American War, advised that the American Revolution be taught as an organic Anglo-Saxon movement in which neither side was thoroughly culpable. English teachers also recognized the need for "inculcating more clear-cut ideals of Americanism in our literature classes," since they were "entrusted with the sacred responsibility of handing down the imperial heritage of the English-speaking world."[43]

The political content of academic war propaganda can be inferred from the comments of C.L. Broadwater, principal of Tyler County High School. Broadwater, who often spoke at West Virginia teacher institutes, outlined competing motives for studying history. The pure purpose, which was to make the world intelligible to the pupil, prevailed in a democratic state, since students were taught to "discern between fact and opinion, inference and conjecture, truth and falsehood." The reverse of the democratic impulse was statist in implication, teaching that "the state is everything and the individual is nothing except a unit in the state." Germany, said Broadwater, had "used history as a very formidable tool to train the individual citizens for the interests of the state." German history books were carefully edited to prevent the people from learning "what the rulers do not wish them to learn." The history they absorbed did not always correspond to the facts but did accomplish "the exaltation of the state." The task of the teacher in a democracy, on the other hand, was to make the present "intelligible to the pupil under his charge." The "great questions of the present" must therefore be integrated into history lessons:

> Newspapers and magazines may be used at these times with advantage, if the teacher remembers to train the pupils a little in judging historical evidence. The pamphlets and papers issued by the Committee on Public Information are very good for such use, as many of those are well-annotated. There are also many documents sent out by patriotic leagues and organizations which are of use. Proper teaching of this kind will result in a clearer understanding of our national aims and every citizen of democracy should know them in order that he as an individual unit of that democracy may show no weakness of will which would break the solid wall of determination to win this war at whatever cost.
>
> A knowledge of individuals that we are right in our causes and aim will strengthen the national aim for defense against a menace that threatens to engulf the world and not only for defense against menace, but this knowledge will stimulate the people of this nation to pursue into utter destruction the destroyer of the world's peace, of national faith, of innocent children, of unprotected women, or to die both individually and nationally in the hope of democracy and Christianity that gave our nation birth. German militarism must die or we shall not live, unless we choose slavery.[44]

One of West Virginia's leading academic figures in the war propaganda drives was James M. Callahan. Callahan was born in Bedford, Indiana, in 1864. He earned his Doctorate of Philosophy in 1897 at Johns Hopkins, studying under Herbert Baxter Adams, and his WVU colleague Oliver Chitwood also earned the Doctorate of Philosophy at Johns Hopkins. While at

Hopkins, Callahan was influenced by the scholarship of Woodrow Wilson, another Hopkins graduate and Adams's first doctoral student, who lectured there while Callahan was a student.[45] In an 1899 monograph published by the Johns Hopkins University Press, *Cuba and International Relations*, Callahan expressed a firm belief in the superiority of Anglo-Saxon principles and institutions as the model for the modern world, urging Americans to teach Anglo-Saxon values to the "Spanish children" inherited from Spain in the Spanish-American War.[46] Callahan later described American territorial expansion as a "heroic, sublime migrating procession," stating that "the mission of the age was to subdue the wilderness and carry the Anglo-Saxon frontier farther and farther westward."[47]

Callahan apparently shared the prevalent notion among American historians, and supported by the era's dominant scientific consensus, that people of color were genetically and socially inferior to whites. Fueled by the authority of "scientific racialism," the doctrine of Anglo-Saxonism dominated the profession by the turn of the century, endowing the "English race" with full responsibility for America's political and social development and supporting American imperialism and immigration restriction.[48] The preparedness movement had capitalized on this spirit, claiming that the war promised a renewal of Anglo-Saxon cultural leadership internationally, and "from the earliest days of the war, there was little doubt that U.S. elites were Anglophilic."[49] Callahan's colleague Albert Bushnell Hart of Harvard, descended from an abolitionist family, was convinced by contemporary arguments of black inferiority that white superiority, in retrospect, had justified slavery and black political and social dependence. "Race measured by race," said Hart, "the Negro is inferior, and his past history in Africa, and in America, leads to the belief that he will remain inferior."[50] Hart's observation echoes that of Madison Grant in one of the decade's most influential racial polemics, *The Passing of the Great Race*, published in 1916. Grant scoffed at the "fatuous belief" of Civil War era "sentimentalists" who claimed that environment, education, and opportunity could "alter heredity." It had taken fifty years, said Grant, to realize that "speaking English, wearing good clothes and going to school and to church do not transform a Negro into a white man."[51]

Grant's well-received work was one of hundreds, beginning in the 1890s, that blended tenets of racial superiority with apprehension about the new immigration from southern and eastern Europe. The concurrent migration of American blacks to southern and northern urban areas further galvanized the Anglo-Saxon racial consensus on the natural intellectual and moral advantage of Anglo racial stock.[52] American expansionism broadened the racist consensus. It was America's destiny, said James M. Callahan, "to lead in new paths" and to "domesticate nature and develop ideas of liberty and self-government," guided by the "strong American combination of Norse, Celt, Norman, and Saxon" stock. Economic strength followed political benevolence. American interests demanded the possession of "distant islands," to "provide for naval stations and commercial interests in the Pacific." America would lead the world in trade and industrial expansion, said Callahan, and must acknowledge the trend of modern history toward colonization and protectorates for "less civilized peoples." Americans must "reach out in helpfulness to lift the less enlightened to liberty's plane, to search for fresh resources, to transform seas into paths for ships, and yoke nature to serve man." Callahan dismissed those critics who warned that authoritarianism might accompany imperial growth, "as if empire could grow on freedom's soil."[53]

The inevitability of Anglo-Saxon cultural expansion exalted by Callahan seemingly drew on several interrelated theoretical formulas that sought to rationalize international imperialism. Callahan's work, for example, reflects the popular philosophical principles of August Comte's (1798–1857) Positivist theory of development and English philosopher Herbert Spencer's (1820–1903) application of Darwinian theory to human society. Positivism envisioned interventionist modern states directing progress, maintaining order, and imposing social and political stability on the developing nations. Positivism reached the height of its influence between 1880 and 1900, formative years intellectually for Woodrow Wilson, A.B. Hart, and Callahan. Comte and Spencer proposed that modern, or industrial and scientific, society evolved from traditional culture through a series of complex stages. Leading the transformation to modern civilization were, as Madison Grant believed, "selected individuals" who brought mankind from savagery and barbarism, based on natural capacity that "gave them the right to lead and the power to compel obedience."[54]

Callahan's Anglophilia also drew upon his mentor Herbert Baxter Adams's "Teutonic Germ" theory, which flourished briefly during Callahan's tenure at Johns Hopkins, and its successor, Frederick Jackson Turner's frontier thesis of the expansion of American institutions. Adams's idea proposed that English and American liberal democratic institutions grew from an institutional germ within prehistoric German forest cultures, which was carried to Britain by Teutonic tribes in the fifth and sixth centuries. The purity of the institutions was preserved by the extermination of racially inferior Celtic Britons and reinvigorated in North America by the development of the New England town meeting. In 1893 Turner, who was also trained at Johns Hopkins by Adams, altered his mentor's emphasis on the direct Germanic influence on American institutions, promoting instead the singular environmental forces of the wilderness that made the frontier "the line of rapid and effective Americanization."[55] Callahan's writing and actions imply a synthesis of the conservative and evolutionary nature of both interpretations, which stressed the continuous growth of political and social institutions and harbored suspicions of mass action, popular agitation, and rebellion.[56]

Callahan was also influenced by the functionalist views of the progressive era's "New Historians," positing that history "is a social instrument, helpful in getting the world's work more effectively done," that the study of the past was justified by its service to the present. This was not a new concept, but the war gave it expanded activist dimensions. New fields of social and intellectual history had directed scholarly attention to the abuses of class privilege, poverty, and industrial exploitation, but both conservative and progressive historians shared a consensus in the superiority of American institutions and rushed to use history to promote patriotism and the Allied cause. While traditionalists justified the war as the defense and preservation of Anglo-Saxon civilization, progressives envisioned an opportunity to defeat imperialism and German militarism, and achieve the "real democratization of our industrial as well as of our political life."[57]

James M. Callahan's sense of American mission steered him to a fiercely moralistic embrace of the war effort. He wrote his brother that while personal sacrifices might be painful, "we are paying the cost of a war in a good cause—to protect the weak, to defend our rights against the brutal military masters of Germany and to save civilization from the curse of German Kultur."[58] An early advocate of the preparedness movement, Callahan heartily endorsed the principles of the Roosevelt Non-Partisan League, a private patriotic organization that sought to unseat Wilson in 1916 and reinstate Theodore Roosevelt as president. The Roosevelt League presented a platform of national honor, peace without sacrifice of national rights, and preparation for anticipated industrial upheaval following the European war.[59] Historian Alan Dawley identifies such militant preparedness supporters as "the cream of the Yankee Protestant establishment," who saw military readiness as the keystone of national unity. Led by General Leonard Wood, Elihu Root, and Roosevelt, extreme preparedness backers abandoned social justice reform, emerging, according to Dawley, as the first American embodiment of the twentieth-century authoritarian right.[60] The Roosevelt League, frustrated with Wilson's belated embrace of military preparedness, charged that it was time for a president "whose creed and deed are *straight Americanism*." After America entered the war, Callahan wrote that pro-interventionists should congratulate themselves that the Wilson administration had at last adopted Roosevelt's vigorous policy. Roosevelt, Callahan affirmed, had directed the nation to its "true course of duty in this greatest crisis," and Callahan hoped that the United States would demonstrate to the world "that we are ready efficiently to do our part to stay the menace of militarism made in Germany."

He wrote to a friend that "I am sorry that we are too old to fight for we know that we never could hope to find a nobler cause."[61]

Callahan's specialty in Latin American and United States diplomacy attracted the attention of the Foreign Press Bureau of the Committee on Public Information. He produced several articles for distribution in the Latin American press, hoping they "may prove useful in connection with the great cause of right for which we are struggling."[62] Callahan was approached by Edward L. Bernays and Paul Kennaday, who served as chief of staff to the bureau's director, Ernest Poole, for contributions to the CPI's news and feature service in the Latin American republics. Kennaday outlined the content of the features for the distinguished diplomatic historian:

> Briefly, our general policy is to send news and stories to drive home five big points: First, that we are getting ready to fight for years, if need be; 2nd, Wilson's liberal peace terms; 3rd, we are not imperialists; 4th, although by no means a perfect democracy, we are constantly struggling toward greater social justice and the present crisis is bringing sweeping changes that will make us still more democratic; 5th, the war is giving us a broader interest in the world, especially in Latin America.[63]

Callahan sent a manuscript to the Foreign Press Bureau, which was later released as four short articles. These articles focused on German intrigues to incite Mexico against the United States and to challenge the Monroe Doctrine. The articles were part of a national series prepared with instructions from the Foreign Press Bureau of the CPI for distribution in Latin American newspapers. Callahan assured the Latin American nations that United States war aims were driven by passion for democracy and protection of the sovereignty and independence of "small states."[64]

Callahan also was the most prominent link between the war effort in West Virginia and the National Security League, identified by one historian as "the most extreme and vitriolic of the patriotic wartime organizations."[65] The league was organized in 1914 by S. Stanwood Menken, a New York corporate lawyer who was stranded in Europe at the outbreak of the war. Although the League claimed not to accept contributions from any "whose financial interests might be furthered by a programme of preparedness," a 1918–19 congressional investigation revealed that the league's contributors were powerful leaders in northern financial and industrial circles, who profited mightily from the war.[66] Among the large contributors were Cornelius Vanderbilt, Mortimer Schiff, George W. Perkins, Bernard Baruch, Henry Clay Frick, Simon Guggenheim, H.H. Rogers, Charles Deering, J.P. Morgan, and John D. Rockefeller. Well-known public figures such as Elihu Root and Alton B. Parker were recruited and advertised as honorary officers of the organization.[67]

Founded to lobby for military preparedness, the league soon expanded its preparedness goals to promote its version of patriotic education, including universal military training as means of "Americanizing" the youth of the country, employing modern means of publicity and appeal.[68] Robert McElroy, the league's education director, worked closely with Guy Stanton Ford of the CPI and secured government franking privileges for mailing campaigns, and the league's publishing format and logo parroted the style of the CPI. The National Board for Historical Service recommended NSL literature to school administrators and teachers. The league claimed more than one hundred thousand members in late 1916, with 270–280 branches covering every section of the country. A league dispatch to Callahan announced that the time had come to transcend agitation for military preparedness, by means of "more systematic propaganda" to assist "the organization of national resources."[69]

With the nation at war, NSL leaders capitalized on widespread exposure and acceptance of their views to redefine patriotism, using the war crisis to promote a more rigid concept of social order and discipline than would have been acceptable in peacetime. The league's emphasis therefore shifted from military preparedness to regulating standards of complete national unity of thought and action, seeking to insure conformity by eliminating dissent. Thus, the governing board of the league resolved, as earlier mentioned by the *Daily Athenaeum*, that educational institutions should scrutinize the loyalty of their faculty and staff and be alert for evidence of "sympathy with the Nation's enemies."[70] As documented by George T. Blakey, preparedness campaigns gave way to loyalty crusades, league-sponsored Americanization programs for immigrant groups, and civic education in schools. By 1918 a clear economic ideology pervaded league policies and statements, equating patriotism and loyalty with support for industrial capitalism.[71]

NSL speakers crossed the country, speaking to local chambers of commerce, Rotary and Kiwanis clubs, and schools, first about preparedness and then the league's particular brand of Amerciansim.[72] The league's Committee on Patriotism through Education was dominated by historians such as Albert Bushnell Hart of Harvard and Robert McElroy of Princeton, who, like Callahan, were too old for active service and sought the "moral equivalent of combat" in national service.[73]

Hart energetically sought other historians to educate the nation about the causes and aims of the war. Within a few months of Wilson's war message, Hart had arranged a speakers training camp at Chautauqua, New York. The camp was attended by political leaders, businessmen, reformers, clergymen, and educators from around the nation, including West Virginia Superintendent of Schools Morris P. Shawkey; C.P. Snow, chair of publicity for the West Virginia Council of Defense, and Attorney General E.T. England, all representing the council. At the camp, Shawkey met with Thomas Wood Stevens, and they made plans for the West Virginia tour of the Drawing of the Sword pageant (see chapter 1), to "stimulate interest in the successful prosecution of the war."[74] The camp was designed to "inform and arouse" a country that needed "clear, definite, authentic information of the situation of the world and our own position as a belligerent power." Hart wrote that the American people must recognize the need to organize men, resources, and government to offset the "terrifically concentrated force of our great enemy, Germany."[75]

Hart, who was instrumental in establishing the *American Historical Review* and had served as president of the American Historical Association and the American Political Science Association, capitalized on his extensive network of political and academic contacts to promote the work of his committee.[76] A frequent visiting summer professor at WVU, it was probably Hart who drew Callahan into the NSL sphere.[77] University President Frank Trotter appointed Callahan a WVU delegate to the league's Congress of Constructive Patriotism, held in Washington on January 25–27, 1917, and Callahan served on Hart's Committee on Patriotism through Education.[78] Callahan was joined by WVU delegates E.H. Vickers of economics and Robert A. Armstrong of English at the congress, where the NSL hoped to set in motion the cultivation of "an efficient national spirit." Organizers envisioned perpetual industrial preparedness for peace and war, driven by government and private cooperation.[79]

National unity demanded "educational preparedness" that extended to even the youngest of the nation's children, since "the imagination of a little child is very sensitive, and his memory very retentive." Educator Frederick Windsor explained the importance of early training to delegates at the NSL conference:

> Children of the grammar school age are not too young to face the fact that there are forces for evil in the world which look with hatred on the ideals for which this country stands, and that loyalty to those ideals may mean standing armed in the face of the danger of death to protect them against assault. Education should prepare them gladly so to stand.[80]

Part of the National Security League's agenda was the training of public school teachers for patriotic service, and it joined local and state councils of defense, the NBHS, the CPI, the national Chamber of Commerce, the International Rotary, and scores of other private and public bodies to cover the country with "a fine web."[81] The NSL redirected much of its early wartime energy away from ferreting out suspected disloyal teachers toward more systematic attempts to coordinate historical training in the schools. The commitment of the NSL, NBHS, and CPI to classroom propaganda expanded as the war lengthened.[82]

James M. Callahan assisted greatly in the dissemination of the NSL agenda in West Virginia. Callahan wrote A.B. Hart that he was in "hearty sympathy" with the goals of the league's patriotic education committee and would be glad to help "in any way which you think desirable." In March and April 1917, he delivered about a dozen addresses to high schools, normal schools, and community meetings, speaking on the general subject of America's war goals and "the need of a larger and more active patriotism." He also informed Hart that he would address these themes at several impending high-school commencements.[83] Callahan suggested that the NSL participate in summer teacher meetings, college and university summer schools, and county teacher institutes, requesting that the NSL send him a copy of Hart's *America at War*, an NSL guidebook for public speakers, for use at West Virginia teacher institutes.[84] Callahan repeated his suggestions in a letter to Waldo G. Leland, secretary of the American Historical Association, telling him that throughout West Virginia the subjects of war policy and patriotic education had been included in numerous flag presentations and loyalty meetings.[85]

The NSL organized its historians and other professors to visit summer school classes of teacher colleges to lead workshops on patriotism and civic education. NSL coordinators visited over 250 summer schools in forty-three states, holding sessions lasting from a few days to several weeks. NSL lecturers outlined suggestions for patriotic education to groups of teachers and students in classroom settings. They followed up the summer training with correspondence with teachers regarding practical application. The few records kept on the summer sessions "concentrate on publicity and planning rather than implementation," says historian George Blakey, who concludes that, although records for the summer terms are meager, "the NSL philosophy of '100 per cent Americanism' probably filtered into an increasingly large number of classrooms."[86]

Unfortunately, the NSL's planned summer course at West Virginia University in 1918 left little documentation beyond the plans and guidelines for the course. Responding to an inquiry from Callahan, the league's educational secretary informed the professor that the NSL was well-stocked with "inspirational speakers" for summer schools.[87] English professor Waitman Barbe, director of the West Virginia University summer school, announced that the NSL would supply an instructor and literature for a six-week course in teacher training. The object of the course was to train teachers to convey the "right relation of every individual to the government" and create the intelligent public opinion needed for victory. NSL Educational Director Robert

McElroy affirmed that the course, which enjoyed the support of Governor Cornwell and State Superintendent Shawkey, would aid the university in making every teacher a "sound and intelligent expounder of the meaning and mission of America" in the war crisis.[88]

The *West Virginia School Journal* described NSL courses as part of a national "movement of importance," made possible by the league's connection to tens of thousands of city, county, and state school superintendents in every school system in the country. All educational forces in the state should cooperate so that the NSL material would reach as many West Virginia teachers as possible, and "through them the parents and children." In this manner, the NSL would help West Virginia teachers disseminate its patriotic suggestions to each community and "form the impregnable bulwark of future Americanism."[89]

Director McElroy was a popular figure in West Virginia, not only in planning the summer course at WVU, but as a scheduled featured speaker at the annual meeting of the West Virginia Education Association at Wheeling, November 27–28, 1918, which was canceled due to the influenza epidemic.[90] McElroy earlier told delegates to the National Education Association convention in Pittsburgh that America was "designed by Providence to construct a platform of patriotism world-wide in its scope." He credited the NSL and other preparedness advocates, the "men who roused this nation to its danger," with glory second only to that due the American men who fought in France.[91]

The patriotic mission of the nation's educators had as its immediate goal the destruction of the German Empire, but infused was the longer-term social and industrial reconstruction of the nation as the moral and commercial leader of the world. One educator encouraged training pupils at all levels in the spirit of loyalty, sacrifice, courage, and "national and racial solidarity," affirming that the nation's schoolchildren "will win or lose the Great War after the war."[92] The "New Americanism" envisioned a postwar international state, merging religion with patriotism, allowing Americans to "serve God and the nation at the same time. Our patriotism will take in all humanity."[93]

West Virginia educators realized that the war would have long-term effects on the curricula, "even in the remotest school in the mountains." Schools should endeavor to make children "socially efficient as never before," through the integration of patriotic and civic training, English skills, vocational guidance, and other "character-forming activities." Florence Kellogg, professor of education at Davis and Elkins College, advised that industrial occupations be taught from kindergarten through the eighth grade and that prevocational courses should be provided to pupils who would soon enter industry to guarantee that they chose a type of work amenable to their capacities.[94] The wartime industrial mobilization had proved the value of industrial education for developing efficient, loyal, and productive citizens, and educational leaders were to develop curricula to prepare boys and girls for different vocations and industries.[95] The happiness and welfare of the community depended upon individuals finding the work "for which they are best suited."[96] Underlying all social and vocational training was the goal of infusing the child with "obedience to recognized authority." Most West Virginia educators probably agreed that, in all situations, there must be a recognized voice to say "with absolute finality, 'This shalt thou do.'"[97]

Most commentators declined to acknowledge, however, that instilling absolute submission to institutional authority into "the plastic mold of youth" could lead to manifestations of state power similar to those against which America fought.[98] One of the recurrent criticisms of Germany was the charge that German *Kultur* dictated the manipulation of the individual consciousness to the demands of the state. The vestment of autocratic power in the German Empire, the German ideal that the individual works for the service of the whole state, was organized by the "chief instrument" of education. In the authoritarian state, said WVU education professor L.B. Hill, the aim of the elementary school was to turn the masses of German children into patriotic, efficient German citizens so that each individual would willingly fill "his particular niche as carved out by the state."[99] Hill was just one of many who attacked the German industrial state while acknowledging its efficiency. W.A. Chamberlin wrote in *The Historical Outlook* (formerly *History Teacher's Magazine*) that the German autocracy's influence on public opinion, evolving for a century, had been achieved by "active agencies, inculcating certain leading ideas, and by repressive measures to restrict discordant sentiments. . . . there is consequently no public opinion in our sense of the word. German national ideals are not shaped by the free interchange of thought, but are moulded by the Government." The German state had succeeded in securing a "complete grasp on the public mind."[100]

Authoritarianism dominated Germany, Chamberlin wrote, by means of a system of universal education through which the state coerced absolute loyalty. Over time the state incrementally gained control of the educational system by legislating curriculum and teaching standards. Only the state could determine a teaching candidate's fitness and grant teaching certificates. Once appointed the teacher became a state official, part of "the large army of the German bureaucracy." The teacher swore an oath of submission, loyalty, and obedience to the German state and constitution:

> By this cast-iron regulation of the teachers the State has complete control of the training of its growing citizens. So long as it prescribes the subjects of study and the methods to be pursued, it can shape almost to a certainty the character of its people. Loyalty is one of the principles constantly hammered into their minds. The rules for Prus-

sian teachers emphasize thorough instruction in German national history, especially the achievements of the Hohenzollerns. Patriotism is drummed up on anniversary days of great national victories, which are made the occasions for speech-making and conviviality.[101]

For those American progressives who believed the enlightened state to be the trustee of the public good, the directed mobilization offered a window of opportunity.[102] The great educational philosopher John Dewey, who dreamed of the United States leading "all nations of the earth into an organized international life," defined the war as a progressive hope. Dewey feared that many American intellectual pacifists misunderstood the "immense impetus to reorganization given by this war." He accused them of having squandered energies by opposing American participation in a war that was already "all but universal," imploring American reformers instead "to form, at a plastic juncture, the conditions and objects of our entrance."[103] To Dewey and many other progressives, America's participation in the war brought a chance to shape the world's future through an international organization to outlaw war and to realize enlightened public administration of society that overcame nationalistic interests.[104]

There was no guarantee, of course, that the expected recasting of political, social, and industrial relationships would make the plastic juncture one leading to Dewey's vision of the good society. The irony, and dangers, of the growth of statism in the name of democracy were not lost on all American intellectuals. The war crisis fostered an unprecedented intervention by the state and national governments in the regulation and mobilization of resources, production, and public opinion in the United States. Government efforts to achieve unity of thought and purpose were rhetorically grounded in democratic ideals but depended on the subordination of the individual will to strengthen the industrial state. This inconsistency was attacked by some of Dewey's disciples, notably essayist Randolph Bourne. Bourne and other critics, horrified by the statist and emotionalist turns the war catalyzed in America, charged Dewey and others with "a philosophical sellout." Even progressives, Dewey included, who applauded the opportunities for beneficent statecraft wrought by the war, struggled with the awareness that Germany itself represented the undesirable extreme of state control at "the opposite pole to the equally undesirable extreme of laissez-faire individualism."[105]

The fear of the authoritarian state, therefore, stalked progressives even as they encouraged state intervention. "Progressive statecraft" in America did not parallel the kind of statist authority found in Germany, but did assume the German ideals of unity of national purpose, educational efficiency, and military strength. Social justice progressives and the New Nationalists of the Roosevelt preparedness school alike admired the scientific centralization of

Germany's urban administration. It was, said Herbert Croly of *The New Republic*, a decided improvement over America's urban political machines and "infinitely divided system of 'democratic' powers." Alan Dawley notes that New Nationalists had an authoritarian streak and thus often admiringly referred to Theodore Roosevelt as an American Bismarck.[106] Before the war, some also praised the pragmatism of "Prussianized, paternalistic, undemocratic, impossible Germany," which knew how to compel the "self-organization of the community" for the benefit of "the administrative program, either through encouragement or coercion. Free America needs this lesson badly."[107] According to the *Wheeling Intelligencer*:

> We may berate the autocratic rule of the Kaiser, but we cannot escape the fact that the great advantage the German government has had has been a thoroughly organized efficiency, in getting things done when they were needed to be done, and we can't amble along in this country on the very pleasant pathway of the old theory of division of powers, so that one organ of government vetoes another and we have difficulty in getting anywhere.[108]

The war fed such authoritarian impulses, and only traditions of civilian supremacy and checks and balances, says Dawley, prevented American nationalists from replicating some European ultranationalists' march into state fascism. Rather than a thorough authoritarian bureaucracy, the Wilsonian war government constructed a "corporate-regulatory complex within the liberal state," in which big business, the market society's most powerful element, reinforced and expanded its dominant position in the social order.[109] The mechanics of that process in West Virginia and the positioning of big business in the state to protect its postwar interests are discussed in the following chapter. Subsequent chapters will carry that discussion into the political economy of the state in the early 1920s.

3

National and State War
Bureaucracies and the American
Regulatory Consensus

America's growth as an industrial and military power in the early twentieth century was accompanied by a regulatory consensus, redefining the relationships of government, labor, and business, which matured during the war years. This period was marked by many interrelated long-term social and political trends, including the emergence of large corporations as the dominant form of business organization, a decline in the autonomy of local market relations, and the growth of regional, national, and international market and political associations. The role of the federal government in regulating market relations expanded, complementing the spread of bureaucratic standards and forms of organization developed to rationalize business and municipal government.[1]

Laissez-faire, corporate, and social welfare theories of social organization, which sometimes intersected, competed to control the emerging industrial order. The distinctiveness of competing social visions for America's future was often blurred during the wartime mobilization. As the United States martialed its industrial and human resources for war, some analysts were alarmed about the damage to democracy that seemed possible with the consolidation of state and industrial forces. One of the most outspoken of these was essayist Randolph Bourne, a frequent contributor to the progressive journal, *The New Republic*. An embittered disciple of philosopher John Dewey, Bourne expressed contempt for intellectuals who embraced the war effort, directing his strongest invective at Dewey and *New Republic* editor Herbert Croly.[2]

Croly, an architect of the New Nationalism, had advocated for some years the efficient concentration of public power in the hands of impartial elites who would promote the public welfare and embody the national interest.[3] Men of special ability, said Croly, endowed with sweeping management and regulatory powers, would guide an efficient national bureaucracy. The nation would be freed from "Jeffersonian bondage" by the "Hamiltonian practice of constructive national legislation."[4]

Croly, who edited *The New Republic* with Walter Weyel and Walter Lippmann, regularly published John Dewey's defense of the war's social possibilities. Dewey believed that idealists and progressive reformers must support Woodrow Wilson's war goals, define the terms of the peace, and contribute to new economic and political institutions that would elevate the public interest over private greed in matters of production and exchange. Walter Lippmann agreed. Out of the horror of the war could come ideas to possess men's souls, he believed. America would emerge from combat committed to greater democracy. "We shall turn with fresh interest to our own tyrannies," Lippmann wrote, "to our Colorado mines, our autocratic steel industries, our sweatshops and our slums."[5]

Leading educators invoked similar idealistic themes, affirming that progressives must keep the war faithful to President Wilson's lofty aims. The president of Clark University praised the "splendor and the glory" of America's mission to save Europe and the world for democracy. James M. Callahan wrote that the United States fought for a world in which "no brute nation could live by swagger and threat." America sought to defend its rights, and secure "peace with victory for freedom of the seas from national piracy, and for the rights of small nations." To these ends, "the military spirit of her people has slowly awakened and will sustain her just cause."[6]

Randolph Bourne understood the seductive appeal the war held before progressives. Modern war, waged by a democratic republic against an autocratic enemy, seemed to achieve "almost all that the most inflamed political idealist could desire." But Bourne charged Croly, Dewey, and other pro-war progressives with forgoing the peaceful transformation of political and social institutions and aligning themselves with antidemocratic forces.[7] Bourne called war "the health of the State," which he defined as a "repository of force, determiner of law, [and] arbiter of justice," distinct from the nation or country, which embodied a peoples' customs and ways of life. In a healthy country, citizens tolerated and obeyed the government, but patriotism suggested dominant sentiments "of peace, of tolerance, of living and letting live."[8]

These sentiments disappeared in wartime, however, when "the State comes into its own" and the country is transformed into a political unit. The moment war is declared, "the mass of the people, through some spiritual alchemy, become convinced that they have willed and executed the deed themselves." The people with few exceptions then permit themselves to be regimented and coerced and "turned into a solid manufactory of destruction." All the activities of society are joined to the central purpose of conquest, and the state becomes the regulator of men's business, attitudes, and opinions, demanding "100 percent Americanism among 100 percent of the population." Academic, political, and economic leaders tailor national ideals to war purposes. Minority or dissenting opinion becomes "a case for outlawry," and war orthodoxy becomes the requirement for all professions, opinions, and occupations.[9]

Bourne's warnings were outshone by the zealous light of the war to end wars, in a process that, according to George Creel, would "weld the people of the United States into one white-hot mass instinct with fraternity, devotion, courage, and deathless determination."[10] Woodrow Wilson's success in casting the war in idealistic terms, fortified by the appropriate propaganda machinery, built the ideological engine that drove the bureaucratic organization of the country for war purposes. Success would depend, said Theodore Roosevelt, on the unified use of the nation's entire social, industrial, and military power. Wilson told Americans that modern wars were not won by mere numbers, enthusiasm, or national spirit, but by the scientific conduct of tactics and the scientific application of industrial forces.[11] The emergency demanded the mobilization of civilian populations and the national control of industry, food production, and consumption. The winning side would exhibit "the greatest manpower, the best organized production and consumption, the largest financial resources."[12] At war's end, American industrial mobilization had earned the admiration of its most esteemed enemies, including General Paul von Hindenburg, chief of the German army's high command. Under pressure of military necessity, said von Hindenburg, "a ruthless autocracy was at work, and rightly." Of the Americans von Hindenburg commented approvingly, "They understood war."[13]

Much of the federal mobilization of industrial manpower and machinery was nominally overseen by the Council of National Defense, whose director was Grosvenor B. Clarkson. The council was established in August 1916, comprised of the secretaries of war, navy, agriculture, commerce, labor, and interior. The council relied on a Civilian Advisory Commission to regulate relations between business, labor, and government to insure productive harmony. Representing transportation, labor, industry, finance, mining, merchandise, and medicine, President Wilson defined the advisory commission's purpose as establishing direct communication and cooperation "between business and scientific men and all departments of the Government." Advisory members were selected on a nonpartisan basis, with, said Wilson, "efficiency being their sole objective and Americanism their only motive." Clarkson wrote that the advisory council precipitated an unprecedented involvement of engineers and professionals in the affairs of government.[14]

Progressive ideals of public service and efficiency blended with the single-minded pursuit of productivity in 1917 to create, in the words of historian Robert Wiebe, "the America of Herbert Croly's dreams, a corporate society led by the federal government." Seeking a systematic approach to production and distribution, the Wilson government organized a network of federal agencies for specific economic sectors. The 1917 Lever Food and Fuel Control Act authorized, after the fact, Wilson and the Council of

National Defense to regulate the production, distribution, and prices of food and fuel. Wilson appointed Harry Garfield, president of Williams College, to head the Fuel Administration, and Herbert Hoover to lead the Food Administration.[15]

One of the most powerful wartime agencies was the War Industries Board (WIB), which became the principal coordinating body of the American economy. Representatives of most of the nation's major economic sectors sat on the board, dominated by industrialists. The board was created in July 1917 as an arm of the Council of National Defense, although Wilson put it under his personal supervision in March 1918. The president selected financier Bernard Baruch to guide the WIB, partly to appease industrialists troubled about federal meddling with laissez-faire business practices. Baruch and Wilson were of like mind in their belief that "cooperative committees of industry" should override the "disutility of free-wheeling competition," yet Baruch's familiarity with the leaders of industrial capitalism assured them they had an ally directing the WIB.[16]

Baruch and Wilson agreed that modern America's political economy was defined by the role of the industrial corporation and its relation to the state. Wilson repeatedly stressed that corporate organization was the natural and dominant mode of modern capitalism, reflecting society's modern means of collectivizing its resources and entrepreneurial power. Corporations were the legacy of irresistible forces, said Wilson, and could therefore not be considered immoral. Concentration of corporate power, and the large-scale cooperative organization of business was normal and inevitable, said Wilson, and did not threaten the personal and economic liberties of average citizens. Dissolution of large corporations would cause economic chaos and social instability. The task of enlightened government was, therefore, to guarantee that corporations reflected and responded to the public interest.[17]

The War Industries Board, said Grosvenor Clarkson, succeeded in establishing a uniquely American war machine to regulate resources yet respect the American peoples' devotion to individualism.[18] Alan Dawley notes, however, that the implementation of American-style "war collectivism" was less a function of the government bureaucracies themselves than of the giant industrial and commercial corporations upon whom the administration depended. Essentially, says Dawley, the WIB was a combination of industrial leaders devising their own cooperative policies, sponsored by the state. Only in the operation of railroads and telegraph communications did the government assume direct control, with Secretary of the Treasury Robert McAdoo, Wilson's son-in-law, as "the only government official who actually got to boss corporate presidents around." McAdoo's "thorough and ruthless" rationalization of the nation's rail systems regulated car allocation, passenger service, shipping routes, and coal distribution. It initiated pay raises for railroad employees to insure labor stability. The Railroad Administration was held up as a model of scientific management by progressive reformers, including McAdoo, who applauded the efficiency of a federally controlled rail system.[19]

The War Industries Board constructed a maze of commodity committees, which communicated with war service committees, or private trade associations, to insure cooperative war production. Although defined as strictly advisory by the WIB, the trade associations in fact set war management policy in areas such as awarding contracts, setting prices, and determining distribution priorities. Opportunistic business leaders soon recognized in the wartime managed economy the vast potential for a form of business enterprise relatively free of the insecurity, inefficiency, and unpredictability of nineteenth-century competitive market practices.[20]

By war's end, the Wilson government had pieced together "as complete a military machine as the world has ever seen."[21] In so doing, it helped lay the foundation for a formal political-legal order favorable to corporate capitalism, with the state and the great corporations intertwined. The corporate-regulatory complex that matured during the war left the most powerful element in the regulated market, big business, the dominant force in postwar America. President Wilson confided to Secretary of War Newton D. Baker that the wartime "autocracy" would inevitably leave industrial leaders in control of the country. "They will run the nation," Wilson said.[22]

Wartime management required, said Robert McElroy of the National Security League, proof that a democracy could train its people to perform "with equal efficiency and devotion, everything which autocracy has been able to do." Much of the responsibility for that task in West Virginia fell to its newly inaugurated governor, John Jacob Cornwell, a Hampshire County Democrat who took the oath of office only thirty-three days before the declaration of war. Morris P. Shawkey designated the election of Cornwell, who had served in the West Virginia Senate before the governorship, as "a providential turn" in the state's history.[23] Cornwell was born in 1867 near the village of Mole Hill (now Mountain), West Virginia, in Ritchie County. Educated as a teacher and lawyer, Cornwell also owned and operated apple orchards in Hampshire County and invested in railroad building. As a successful attorney and editor of the *Hampshire Review* in Romney, West Virginia, Cornwell laid the foundation for his political career.[24]

Cornwell was an early advocate of military readiness, expressing his hope that Wilson and the Congress would "do what is necessary for reasonable and proper, but not sporadic and hysterical, preparedness, such as is advocated by extremists in both parties." He once warned that Wilson's belated preparedness plans would fail if the president did not arouse Americans to the country's eminent danger. Cornwell affirmed that he had "never been crazy about Wilson," but was with the President "heart and soul" on preparedness and had "no patience with those who have neither statesmanship nor patriotism enough to follow his lead."[25]

Cornwell reported that his first twenty months as governor were consumed with war matters. His chief desire had been to promote the state's economic development by advertising West Virginia's mineral and agricultural resources, but these considerations were rendered secondary to the demands of war.[26] Cornwell called the state legislature into extraordinary session on May 14, 1917, encouraged by reports that he would encounter little difficulty in securing the cooperation of West Virginia's politically divided legislature, in which Republican lawmakers outnumbered Democrats. In the war crisis, partisan differences would be cast aside in all matters of importance to the war emergency. The governor could expect the legislature "to pass legislation to strengthen the state in dealing with any situation that might arise as a result of the war."[27]

Cornwell appeared before the joint assembly of the legislature to plea for emergency wartime legislation. The legislature promptly responded to Cornwell's request to set aside a West Virginia law forbidding federal acquisition of parcels of land over twenty-five acres, facilitating the construction of a federal armory near Charleston. Cornwell informed the session of his appointment of the executive board of the West Virginia Council of Defense in conjunction with the National Defense Act, and was granted legislative approval empowering the board with broad emergency authority for the executive board and advisory state councils. He welcomed extensive authority for the executive board, urging the legislature to expand state powers to meet any war emergency.[28] Another act penalized speculation in foodstuffs and fuel; still another granted sheriffs and county courts the power to appoint special deputies "for the protection of the lives and properties of the people of West Virginia." The legislature approved a two-cent property tax and an excise corporation tax of one-fourth of 1 percent on net corporate earnings to supply the state defense council's war defense fund.[29]

National and state leaders realized that West Virginia coal, steel, farm products, and livestock were of utmost importance to the war effort. Governor Cornwell expressed the urgency of the demand for West Virginia resources when he told the West Virginia Coal Mining Institute that the motto of every West Virginia worker must be "produce, produce, for God's sake, produce." Not only did the country need maximum production now, said the governor, but following the war there would likely be a demand for West Virginia coal "greater than any of you can imagine."[30]

Believing that voluntary productivity must be reinforced with coercive power, Cornwell asked for and received legislative approval for the nation's first compulsory work law, drafted to "prevent idleness and vagrancy in West Virginia during the continuance of the war." The law ordered all able-bodied West Virginia males except students, ages sixteen to sixty, to work at least thirty-six hours weekly "in some lawful, useful, and recognized business, profession, occupation or employment." The bill's sponsor, Republican William S. John of Monongalia County, proclaimed that any able-bodied men who failed to produce commodities or support for the war would be guilty of moral neglect. John believed that a nonproducer was "a dead weight on society and a slacker," and it was the duty of the state to "impress upon the minds and hearts of the people the idea that failure to engage in useful occupation is unpatriotic."[31]

The enactment of the compulsory work law reflected on a state level the national consensus among preparedness advocates, consistent with progressive values that made devotion to productive work imperative, that loafing was "unfashionable."[32] With the onset of war, loafing became not only unfashionable but disloyal and, in West Virginia, illegal. The compulsory work law was in part the legacy of a "census of idlers" that Cornwell ordered when he took office, taken by the municipal police in West Virginia's towns and cities. The census showed an "amazing number of idlers and unemployed," prompting Cornwell to announce that idleness would be penalized. "Public sentiment will be so aroused," said the governor, "that it will be impossible for the idle person to live content in any community. In this crisis, idleness is unpatriotic."[33] Cornwell credited the census of idlers with much of the eventual success of the compulsory work law, since many loafers had feared their inclusion in the census would get them drafted into the army. These fears were reinforced by the compulsory work law, and, Cornwell believed, forced many "street corner loafers" into gainful employment. Cornwell affirmed that governors in several states had inquired about the mechanics of the law and were taking similar steps.[34] By late summer 1918, Maryland, Kansas, Minnesota, South Dakota, and New York had indeed enacted similar statutes, and President Wilson had asked all states to do the same. The Council of Canada made idleness a crime on April 4, 1918.[35]

The work or fight law became a rallying point for West Virginia county and local councils of defense. Local councils announced that every citizen was expected to report enemies of the government and vagrants as part of his or her patriotic duty.[36] *Our Own People*, a publication of the Davis Coal Company, suggested that any man so cowardly as to refuse to work long hours should "be put in the front line trenches, where he could get as close to his friends, the Huns, as it is possible." All who did not sacrifice willingly "should be COMPELLED to so serve liberty."[37] Cornwell affirmed that "public sentiment should be invoked to drive the loafer to the field, the factory, or the mine." He successfully appealed to the West Virginia press to devote editorial comment for enforcement of the act.[38] The *Wheeling Intelligencer* applauded the law for guaranteeing efficient conservation of resources and for making progress toward eliminating "the non-producing consumer." Just as there "is no room for the drones in a beehive, neither can there now be patience with the do-nothing human." *The Intelligencer* suggested that permanent retention of the law, in peace as well as war, might make West Virginians "more efficient and happier people." Sullivan attested to unanimity among municipal authorities as to the law's effectiveness, many of whom advocated that the law become permanent.[39]

The West Virginia Education Association also tacitly approved coercive productivity at its 1917 meeting. The association advised school officials to track the whereabouts not only of school-age children but of those beyond compulsory school-age, to determine whether they were workers or loafers, and, if employed, whether they were "legally employed?"[40] A positive state effort to guarantee the loyalty of West Virginia youth was Cornwell's establishment, at the recommendation of the U.S. secretary of labor, of the Boys' Working Reserve, for "patriotic service in the field and factory." Sunday school superintendents were charged with enrolling boys aged sixteen to twenty-one in the reserve, and filing their records with the West Virginia secretary of state. The *West Virginia War Bulletin* announced that "225 colored boys" were the first to enroll in the Boys' Reserve.[41]

Oliver Chitwood wrote that the work-or-fight law was not merely a symbolic protest against industrial slackers, but also "had teeth in it." Justices of the peace, mayors, and police judges had jurisdiction to try and punish all offenders, who were penalized as vagrants. In addition to fines of up to one hundred dollars, offenders were ordered by the local trial court to work up to sixty days on some public project. Slackers included habitual street loiterers and pool room, hotel, and depot loafers. Habitual drinkers, gamblers, or narcotics users were also declared criminal by the law. Any able-bodied man proven to be supported "in whole or in part by the labor of any woman or child" was *prima facie* guilty of vagrancy under the law.[42]

Jesse Sullivan, secretary of the West Virginia Council of Defense, issued a report in June 1918 on the first year's operation of the Idleness and Vagrancy Act (the designation most used by state officials). Under the headings "Idleness Aids the Enemy" and "Taking the Slack out of Slackers," Sullivan estimated 811 arrests in 143 West Virginia cities and towns (sixty municipalities filed no report); his figures did not include arrests made by justices of the peace. Sullivan also determined that at least 2,705 loafers, fearing arrest, were compelled to work. He credited an opinion by Attorney General England that the burden of proof rested upon the alleged offender to demonstrate that he had worked the required thirty-six hours, rather than on local authorities to prove that he had not, with securing uniform enforcement of the act. England also declared that "rich idlers," living on inherited wealth, could be prosecuted under the law. If a man's property did not require his "personal attention, he could not use it as a subterfuge to evade the penalties of the vagrancy law." A man with "a large amount of property," however, was exempt from prosecution if managing his money and property demanded a great deal of his time.[43]

Sullivan scored some mayors for lax enforcement of the act, reserving special condemnation for underzealous enforcement in some mining communities. To combat this, the West Virginia Council of Defense adopted a resolution requiring any business employing twenty or more men to submit weekly reports with the names and addresses of their employees who failed to work the minimum thirty-six hours, and Governor Cornwell encouraged the posting of weekly reports of hours worked at mine entrances. The law's coercive effect in coal communities therefore aided in the prosecution of the war, Sullivan reported, as it discouraged miners "who are disposed to remain idle."[44]

Wartime worker productivity was inextricably tied to wartime patriotism, and maximizing coal production required the Cornwell war administration to cultivate the support of West Virginia's black citizens, who were concentrated in the coal regions. Black migrants had been drawn to the southern West Virginia coalfields in a steady stream since the 1880s, coming for industrial employment as well as the relative political equality in the state. Unlike other Appalachian and southern industrial areas, West Virginia had not imposed rigid Jim Crow segregation laws; only in education and marriage was racial integration legally barred.[45] Black coal miners were crucial to coal production, and Edward T. Hill, secretary of the West Virginia Negro Bar Association, wrote Governor Cornwell that his organization was involved in a publicity campaign "to get the miners to work regularly and load more coal, to somewhat make up for the loss of the services of nearly 400 coal miners" who had enlisted in the armed forces.[46]

Hill spoke for an expanding black bourgeoisie in southern West Virginia, who, led by black women teachers, were "harbingers of the new industrial ideology" of progress, emphasizing thrift, economic development, and individual responsibility. Even with the relative lack of legal forms of segregation in southern West Virginia, the infusion of blacks into the coal economy had precipitated incidents of violence and discrimination against blacks. West Virginia blacks capitalized on their political enfranchisement in the state to resist private and public manifestations of racial bigotry, using their political leverage to considerable effect in the Republican party's local machinery in the southern counties.[47]

Cornwell, a Democrat, held no political loyalties to the state's black voters, and his Republican opponent in the 1916 election, Judge Ira Robinson, had swept most black precincts. Once in office, Cornwell embarked on a purge of black Republican appointees to the state's bureaucracy and cut state appropriations to black institutions. As with all other local aspects of the wartime mobilization, however, race relations were tied to the Wilson administration's pursuit of a unified front. Cornwell, if for no other reason than to maintain wartime harmony with the Republican majority in the West Virginia legislature, was therefore compelled to paper over his party's poor relationship with West Virginia blacks.[48]

Nationally, the Wilson administration also sought to assuage black suspicions of the party of white supremacy. Rumors of a German plot to foment black insurrection engendered fears of preemptive patriotic lynching and terrorism in black communities.[49] The Committee on Public Information worried that blacks would be particularly susceptible to German propaganda because of their "illiteracy and consequent credulity." One intellectual feared that even though blacks had adopted the rudimentary cultural standards of whites, their lack of economic and educational opportunities meant "they have not yet reached a level where they fully appreciate Americanism."[50] Facing such widely held biases, many blacks saw wartime service as an opportunity to advance the standing of their people. Over three hundred thousand blacks were drafted, and black men enlisted in great numbers, partly from national allegiance, and in part in hope that the fruits of the war for democracy would be the fulfillment of the United States promise of equality, rights, and fair treatment. The intellectual activist W. E. B. DuBois wrote in the July 1918 *The Crisis* that while the war lasted, American blacks should "forget our special grievances and close our ranks shoulder to shoulder with our white fellow citizens."[51]

Black dreams for the transformation of Americanism into an inclusive rather than racist ideology, however, were not well served by Woodrow Wilson or his administration. Few sectors of the American public had less reason to trust the idealistic nostrums of the president, and black support for the war effort was probably more in spite of Wilson than because of him. Wilson's devotion to Anglo-Saxon culture was grounded in his unshakable belief in white supremacy, reinforced by his personal internalization of the American South's traditional racial assumptions. Wilson introduced movies, which became one of the major propaganda tools of the mobilization, to the White House by showing *The Birth of a Nation*, and he strongly endorsed its pro-Ku Klux Klan interpretation of Reconstruction as "history written with lightning."[52]

Democrat Wilson had convinced some black voters of his devotion to justice in race relations, prompting a modest swing in traditional political loyalties among enfranchised blacks in 1912. Black faith in Wilson receded, however, with a progression of racist actions. In addition to the *Birth of a*

Nation incident, Wilson segregated federal office buildings and stirred race hatred in East St. Louis, Illinois, by charging the Republican party there with importing black voters in 1916. The president responded to criticism by announcing that if "the colored people made a mistake in voting for me, they ought to correct it."[53]

John J. Cornwell's association with the party of Wilson exacerbated his chilly relations with the state's black political base, but the state defense council was determined to make blacks a "potent factor" in the industrial mobilization. If blacks were to contribute to the Allies' victory as food conservators, soldiers, industrial workers, and buyers of Liberty Bonds, they should be represented in the war-management bureaucracy. Consequently, to guarantee "the complete and thorough organization of the Negroes of the State," the state defense council formed an Auxiliary Council of Defense. Cornwell and his colleagues recommended "the employment of a colored man" to impress upon the state's black citizens the importance of giving their labor and financial support to the national army.[54]

The executive board appointed J.C. Gilmer as secretary of the Auxiliary Council, at a salary of one hundred per month, less than half the salary of Jesse Sullivan.[55] The Auxiliary Council included the presiding officers of religious and fraternal organizations and "other prominent members of the race," including ministers, physicians, businessmen, and women's lodge and club leaders. The Auxiliary Council soon organized county councils, "as used with so much success among the white people." The Auxiliary Council took a stand against idleness, with each member pledging to resist "this particular nuisance in his neighborhood," and black women and girls entered wartime industrial occupations and ran food conservation campaigns. Gilmer defined the main mission of the county auxiliaries as "enlightening the masses" about the aims of the wartime agencies. In all wartime campaigns, Gilmer credited the Auxiliary Council and its subsidiaries with a

> leading part, organizing and directing forces which awaited only to be told what and how to do. It found a willing constituency, loyal to the core and almost pathetic in its eagerness to give its men, its money and its labor with the hope that it might share fully in the glory of the victory and the blessings of peace.[56]

As a political message to the party of Cornwell and Wilson, West Virginia blacks in the spring of 1918 joined a national campaign by the National Association for the Advancement of Colored People to protest the screening in West Virginia of *The Birth of a Nation*. The West Virginia protest was launched when the McDowell County Auxiliary Council, led by Rev.

J.W. Robinson and Dr. A.S. Adams, combined forces with the West Virginia State Civic League, a black activist group founded in 1915.[57] Reacting to its pressure, the State Defense Council prohibited any showing of *The Birth of a Nation* or any similar play or picture for the duration of the war. Such movies, the council proclaimed, were "calculated to arouse hatred and prejudice between races" and therefore were likely to obstruct racial cooperation for efficient war work.[58]

The West Virginia Council of Defense's overtures reflect its concerns that issues of race not obstruct maximum cooperation and productivity in West Virginia. Coal mining was by far the major occupation for black males in the state, with blacks comprising more than 19 percent of West Virginia's miners in 1918.[59] The loyalty and productivity of all miners was a prime concern to the Wilson administration. When the United States entered the war, coal provided nearly three-quarters of the mechanical energy in the country, and West Virginia miners produced 25 percent of the total.[60] Coal production in the state was stimulated by Allied purchasers prior to U.S. entry, growing by more than 20 percent from 1915 to 1916.[61] The United States Navy almost always used southern West Virginia's high quality smokeless coal. In the latter stages of the war, the U.S. War Department ordered southern West Virginia draft boards to stop drafting coal miners, and President Wilson informed coal diggers that their patriotic duty was more to mine coal than to fight overseas. Nonetheless, more than fifty thousand miners nationwide enlisted, and three thousand died in combat.[62]

The status of coal producers illustrates the admixture of patriotic propaganda, industrial production, and business promotion that characterized the war management bureaucracy's pursuit of autarky. Coal operators and United Mine Workers of America (UMWA) spokesmen alike emphasized the patriotic obligation of miners to produce, appropriating the idealistic pronouncements of Wilson and the propagandists that the war was a fight to establish liberty and democracy throughout the world.[63] The *United Mine Workers Journal* (UMWJ) pointed out that wars were no longer fought only by armies but that "millions of men manage the machinery of destruction," and "every human unit in America has its burden to bear." The lives of soldiers were in the keeping of industrial workers, each of whom represented a part of the fighting force. "This is labor's part in the war machine."[64] UMWA District 17 President Frank Keeney implored miners to push for maximum production. He served as grand marshal for a massive bond drive parade in Charleston in April 1918.[65] The Department of Labor hopefully announced that the spirit of common sacrifice that united Americans foretold employer-employee compatibility that, if nurtured, could build a new industrial partnership after the war. Governor John Cornwell wrote that sporadic early wartime unrest in some coalfields soon vanished, in the face of "public discussion," and wage workers and labor leaders had "constituted—with a very few exceptions—a potent army of defensive support of the men in uniform."[66]

These optimistic reports gloss over the serious concerns the Wilson and Cornwell governments had about their ability to marshal universal labor support for war production. The Wilson government's centralized war bureaucracy was in the formative stages in the spring and early summer of 1917, seemingly powerless to control work stoppages to protest the rising prices that accompanied the war boom. Despite pay increases for many workers, work stoppages over the cost of living or work hours rose from 2,036 in 1916 to 2,268 in 1917, many in vital war industries.[67] Cornwell often employed the emergency Special Police Deputies Act to intervene in work stoppages or in "locating slackers." Labor "riots" in Gilmer County in August 1917 and a Raleigh County strike in October of the same year prompted the governor to send special deputies to those counties for several weeks.[68] Special deputies were requested at Gilmer by C.H. Workman of the Executive Council of UMWA District 17, who alleged that private guards employed by the West Virginia Coal and Coke Company were vandalizing the homes of striking employees. But striking miners in Raleigh County may have questioned the impartiality of the special deputies, appointed by the county sheriff and county court and empowered to carry unlicensed firearms, when the deputies were quartered in buildings owned by the Raleigh Coal and Coke Company.[69]

To block possible industrial unrest, the State Defense Council also authorized the formation of voluntary Home Guards or Home Reserves, paramilitary groups of "citizens of good standing."[70] Official fears of widespread wartime labor rebellion in West Virginia, however, were baseless. Leaders of organized labor in the state fully realized the crucial demand for worker productivity, but some expressed concern that their traditional adversaries in government and industry would use the war crisis to destroy the union movement in the state. Fred Mooney, secretary-treasurer of District 17 of the UMWA, charged the Cornwell government with using the compulsory work law to harass the miners' union. Cornwell personally ordered Mingo County coal operators to keep accurate records of hours worked by their miners, and to post copies at their mines each week. He also issued a blistering missive against unproductive miners. "The slacker," said the governor, "has increased the chance that the boy who worked by his side before he was called to arms will not come back. . . . He is making it harder for the American soldier to save the world from autocracy."[71]

In the war's first year, some West Virginia operators sought to use the work-or-fight law to deny rights of free association to striking miners, whom the law defined as vagrants. Mooney complained that the UMWA spent more money keeping alleged slackers out of jail than it did feeding strikers. A consortium of mining companies in Kanawha and Raleigh counties used a "slacker board," posting the productivity of working miners and the names of strikers. If quotas per man were not filled, the offenders were fired and lost their draft-exempt status. One miner alleged that if the company believed a worker was slacking, company guards would march him to the local draft board and have his exemption removed.[72] Justus Collins, president of the Winding Gulf Colliery Company, periodically received "a digest of slackers" from his managers. Collins wrote personally to the accused slackers, accusing them of treasonous behavior and of abandoning American soldiers. "Every ton you fail to produce aids our enemies and you must realize this is the case," Collins accused. "If you are not in sympathy with our country in its desperate situation, then you should get out of it and go to Germany. There you would get a taste of the real thing if you were a slacker."[73]

In the early months of the war, some nonunion or anti-union operators sought to use production demands to destroy the miners' union. Collins believed that the West Virginia legislature, meeting to draft the emergency wartime bills, was eager to suppress all agitation and disturbance in the coalfields. Perhaps, he concluded, this state of affairs could be used to get union leaders to "back off gracefully" from organizing the New River and Winding Gulf coalfields. Collins, apparently unconcerned about possible legislators' objections, ordered one of his superintendents to "keep a sharp eye" on his employees, and if "anyone among them is agitating and creating unrest, or is a sore head, discharge him summarily without further consideration."[74] Mine superintendent George Wolfe assured Collins that "the very minute" a Winding Gulf miner joined the UMWA, "either in fact or in spirit, he is promptly discharged and gotten off the job." Collins huffed at UMWA demands at his mines for the checkoff, recognition of union committees, "and all that sort of stuff." He advised his managers that "I think that while the political complexion of the State is in the shape it is in, we should drive the Union out of the State from one end to the other, as far as the coal fields are concerned."[75]

This type of contentiousness, however, was anathema to the war bureaucracy. Desperate to stabilize industrial relations, the Washington war management complex made several overtures to labor. President Wilson appointed American Federation of Labor President Samuel Gompers, a loyal Wilson supporter, to the advisory council for the Council of National Defense.[76] Alarmed at appeals to labor by the antiwar People's Council of America, led by Socialists and leftist intellectuals like Morris Hillquit, Rebecca Shelly, Roger Baldwin, and Scott Nearing, and at membership gains on the West Coast by the anarchist Industrial Workers of the World, Gompers guided the AFL into the pro-war American Alliance for Labor and Democracy.[77] The alliance welcomed any pro-war worker or organizer, and was joined soon after its July 1917 formation by Socialists J.G. Phelps, Charles Russell, William Walling, and John Spargo, who all had bolted the Socialist party at its May convention in St. Louis when it adopted an antiwar position. The convention featured a major address by the prominent West Virginia Socialist, Dr. Matthew Holt. Holt vigorously condemned American participation in the war and announced that he and his wife had sent one of their sons to South America to prevent his sacrifice in an immoral war.[78]

The war issue mortally divided West Virginia's vibrant Socialist party. Holt's dramatic actions served as counterpoint to the abandonment of the longstanding antiwar position by Walter Hilton, the influential Socialist editor of the *Wheeling Majority*. Hilton explained that Americans were obliged to support the country's commitment to the war in spite of personal objections. *The Majority* featured articles by the Alliance for Labor and Democracy, agreeing that the war, however regrettable, could lead to the fulfillment of many Socialist goals if its idealistic principles were maintained. Robert Maisel, director of the alliance, announced that the Committee on Public Information would sponsor the agency by supplying propaganda outlines and paying salaries, rents, and other expenses.[79]

Samuel Gompers, like Hilton and John Dewey, embraced the notion of the social possibilities of the war, believing it would usher in a new era that would recognize the labor movement as an equal partner with industry and government in postwar America. His vision of an industrial partnership compelled Gompers to pressure the AFL to compromise on the issue of the open shop, the AFL's primary negotiating demand, foreshadowing the crippling anti-union movement after the war. Gompers won gains for many workers by obtaining union wages, hours, and recognition from the war government, but he secured no firm commitment for government support or business cooperation on unionization when the war ended.[80] Gompers understood the essentially status quo posture of the government, which was clearly stated by the Council of National Defense. The council took the position that "during the war there should be a truce between conflicting industrial interests, for the period of which each side should hold the ground it held at the beginning of hostilities" and that any alterations would be solely for the promotion of industrial efficiency during the war. Grosvenor Clarkson candidly acknowledged the government's noncommittal position. When the War Industries Board was formed to manipulate industrial resources, its labor member, Hugh Frayne, was "not on the Board to represent labor, but to manage it."[81]

Gompers sought to administer a national labor policy through his Committee on Labor of the Advisory Commission to the National Council of Defense. President Wilson, however, assigned the formulation of such a policy to the War Labor Administration (WLA), controlled by Secretary of Labor William B. Wilson, and integrated the Gompers committee into this agency. The WLA soon formed the National War Labor Board (NWLB), chaired by former president William Howard Taft and attorney Frank P. Walsh, to serve as a court of last resort in labor-management disputes. The NWLB recognized the right of workers to organize and bargain collectively, forbade strikes and lockouts, and preserved the union shop and union conditions where they existed. The board, however, had no statutory power and assumed no responsibility for protecting labor's rights after the war.[82] The NWLB plainly stated that it stood for securing maximum production for the employer, and for protecting workers' economic welfare and right to organization *while the war for human liberty everywhere is being waged*" [emphasis added].[83]

Although this ostensible federal neutrality boded ill for the UMWA in southern West Virginia after the war, American coal miners were justifiably encouraged by the actions of President Wilson's Fuel Administration in its pursuit of labor loyalty. The Fuel Administration, given broad authority by the Lever Act over the price and distribution of coal, brought the UMWA and the coal industry to the table to negotiate the Washington Agreement in October 1917. To be in effect for the duration of the war, or until April 1, 1920, whichever came first, the agreement granted wage increases to miners in return for a no-strike pledge. Southern West Virginia operators consented to the Washington Agreement in part because they feared government seizure of their operations, and reluctantly agreed, according to Justus Collins, to "arrange some kind of a working agreement with the Government along lines that will be fair."[84]

The Washington Agreement prohibited the firing of miners for union membership, thus encouraging the rapid advance of unionism in areas under tight company control, such as southern West Virginia.[85] With federal protection, Districts 17 and 29 of the UMWA grew dramatically during the war years. Many West Virginia miners won the checkoff and the union shop, including those in the northern West Virginia district. District 17 president Frank Keeney, assisted by Fred Mooney and local organizers, seized the moment to invade the industry in radically anti-union McDowell County, with plans to organize Logan and Mingo counties as well.[86] Coal operator William D. Ord complained about the "evident determination" of the Fuel Administration and some politicians "to organize labor in nonunion fields." The UMWA, Ord said, was exploiting "under cloak of war" the patriotic spirit of the coal operators, who, to preserve industrial peace, could not resist when the union sent "secret agents" into non-union fields. Ord wrote that union gains would leave coal operators' property "worth only a fraction of its present value" at war's end.[87]

In addition to UMWA gains, anti-union operators also were cool to the Fuel Administration's power to fix prices. Governor Cornwell noted that West Virginia coal operators resented any interference in pricing, and some sought exemption from the wartime controls, or delayed coal shipments, hoping for a price increase. This irritated the governor, who although a friend to the industry (he had asked Secretary of Labor Wilson to order UMWA organizers out of West Virginia, prior to the Washington Agreement) nonetheless was determined to keep coal production and distribution flowing.[88]

West Virginia operators upset by UMWA wartime advances, however, were not without sources of comfort. Once the crisis of the war passed and the federal government retreated into its neutral stance on labor-management issues, the industry would be free to enforce the proscriptions against unionism inherent in the U.S. Supreme Court's December 10, 1917 decision in *Hitchman Coal and Coke* vs. *Mitchell*.[89] *Hitchman*, which had been in the courts since 1907, grew from the claims of coal operators that the UMWA was an illegal combination in restraint of trade, with union contracts interfering with the property and contractual rights of the operators. Federal District Judge Alston Dayton of West Virginia had issued injunctions against the union, prohibiting it from organizing in some districts. Dayton's history of intransigence on labor rights frustrated some industrial and political leaders who believed the judge contributed to unstable industrial relations. In the ten-year controversy over *Hitchman*, Dayton had survived impeachment proceedings by the United States House of Representatives, ably served by his attorney John J. Cornwell. The Supreme Court finally vindicated Dayton, ruling in 1917 that the so-called yellow-dog contract used by employers, forbidding union membership by their workers, was legal. The working man was "free to join the union," said the court, but the employer was free to deny employment to any worker who exercised that freedom.[90] Overshadowed by the compulsory truce between the miners and the industrialists during the war, *Hitchman* was unleashed with a vengeance against the UMWA when the war for democracy ended (see chapters 5 and 6).

The coal operators had other friends in powerful positions. While the UMWA realized temporary membership gains during the war, coal operators redoubled their practice of combining to protect their interests. In northern West Virginia, for example, the Fairmont Coal Club organized to promote harmony among the region's coal operators. The club included representatives from practically every coal producer in the Fairmont field and would meet weekly to exchange ideas and discuss policy.[91] The coal executives, said the *Fairmont Times*, had "relegated personal desires and ambitions to the background while their country is in such dire need of their assistance." A. Brooks Fleming, Jr., production manager of the northern West Virginia section of the Fuel Administration, was active in the formation of the club.[92]

Fleming was a director of the Consolidation Coal Company and an assistant to the company's president. Son of the eighth governor of West Virginia, Fleming also served as a director of the Northern West Virginia Coal Operators Association, the Fairmont Land and Building Corporation, the National Bank of Fairmont, and many other corporate enterprises. As fuel administrator, Fleming's duty was to forward information and recommendations on coal production to the U.S. fuel administrator in Washington. Fleming and other West Virginia fuel managers often fielded charges by West Virginia miners that some state operators were engaging in "less than patriotic practices" when they sought to circumvent federally sponsored wage agreements and some raised company store prices to offset wage increases.[93] Suggestions of conflict of interest were refuted, however, by West Virginia's chief fuel administrator, J. Walter Barnes, who assured the public that the regional and county fuel administrators were "all men of high grade, and patriotic motives, and have willingly given their time to carry on the work of the Administration, and deserve thanks for their earnest labor and helpful advice."[94]

At the core of the rapid wartime expansion of America's regulatory consensus were the long-term, market-oriented principles with which political, industrial, and conservative union leaders viewed the world. Accumulation and reinvestment of capital, accomplished by the rational organization and productivity of modern industrial culture, would lead to sustained economic growth and distribution of services. To guarantee this, law, statecraft, and personal relations must conform to the dictates of the market and capitalist property relations. Economic activity thus dominated social and political spheres, and business became, says economic historian Martin Sklar, "activity that presupposes and is permeated by a complex mode of consciousness" that determined values, behavior, and status relationships. The Wilson administration's regulatory complex definitively established corporate capitalism as the most powerful element in American society, overpowering socialist and social-democratic movements.[95] According to George Creel, the war occurred at a crucial juncture for America's social and political organization, when oppositional voices to the business culture were "interpreting America from a class or sectional or selfish standpoint." If war had to come, Creel implied, at least it had come at the right moment for the preservation of American corporate ideals.[96]

John J. Cornwell and the war management bureaucracy in West Virginia were conscious of the market opportunities for West Virginia coal in the postwar world. As the governor instructed West Virginia mines to suspend operations to engage in a day of patriotic celebrations to begin the Third Liberty Loan campaign, he arranged to confer with coal associations at a special meeting in Charleston. The purpose of the meeting was to devise strategies for extending West Virginia's coal exports into South America. It would be shortsighted, the governor said, to wait until the war was over before making plans.[97] Earlier, the executive board of the West Virginia Council of Defense had warmed to the idea of the patriotic value of making a propaganda film for the West Virginia coal industry. Roughly $21,000 had been subscribed by some of the state's coal operators to produce such a film, illustrating the development of the coal industry and the mining conditions in West Virginia.[98] Informed by the producers, the Gentry Film Company of Charleston, that the movie would have "a patriotic feature illustrating how the coal industry is essential to the winning of the war," the executive board authorized the needed $4,000 from the war fund so that the picture could be exhibited in moviehouses nationwide and overseas.[99]

The rationalist ideals for the corporate model of industrial and social organization were well broadcast by the industrial, political, and educational elites in West Virginia. Editor and legislator Hugh Isaac Shott advocated the "science of man-power," which had to be coordinated "to continue our growth in industrial, agricultural, mining and manufacturing enterprises in time of universal demand. . . . The future greatness of our people will be measured by their ability and facility to adopt themselves to the new era that is dawning." Shott noted that "the time-honored system of work and wages, the established measurement of enterprise and reward are shifting, the basis of power is changing." America would realize the full measure of its power only if its people were committed to "unifying the man-power we have at home and making it efficient and potent to reorganize along the lines that advancing civilization demands." If the country failed, "some other nation will outstrip us in everything that goes to make a people prosperous and contented."[100]

4

Postwar Strategies for Promoting Industrial Americanization, Antiradicalism, and Habits of Industry

War management leaders often spoke of the importance of coordinated efforts to seize the trade, manufacturing, and commercial opportunities presented by the World War. Governor Cornwell's call to West Virginia coal operators to confer about expanding the state's coal markets into South America suggests that the governor had not lost sight of his primary goal at inauguration, that of promoting West Virginia's mineral and agricultural resources. Cornwell accurately contended that the country's war program had to a great extent depended on West Virginia's coal, gas, and oil resources, and he was determined that that status be maintained. The spirit of wartime unity should continue permanently, without "lapsing into partisan schemes and partisan wrangles." In such an environment, the state would "come into its own," and its people would be "finer and happier."[1] The integration of West Virginia coal into South American markets would, Cornwell hoped, generate favorable reciprocal trade in products such as leather, candy ingredients, cocaine, platinum, and tin from Latin American producers. These raw materials ideally would be processed in new West Virginia manufactories, allowing the state to play dynamic roles as both exporter of raw materials and manufacturer of finished goods in the world's postwar commercial reorganization.[2]

Cornwell shared in the hope that the United States would use its wealth and resources to "guide the footsteps of all nations." But the fulfillment of the nation's destiny would be played out in the context of a struggle for industrial supremacy equal in intensity to the war itself. In this struggle, many influential Americans believed the survival of the fittest applied. In the competition for world markets, victory would depend upon the commercial and industrial education provided for future generations. No nation could compete in the economic struggle whose citizens were "shiftless, inefficient, and inadequately trained and educated." A leading spokesman for the National Security League voiced the conviction of most corporate elites that business and professional men, as leaders of public opinion, should influence educational institutions to train young men and women "to market our products" worldwide.[3]

Unity of purpose was considered as essential to the impending commercial competition as it had been to the war. Historian John Higham writes that the all-encompassing nature of the Great War spawned an emotional climate wherein even slight wavering of purpose or lack of enthusiasm appeared intolerable to the cause. Only single-minded dedication to national objectives could insure that other loyalties would not conflict with the will of the nation.[4] The collective pursuit of common aims, manufactured and reinforced by the war management networks, was consistent with traditional American ideals of freedom as defined by Woodrow Wilson. Wilson defined individual freedom in terms of a piston in a well-tuned engine, which would run smoothly "not because it is left alone or isolated, but because it has been associated most skillfully and carefully with the other parts of the great structure."[5] Such an operational view of freedom and obligation, which formed the core of "one hundred per cent Americanism," equated freedom with conformity and treated as suspect any deviation from the existing social order.[6]

The ideals of the freedom of conformity had contributed by war's end to an apparent understanding in elite educational, political, and industrial circles that the world was a base and dangerous place, divided between good and evil. This dichotomous ideological premise is generally more closely associated with the post–World War II Cold War consensus, pitting "Free World ideals" versus "Marxist delusions," with the attendant destiny of the United States to disseminate free-market economic principles to the rest of the world.[7] When President Harry S. Truman said in 1947, however, that at that moment in history, "nearly every nation must choose between alternative ways of life," he was updating the sentiments of World War I military and civilian leaders.[8] Woodrow Wilson's interior secretary, Franklin K. Lane, likened the war to a holy struggle between the forces of Christ and barbarism. Secretary of War Newton D. Baker announced that the World War demanded that mankind choose between militaristic autocracy and democratic justice.[9] The continuing postwar world struggle required that Americans accept the "kinds of discipline and control" necessary to fight for world democracy.[10] A War Department spokesman told NEA delegates that a major task of education was "to assimilate the peoples of other nations" by instilling in them a democratic vision.[11] Albert Bushnell Hart believed that Americans should be somehow induced to understand their universal democratic mission, and apply wartime organizational skills to "any great national purpose."[12]

Organizing postwar society politically and socially for sustained commercial and industrial expansion required a fusion of emotional commitment to mundane principles of order, productivity, and efficiency. Accepting historian Alan Dawley's observation, as I do, that the war's corporate regulatory complex left business as the most powerful influence in American society, it is reasonable to define representatives of industrial capitalism as dominant arbiters of social norms and values. It is then important to address how business interests sought to identify their principles as American and shape the contours of public discourse and education. It is important to investigate how they went about transforming a set of ideological assumptions and economic practices into accepted cultural values that were beyond the realm of meaningful debate. The task was essentially to equate loyalty to the nation with obedience to one's employer, or, in a broader sense, to corporate capitalism. Workers were therefore often informed, as in the journal of the Consolidation Coal Company, that "Obedience helps make men truly great."[13]

The postwar campaign by business interests and organizations to mold public opinion was "a class movement, built upon the concept that the employers' interests are those of society, including its working class members."[14] This movement used methods of persuasion perfected during the Great War, entailing the conscious manipulation of the language and symbols of that conflict, patriotism, and nationalism generally. This manipulation exalted specific values and beliefs in processes of "mobilization of bias," a modern expression meaning that institutional rules and procedures operate systematically to benefit certain persons or groups at the expense of others, leaving the dominant groups in "a preferred position to defend and promote their vested interests."[15]

Business interests were not alone in appropriating the words and iconography of Americanism. Historian Gary Gerstle has shown that a preoccupation with being "American" compelled all groups interested in social or political power—including capitalists, unionists, and ethnic and religious groups—to articulate their programs in the language of Americanism. But business organizations were arguably the most successful, and had ready access to the means to disseminate a nationalist, conservative ideology of Americanization. Pro-business Americanization infiltrated industrial relations, educational institutions, and modern channels of mass media, such as movies, radio, and national magazines. The combination of these forces resulted in a pervasive national emphasis on pledging loyalty to American institutions and defining appropriate American behavior.[16]

Just as in the war effort, public education played a critical role in the transmission of national, corporate, and state goals to the public. Recognizing this, Consolidation Coal told its employees that whoever wished to promote the company's interest should use the schoolroom as a forum. Teachers were particularly well-positioned to "create a sentiment" for cooperation and business success.[17] Their experience in the war mobilization could also be applied to casting out "the rabble, the anarchists, the disturbers of industrial peace," such as "I.W.Ws., Socialists, Bolshevists, or Union of Russian Workers" sympathizers. These agitators should be "informed upon whenever and wherever they are known to exist. . . . Law and order must prevail in our land." *School and Society* encouraged teachers to watch their pupils for "incipient signs of disloyalty." In like spirit, *West Virginia School Journal* asked less than two months after the Armistice if teachers displayed "signs of Bolshevism in your school?" If so, the editors mused, Russia needed "a few thousand good school teachers." Loyal teachers, however, understood that "the true patriots and real soldiers recognize that the best way to serve the country now is to go to work with all of one's might at the routine duties of daily life."[18]

It was largely the postwar Red Scare that provided the emotional tinder to spark the transfer of passion from the Hun to less tangible, but perhaps even more fearful, suspected new threats to American security. The Bolshevik triumph in Russia inspired later European revolutionary outbreaks, and a February 1919 general strike in Seattle raised alarms that the virus of revolutionary radicalism had emigrated to the United States.[19] The premature withdrawal of Bolshevik Russia from the World War, and civil war between the Bolshevik Red Army and White forces in Siberia, had prompted the 1918 Siberian intervention by some twenty-two thousand United States and Allied forces, the first American attempt to contain communism.[20] These developments—together with the formation of the Third International, or Comintern, in March 1919, urging the world's workers to form workers' soviets—vested "even the most innocuous events" with the aura of class revolution. Attorney General A. Mitchell Palmer's raids against suspected radicals and grassroots vigilante action against proponents of tainted ideas bespoke a widespread intolerance and uncertainty in the U.S., with anti-German and anti-radical impulses so "interlocked and continuous," says John Higham, "that no date marks the end of one or the beginning of the other."[21]

Higham suggests that the Red Scare can be explained by the psychic gratification provided to millions of Americans by the war's common purpose. They simply transferred their missionary zeal to a new common adversary, reinvigorating the wartime "clamor for absolute loyalty." William Tuttle, analyzing the racial violence of 1919 in the context of international turmoil, calls the Red Scare an extension of the wartime cult of patriotism, characterized by an atmosphere of violence and a definable enemy. The flames of instability were also fanned by the rapid demobilization of American military forces at war's end. As government agencies terminated war orders, the army issued discharges at the rate of fifteen thousand per day. American industries were cutting back, shutting down, or retooling for peacetime production just as veterans glutted the labor market; the result was an unprecedented wave of strikes and lockouts, including the Seattle strike and the bitterly divisive steel strike of 1919. Fears of a proletarian revolt evoked responses similar to those directed against real or imagined German sympathizers during the war.[22]

Shortly after America entered the war, the *Wheeling Intelligencer* predicted that when peace came, the nation's voracious demand for labor would cease, requiring adjustments by workers accustomed to inflated wages. Foreshadowing a persistent theme in postwar years, the *Intelligencer* encouraged labor to exercise rigorous personal economy, so as to be "better prepared for the let down that is sure to prevail." It was, of course, imperative for postwar stability that labor exercise a "just recognition of the rights of capital."[23] The worries of the *Intelligencer* notwithstanding, United Mine Workers of America leadership and most members had no quarrel with the "just rights of capital" nor with the government's hope that the war had ushered in a new era of industrial peace, based on mutual employer-employee understanding that would build "a new world after the war."[24] Within days after the Armistice, the *United Mine Workers Journal* cautioned that every loyal American should "sit steady in the boat," that the time required "safe and sane leadership for labor in America."[25]

A gap between perception and reality appears, however, in the U.S. Labor Department's homiletic reduction of miners' concerns to big-ticket consumer items. "It is better," said the department, "for the workman to have a fur coat and automobile than not. . . . Large production will mean plenty for all, provided there is the tolerance and respect on both sides that will lead to industrial peace."[26] Such pronouncements trivialized the differences between West Virginia miners and their bosses, which led to industrial warfare in the state from 1919 to 1921 and the crippling of the United Mine Workers in West Virginia for over a decade thereafter. When southern West Virginia miners struck for union recognition in 1920, the stakes were considerably higher than a fur coat or a Model T.

Addressing the miners' pursuit of industrial justice, labor historian David Corbin attributes their solidarity largely to the government's effort to market the war. The rhetoric of sacrifice and commitment for democratic principles, says Corbin, awakened class consciousness in the miners, leading to their political education.[27] The miners' struggle for unionization in Logan and Mingo counties culminated in the "Miners March" from Kanawha County to Mingo County in the late summer of 1921. Along the route of the march, the militant miners enjoyed the help and support of many citizens not directly connected with the miners' economic concerns who sensed that the march raised questions of liberty and oppression rather than simply concerns of material comfort. Historian Ronald L. Lewis therefore contends that the march transcended labor/management conflict to encompass a "much broader struggle for democratic ideals, a conflict between freedom and tyranny, an effort to break the all-pervasive power of the coal companies, which owned two-thirds of all privately owned property in the state."[28] Corbin and Lewis, then, place the mass strikes of 1919–21, during an unprecedented period of industrial unrest, in the context not of material comfort but of a militant commitment by American workers to the ideal of freedom.[29] As such, the industrial struggle in West Virginia illuminates the ideological struggle, symbolized by miners and their bosses, to capture the meaning of true "American Ideals" in the volatile postwar climate.

Many influential West Virginians were troubled by the radical possibilities of the rhetoric of democracy. Josiah Keeley of Kayford, president of the West Virginia Coal Mining Institute, worried that coal miners who had fought the Hun or produced mightily for war purposes might take the language of democratic liberation too seriously, like the Boston worker who later declared, "We fought for democracy and got 23 cents an hour."[30] Having made the world safe for democracy, Keeley suspected that workers would turn their minds "to their old enemy, capital." If militant workers, especially those with military training, were to "take the idea of an actual emancipation so literally," isolated coal camps, devoid of effective civil authority, would become "fertile grounds for disorder."[31] Robert Armstrong, an English professor at West Virginia University, feared that the rhetoric of democracy would so arouse the hopes of the masses that power might devolve to "the hands of the selfish and vicious." Democracy then would be "not a blessing, but a curse. Democracy is a blessing only when it brings the rule of justice and righteousness."[32]

Others harbored similar fears. Colonel George S. Wallace, former state adjutant general and West Virginia's first director of Selective Service, later served with the provost marshal's staff in France. Wallace, a Virginia native, claimed in 1919 that he had changed from being a Virginian, "a Provincial, if you please—to Nationalist, and I have nothing in common with, and no sympathy for, the man who does not speak NATION." Wallace's greatest fear was a reaction against the idea of a permanent national army, and he sought a "broad military policy that will be democratic, nationwide, and under Federal control."[33] He expressed these sentiments to Clarksburg native Guy D. Goff, with whom he had served in France. Goff's chief concern was domestic labor conditions. Writing to Wallace at the peak of the 1919 steel strike, Goff could not abide workers' complaints at a time when labor was well paid and had never "enjoyed as many comforts from its earnings as it did during the late war." Goff charged "socialism, slackerism, and unionlaborism" with precipitating a "demoralization of character" by promoting wage equalization over piece-work payments and thereby encouraging like rewards for "the good, the bad and the indifferent." Only with a return to piece work, said Goff, would "the worker be taught efficiency. In no other way can the slacker and the drone be eliminated, and the waste of this great war supplied."[34]

Keely, Armstrong, Wallace, and Goff expressed guidelines for social organization consistent with those voiced earlier at the National Security League's Congress of Constructive Patriotism. In an address to that congress, H.H. Wheaton of the United States Bureau of Education affirmed that government, education, industry, and civic organizations should join forces to form a united front to "Americanize America" under the rubric of "Industrial Americanization." Wheaton announced that the ideals of industrial Americanization were embodied in the slogan "America First," meaning "America efficient," "America before social and industrial justice," and "America for humanity." Finally, industrial Americanization meant "allegiance to a common plan, to a common country."[35] John J. Cornwell, Morris P. Shawkey, and Jesse Sullivan attended one of several national Americanization conferences, sponsored by Wheaton's Bureau of Education, in April 1918, joining delegates from nearly all state councils of defense, commercial and industrial leaders, and educators.[36]

Industrial Americanization included assumptions that economic and social health depended on favorable working and living conditions, merit pay increases, and rewards for efficiency for industrial workers. Employer responsibility for proper housing and plant conditions in industrial communities would reduce turnover and guarantee employee loyalty. Efficient production, standardization of the working force, and plant organization, all key elements of the industrial mechanism, were to be the responsibility of professional engineers, described as the "most important factor" in the industrial equation. These experts in plant management, employee training, housing, and industrial organization, or "social engineers," as described by Wheaton, "hold the key in industry to successful Americanization."[37]

Industrial Americanization as defined in the postwar era therefore embraced the principles of scientific management, promoted by Frederick Winslow Taylor early in the twentieth century. Driving Taylor's philosophy was the dictum, "In the past the man has been first; in the future the system must be first."[38] "Taylorism" influenced the war managers of the regulatory consensus, who then sought to expand the unity and efficiency of the mobilization to the postwar social and economic order. The reorganization of work and social relations that accompanied the expansion of industrial capitalism gave rise to Taylor's theories of efficient industrial organization and control, which proponents believed would "reconcile labor and capital under a 'government of facts and law.'"[39] Taylor envisioned the application of his principles of industrial efficiency to society in general, including home and farm management, churches, universities, and government agencies.[40]

Scientific management's social application would extend factory control over "ever-wider ranges of external variables." One enthusiast proclaimed "our plain duty and opportunity to build up our economic and social order on scientific principles."[41] The scientific reorganization of the factory, the corporation, the government bureau, and the school would, in Taylor's words, benefit the "whole people."[42] Once workers had undergone a "complete mental revolution," which secured their acceptance of the scientific method in the workplace, business would enjoy a rise in profits, labor a rise in wages, and consumers access to more goods. Taylor's use of daily performance slips, standardized tasks, and unit time studies would lead workers through evolutionary stages of industrial efficiency, finally reaching optimal production. Complete efficiency of the workplace, said Taylor, meant that each worker would have to adapt to new standards, covering details of job performance "which in the past have been left to his individual judgement." Especially in routine work, workers' capabilities should be barely equal to the job's requirements. Workers' contentment would reign when their scientifically determined abilities yielded the largest possible financial return.[43]

David Montgomery writes that while many corporate leaders were somewhat skeptical of the claims of universal social application in Taylor's theories, most generally agreed with the *New Republic*'s conclusion that "Mr. Taylor and his followers have made a major contribution to civilization," and incorporated the basic thrust of scientific management into their ideals of organization.[44] Taylor's emphasis on management of industry by neutral experts was well-matched to *New Republic*-style progressvism, which sought to eliminate the deficiencies of American industrial society without revolutionizing the social institutions and values the progressives held dear.[45] The tenets of Taylorism were woven throughout the fabric of American progressivism, perhaps most explicitly in the presumption of neutrality and "exact knowledge" based on the reorganization of "facts." The facts that drove the engine of Taylorism were politically charged, however, based on value judgments assuming that managers, business leaders, and economic elites knew what was best for all social classes, and that some people were justly empowered to control the work and social experiences of others.[46]

Taylor forecast a well-ordered factory system overseen by a benign management hierarchy, where the interests of the company and the worker were identical. Likewise, Walter Lippmann of the *New Republic*, a leading intellect of progressive social engineering, envisioned the impartial management of society by "a specialized class whose personal interests reach beyond the locality." This class would guide the mass of American citizens, most of whom were "mentally children or barbarians," unqualified to envision the nation's common interests. Political decisions were the concern of a few decision-makers, whose "exact and objective" verdicts would serve the common social goals of material well-being and political freedom.[47] Madison Grant's influential 1916 racial exegesis spoke in similar terms, when Grant declared that a true republic represented the interests of the whole community only when governance was left to "those best qualified by antecedents, character and education, in short, of experts."[48]

To its proponents, Lippmann's elitist concept of social management was democratic, since responsible leaders or experts would so inform the masses as to guide them to reasonable judgments. Lippmann employed the expression "manufacture of consent" to describe the guidance of ordinary citizens by dispensers of relevant facts.[49] Through educative processes democratic in form if not in substance, the masses would internalize presuppositions about social organization compatible with the experts' vision. Edward L. Bernays used a similar expression, the "engineering of consent," which was borrowed by historian William Graebner for his 1987 analysis of democracy and authority in twentieth-century America.[50] In terms of public policy, Bernays identified Lippmann's leadership class as "an invisible government," an enlightened minority to whom Bernays attributed the progress, development, and public good of the nation. The public, said Bernays, could only understand and act upon new ideas through the "active energy of the intelligent few."[51] Graebner points out that Bernays sought to integrate the profession of public relations into a general social theory and shared with Lippmann a critique of democracy that sought to establish an intelligent social consensus by using group process techniques generated by the social sciences. Bernays and Lippmann each emphasized the role of leadership, using terminology that obscured the distinction between persuasion and coercion. Bernays made this point succinctly when he said, "Advocacy of what we believe in is education. The advocacy of what we don't believe in is propaganda."[52]

These comments imply that the intertwined social and industrial missions of scientific management rested upon a structure of domination and control. In mass industry, management science extended the managers' control over worker autonomy, using avowedly neutral facts to make hierarchical power appear objective and rational and reducing adult workers to factors of production.[53] At an earlier stage of human development, business, political, and educational institutions also sought to apply Lippmann's ideals of the specialized class and Bernays's intelligent few. These interlocking sectors combined forces to insure that each American child, in order to develop "along the line of its special capacity," learn "habits of industry." If children absorbed "grit, persistency, pluck, determination, fearlessness" in the formative years, the nation would benefit from the predictable development of the future skilled producer.[54]

These views shaped educational opinion and policy at state and local levels. Joseph F. Marsh, secretary of the West Virginia Board of Education, told state teachers gathered in 1919 that it was their chief professional duty to attend to the vocational needs of the "ninety-six in each hundred who must do the main work of the world." He later insisted that West Virginia boys and girls must "be taught to view the world as it is and plan to enter upon some work suited to their training and talents that needs to be done," and that the state must also "use profitably the idle hours and brains of our army of young workers."[55] Defining the nation's children as the capital of civilization, the West Virginia Board of Education identified the duty of schools to train them to "contribute intelligently to the fundamental needs of human welfare: production, exchange, and wise consumption."[56] True Americanism, said West Virginia Superintendent of Schools Morris P. Shawkey, was grounded in order and efficiency. "No agency can do its part in this great work," said Shawkey, "better than the public schools."[57]

These statements reveal a common desire among professionals such as Shawkey and Marsh to regulate social and industrial relations on the basis of values common to middle-class men and women. Shawkey and Marsh were educators but shared social, political, and economic assumptions with a wide range of white-collar workers comprising a self-conscious social class, who "interpreted the job of industrializing the land as their mission" and sought to transmit their values and influence to the larger population.[58] The middle-class individual required a reliable institutional system, based on "the partitioning of space and the scheduling of time." In a well-ordered environment, one was limited only by his lack of ambition and determination. The ambitious citizen who took full advantage of opportunities could expect an ever-rising standard of material consumption, which would continue to rise for his children. At the core of the middle-class ideology was the conviction that economic growth and social progress would flourish only with the preservation of "obedience to the law, order, and conventions necessary for stable civilization."[59]

Those who considered themselves middle-class absorbed corporate standards for the development of a continental economy.[60] Modern educators such as Shawkey and Marsh tailored their principles to fit the production demands of American capitalist expansion and investment in anticipated postwar markets. In so doing, they implicitly agreed to shape laws, customs, and the people's thinking to the requirements of corporate capitalism. Woodrow Wilson described this accommodation in evolutionary terms, noting that laws originally applied to the business of individuals must be adjusted to business done by "great combinations," to assist the country's material development. Domestic and foreign corporate expansion eventually marginalized many middle-class businesses, relegating them to subordinate, peripheral economic roles, but in the postwar years, progressive educators and other professionals supported the belief that large-scale corporate-industrial capitalism, with its required regimentation, was indispensable to the nation's development.[61] The canon of rationalization of the shop floor and the classroom was therefore cast onto the domestic and international political economy, avowedly to benefit the whole people.

Morris P. Shawkey believed that educational leaders were positioned to match West Virginia's impending commercial development, which had been enhanced by wartime productivity, with educational progress. Shawkey agreed with West Virginia's rural school supervisor, L.F. Hanifan, that the efficiency displayed by the schools in "carrying forward the program of the Government" for war purposes could be as effective in peace as in war.[62] As superintendent of schools, Shawkey steered the postwar centralization of educational administration, resulting in a structure of unified control that state educational leaders had long advocated. In 1919 the legislature abolished the state board of regents, the state board of education, the state book commission, and the state vocational board in favor of a seven-member bipartisan state board of education, with the superintendent elected by popular vote and the six other officers appointed by the governor.[63] Shawkey wrote that the 1919 school code assigned all educational affairs of the state, from the kindergarten to the state university, to the new West Virginia State Board of Education. The board had authority over teacher training in private and denominational as well as public institutions, established standards for courses of study, and had broad powers to determine and direct educational policy in the state. In twelve years as state school superintendent, Shawkey, says James Morton Callahan, brought to West Virginia schools a "master mind for organization" and directed the educational energies of the people in a manner that "inspired confidence and forward looking everywhere."[64]

Centralization in West Virginia reflected broader national trends toward consolidation and collective corporate practices in education, part of what Shawkey's biographer describes as a general movement toward concentration of school power in state hands.[65] In the prewar decades school boards, especially in urban areas, became battlegrounds between elite domination and competing community-based Socialist, populist, and ethnic reform groups. In these struggles, school boards often became the "dominion" of businessmen and professionals, and boards of education behaved much like corporate boards of directors, delegating blanket authority to recognized experts such as superintendents. When war came, the Wilson administration, patriotic organizations, and many pro-war Americans viewed public schools as instruments of national defense and preparedness. Educational historian William J. Reese demonstrates that the hysteria of the war years mortally wounded many nonelite or antiwar challengers to business domination of school systems. Patriotic citizens exercised a "blatant abuse of power" by using school facilities and personnel to chill free speech, abolish training in foreign languages, and conduct "an aggressive witch hunt for German sympathizers" among teaching staffs.[66]

School systems emerged from the war crisis as more than ever the object of class-determined administrative reforms wrought by the powerful influence of businessmen, industrialists, and their professional allies on local and state school boards or in school administration.[67] Shawkey could report by 1928 that the modifications of recent years had left West Virginia with "a good school organization. The system is fairly well centralized." He contended that although centralization might appear undemocratic, "the policy has resulted in greater economy and higher efficiency, which means more to the people than the mere forms of democracy."[68]

In 1907, early in his professional career, Shawkey had founded *The Educator*, a privately owned and published journal of educational affairs, published at Charleston. The purpose of the journal was to reach "the masses and the teachers" with suitable news, editorials, and discussion. From this forum, Shawkey successfully campaigned for the state superintendent's office. *The Educator* merged with another private educational journal, *The School Journal*, in 1915, with publication of *The School Journal and Educator* at Morgantown. The journal remained a private operation until 1921–22, after Shawkey had left the superintendency, when it was renamed the *West Virginia School Journal* (herein WVSJ from 1915 on), and became an affiliated publication of the West Virginia Department of Education. Edited at this point by Superintendent George M. Ford and state board of education secretary Joseph F. Marsh, the *WVSJ* was acquired as the official publication of the West Virginia Education Association of teachers in 1923.[69]

From the merger in 1915 until 1921, Shawkey shared editorial duties on the *School Journal* with Dr. Robert A. Armstrong and managing editor Dr. Waitman Barbe. Barbe, former managing editor (1889–95) of the Parkersburg *Daily State Journal*, was one of West Virginia's leading academic propagandists during the war years. A graduate of Harvard and Oxford and an accomplished poet as well as teacher, Barbe directed the West Virginia University summer school from 1910 until shortly before his death in 1925, and he was president of the West Virginia Education Association in 1917–18. Hailed as a "distinguished educator and literary man" and as "one of nature's noblemen," Barbe wrote "Stars of Gold," praised as "one of the best poems produced as a result of the World War," which he introduced in Commencement Hall at WVU on March 6, 1919, and read on many public occasions later. In 1924, the *West Virginia Review* noted that Barbe reached "heights sublime and exquisite when he lauds the boys who left their halls of learning and took their places in the ranks, never to return again."[70]

Barbe often applied his poetic and oratorical talents to the state and national "educational readjustment" that marked the early postwar years. He told delegates to the 1919 West Virginia Education Association meeting at Fairmont that a great campaign was under way in West Virginia, led by Shawkey and his assistants, whom Barbe described as "leaders in the cause of civic righteousness." The goal of the educational campaign, carried on in every schoolhouse, was a "truer and more intelligent Americanism." Barbe offered thanks that John Cornwell, endowed with fearless Americanism, occupied the governor's office rather than "a spineless politician or a tainted Bolshevist." He expressed similar confidence in Shawkey and the state board of education. "Who can over-estimate the power that lies in the hands of these seven excellent men under the new Code? All power is theirs; may theirs likewise be all wisdom. We are in the hands of our leaders."[71]

Anticipating Walter Lippmann, Barbe declared that of one hundred million Americans, only a few, "by the proper development of native gifts," were qualified to "lead the rest of us in the multifarious paths of progress." He cautioned, however, that native ability would bring wise leadership only if the gifted themselves were properly educated. He warned that "sinister and diabolic" men such as Samuel Gompers of the American Federation of Labor, John L. Lewis of the UMWA, and William Haywood of the Industrial Workers of the World were gifted leaders, but their actions threatened "to wreck our Constitution." Their words instilled false knowledge and purpose in the ignorant masses, who "follow where the keen and conscienceless leaders go." The intentions of such false prophets must be conquered by leaders driven by "Christian education." Only such great men, said Barbe, could "lead and guide the wavering, struggling masses of mankind up the rough mountain of life."[72]

Barbe's vocations as professor and poet did not detract him from a conviction that the natural and industrial resources of West Virginia must be exploited by workers with practical industrial education. Only then would "our crude material" contribute to "the higher things of civilization as well as to individual wealth."[73] Barbe probably did not intend that schoolchildren, rather than gas, coal, and oil, be identified as "crude material" for the industrial system, but the irony of the metaphor is unavoidable.

Another commentator on the goals of education in West Virginia noted the factor of production role for schoolchildren and elaborated on Woodrow Wilson's piston analogy of human potential in a 1919 *WVSJ* column. Philip M. Conley—later editor of *West Virginia Review*, historian of the West Virginia coal industry, and managing director of the American Constitutional Association (see chapters 6–8)—wrote that the "business of a school" was to train children that happiness and contentment were the rewards of hard work. Conley told teachers that each child required individual treatment, just as the parts of an automobile required special treatment when in need of adjustment. To successfully run a car, Conley wrote, "you must learn the function of each lever."[74]

Educators' belief in the virtues of industrial education, such as thrift, sobriety, hard work, and obedience, were well-suited to the industrialists' desire for close ties between education and the demands of the market.[75] Only with systematic training would the rank and file "outputs" of the schools prove reliable, resourceful, industrious citizens.[76] Employers agreed with educators that preparing boys and girls for industrial and commercial work in school would adapt them to the market environment. It was the task of the school, said Phil Conley, to shape "the attitude of the boy toward his future work." An industrial welfare director remarked that since "production is the big word in most industrial establishments," future workers must be trained to "produce the goods." Schools must help the nascent industrial worker attain the right mental traits "to adjust himself to his work." Industrial training in school should emphasize accuracy rather than speed, "but if quick thinking can be stimulated in school work it will pave the way for the final development of the future skilled producer."[77] Even kindergarten children should learn industry, loyalty, patriotism, and other social virtues essential to American "political and social industrial democracy."[78]

Many West Virginia business leaders looked approvingly on the emerging modern standards for American industrial leadership as described at the 1921 session of the West Virginia Coal Mining Institute, an association of coal operators, directors, and managers. The participants agreed that industrial leaders must personally solve problems of productivity, efficiency, and labor militancy. They should assume control much as the anonymous mine superintendent who read the newspaper to his men, in order to "place the true interpretation on the news." Working hand-in-hand with the public school system, "the men in responsible positions will be expected to be the interpreters."[79]

Throughout America, the interpreters from business, industry, and education organized the educational state to guide the nation's youth toward their social destiny.[80] Joseph Marsh proclaimed that West Virginia schools, under the guidance of a committee of educators, had joined a nationwide movement to "point our boys and girls to the gateway leading to their most appropriate avenue of service." To the 95 percent of West Virginia students who were not destined for professional occupations, teachers imparted "more drill on the facts needed to back up our theories and practices in government and in life."[81] Marsh's statements echo those of educator G.F. Arps in *School and Society*. National integrity, said Arps, demanded that every youth be habituated, from early childhood, to profitable employment. No capable hand or brain should avoid sharing in the nation's work, or America would falter "in the international struggle for supremacy."[82]

The organization of the educational state was built on a political as well as an economic foundation. Alternative visions to the politics of capitalism were overwhelmed in the postwar era, and the struggle for commercial dominance compelled powerful policymakers at state and national levels to interpret "industrial Americanization" not only as a model for social organization but as the antidote to Bolshevism, or any other un-American doctrines. The National Security League propelled its type of authoritarian Americanization into the Red Scare. "The battle to make the country safe is not won," a league spokesman announced. "The enemy but wears a different guise."[83]

The crusade to withstand radicalism infused West Virginia educators with renewed zeal. F.R. Yoke told elementary school teachers at the 1919 WVEA meeting that as captains in the world's greatest army, that of twenty-two million schoolchildren, they must "get ready for the front" of service to the nation. Above all, the teacher should teach that law and order must be supreme and inculcate in their students "a loathing for that thing which is the antithesis of law and order—Bolshevism." At the same meeting, educator E.F. Scaggs raised a persistent nagging obstacle to the efficient organization of the public for postwar commercial advancement, a problem brought into sharper focus by the war and the consequent suspicion of alien political doctrines. For years, Skaggs declared, America had been collecting an "undigested mass" of foreign-born immigrants, too many of whom retained their language and customs and "associated only with their own class." With the outbreak of the World War, "we found a dangerous element in our midst, who had no sympathy with our Government, our institutions, and our ideals, and only the most drastic laws prevented them from doing much harm."[84]

Skaggs's address to the WVEA revealed the ambivalence with which many middle-class Americans regarded the nation's ethnic populations. While Skaggs voiced suspicion of the approximately sixty thousand foreign-born in West Virginia, he also asked whether America had truly been a land of liberty, equality, and justice for its immigrants. He endorsed unified compulsory education for all Americans, warning that insufficient national training in English, safety, health, and the ideals of American institutions would result in drastic episodes such as the 1919 steel strike[85] (see chapter 5, below).

Skaggs's ambivalence about the immigrant population was not uncommon. Pre–World War commentary on immigrant populations in the state often reflected the racially biased, paternalistic yet generally benign attitudes toward the foreign-born typical of progressive ideals of Americanization. Prewar programs to socialize immigrants, however interventionist in cultural terms, were designed to provide passage out of poverty and into roles as loyal, industrious domestic and industrial operatives. Patriotic and voluntary associations such as the Daughters of the American Revolution and the Young Men's Christian Association assumed the formidable job of schooling immigrants in behavior and principles deemed appropriate by middle-class Americanizers.[86] The West Virginia's Woman's Christian Temperance Union affirmed that large-scale Americanization, combining the efforts of the WCTU, universities, the United States Chamber of Commerce, and other institutions, must be carried to the factory and the home. To eliminate foreign "colonies" through teaching of "American ideas," a "large army of tactful, well-trained women" should train immigrant women in their homes, and join with others to educate industrial workers in the workplace. To dedicated Americanizers, the benevolent purposes of their crusade was grounded in the middle-class principle that the social forces that were reshaping America must be controlled through legislation and education. Leading Americanizer Frances Kellor summarized their mission when she declared that nation building would entail "a deliberate formative process," not a haphazard arrangement.[87]

Early West Virginia Americanizers taught that since foreign immigrants came with no concept of responsible self-government, it was the obligation of the "most purely Anglo-Saxon element" in "the Appalachian strain" to steer immigrants toward responsible American citizenship. Coal and railroad baron Thomas Nelson Page told the 1910 meeting of the West Virginia Mining Association, held in Washington, that while the foreign-born population in the Appalachians was minimal, foreigners would be forever a "disorganizing element" unless assimilated by the indigenous people of the region, "who are of pure American blood." Page told the assembled coal men that they were responsible for "fusing [immigrants] into your own kind, and of uplifting them."[88]

Americanizers agreed that the amalgamation of immigrants into the "American race" was crucial to stability and order, especially since "it would appear that the foreigners violate law more than our own people." West Virginia Tax Commissioner Frederick O. Blue contended in 1916 that from the "mass of ignorance and prejudice" germinating in "these outlanders" grew the ranks of the Industrial Workers of the World and kindred radical organizations. Blue argued that the foreigner must understand he would be accepted if he respected the law and agreed to conform to American ideals and American institutions. If, however, he embraced the ideals and institutions of other nations, "then there is no place for him in America." Blue warned that the immigrants' exaggerated ideas of liberty upon arriving in America would cause them to interpret liberty as license, leading to irresponsible behavior and loss of respect for law and authority. To avoid the chaos of lawlessness, Americanizers sought to implant in immigrants and their children, Anglo-Saxon ideals of government, law, and order.[89]

Internalized elite assumptions about Anglo-Saxon superiority surfaced more virulently among Americanizers during the war crisis, interwoven with the anti-radicalism that carried into the postwar Red Scare. The generally humane values that guided the early Americanization movement were over-whelmed by more coercive impulses that had always shaped its ambiguity. The war, says historian Otis Graham, resolved the ambiguity as the con-formist tendencies of 100 percent Americanism dominated the "permissive, humanitarian side," turning Americanization in a reactionary direction.[90] Americanizers never completely abandoned humanitarian sympathy for aliens. Their sentiments, however, underwent "subtle but profound" changes, as Americanization merged with the preparedness, mobilization, and 100 per-cent Americanism crusades that shaped the political culture of the postwar era. By threat and rhetoric, 100 percent Americanizers launched a "frontal as-sault" on foreign influences in American life, rooted in "unquestioning rever-ence for existing American institutions," culminating in the restrictive immigration legislation passed by Congress in 1921 and 1924.[91]

The equation between radicalism and nativist hysteria, which accom-panied the Americanization shift, says John Higham, grew partly from a tra-ditional American assumption that militant discontent was a thoroughly foreign importation, that, as Frederick Blue stated, "there is no need for a man to be anarchistic to succeed here." This assumption was often articu-lated during the war, as when Hungarian miners in West Virginia were as-sured that they would not be interned or fired if they demonstrated their good will by working steadily and quietly for American war aims.[92] The Na-tional Security League warned, however, that immigrant workers' passivity did not necessarily indicate loyalty among ethnic groups. True Americaniza-tion must reach the "hordes of children" of immigrant parents who have "never in their lives felt the thrill of patriotism . . . and who bring us the di-vided allegiance of the hyphenated American. Such parents are little likely to inspire their children with that love of country which leads men to lay down their lives gladly in its defense." After the war, the league continued its militant Americanization drive, demanding that every good American must protect national security, law, liberty, and progress. Before 1917, the league announced, "Americanization work was philanthropy. Now it is a plain busi-ness of citizenship."[93]

Soon after the war, more than eleven hundred businesses, the Federal Bureau of Education, the Department of the Interior, the Federal Bureau of Naturalization, and a network of community-based organizations carried on Americanization programs.[94] Frances Kellor was perhaps the most ambi-tious architect of Americanization. To break up immigrants' identification with their native ethnic groups, she enlisted corporate supporters in the Inter-Racial Council, whose major Americanization tactic entailed seizing control of the foreign-language press.[95] Kellor sought not to abolish the foreign-language press but to make it pro-American and thereby to facilitate the assimilation process of immigrant groups. Proper use of foreign language newspapers would "get the right ideas about American business and American life and American opportunities before these people" and undercut the appeal of political and economic radicalism. Her corporate supporters secured for Kellor the presidency of the American Association of Foreign Language Newspapers, which handled all advertising in the ethnic papers. "We have taken over the Association," Kellor reported to the National Association of Manufacturers (NAM). "We want to sell you industrial Americanization as a business proposition." Kellor maintained that if seven-tenths of the advertising in foreign-language papers could be made "American instead of foreign, we will begin to get, without any suggestion on our part, pro-American editorials and pro-American news." Kellor told an appreciative NAM audience that this was a "perfectly practical pro-American way of reaching the foreign-language group."[96]

Control of advertising revenues enabled the Inter-Racial Council to inundate foreign-language editorials and news stories with antiradical propaganda. Other propaganda bureaus, such as the America First Publicity Association, filled the country's English newspapers with the litany of industrial Americanization. The Huntington *Herald-Dispatch* often carried the association's half- or full-page advertisements, including one in 1920 announcing that "incoming masses" must be "sterilized in accordance with Uncle Sam's new formula" or face deportation. American labor especially must be protected from "the contaminating influence of Bolshevism and its vicious kin." The true American workman would reject the unscrupulous agitation that accompanied such doctrines, which endangered "the first real opportunity to win the markets of the world for American industry."[97]

In West Virginia, women's clubs, civic groups, trade associations, local boards of education, and patriotic societies joined with the educational establishment in promoting "100 per cent Americanism." Josiah Keeley, president of the West Virginia Coal Mining Institute, summarized the sentiments of most Americanizers when he declared that Americanizing the foreign-born was not sufficient. Trouble in the coal industry, said Keeley, was largely the result of foreigners "following a very few un-American Americans." He emphasized that the task ahead "was to Americanize some of our very un-American Americans." As far as foreigners were concerned, another coal operator claimed, "we need to give the foreigner an American outlook, to let him gradually absorb Americanism without knowing it," to be "inoculated" with "our Americanization."[98]

The inoculation process required a cooperative effort between business, industry, government, and the school system. Morris P. Shawkey agreed that no agency was better suited to the teaching of true patriotism than the schools but that other civic agencies should join educators in teaching the ideals of Americanism. Shawkey emphasized the contribution of wartime mobilization tactics to strategies of Americanization, noting that the "many war campaigns have trained us well in methods of getting action in any cause of general importance." He pledged the support of West Virginia educators in the national Bureau of Education's national Americanization campaign. Shawkey issued a program and song book for West Virginia's 1919 teacher training institutes, subtitled "All of West Virginia 100% American," in which he warned that the nation's deficiencies, including the presence of internal foreign colonies and lack of respect for authority, might escalate dangerously unless teachers could "make America safe by the effective teaching of true Americanism." Therefore, the 1919 summer teacher institutes would focus on the West Virginia campaign for Americanism and industrial Americanization.[99]

Shawkey's plans for the Americanization training of West Virginia teachers reflected nationwide attempts by school administrators, industrialists, and legislators to combat the domestic uncertainties of the postwar order. Lawmakers across the country anxiously approved sweeping laws to resist the perceived threats of Bolshevism and other ideologies at odds with industrial capitalism. The scope of "Bolshevism," however, broadened to include practically all social criticism, and business and educational organizations collaborated to resist perceived subversive ideas of all kinds.[100] In postwar America, dissent in all forms, says Otis Graham, was considered revolutionary and intolerable, and the climate of "credulous complacency" which fed reaction persisted into the 1920s.[101] Elite Americanizers took note of the success of the wartime federal sedition laws, which had succeeded in destroying antiwar and antidraft resistance, as well as the strength of Socialist antiwar political candidates, in some regions of the country.[102] The middle-class Americanizers were determined to head off any burgeoning Americanization movement "from the bottom up." Acculturation based on the institutions of a maturing working class, emphasizing interethnic cooperation to achieve workers' solidarity, was alarming to the orderly vision of the industrial Americanizers. Working-class consciousness, articulated on the shop floor, through independent labor unions or radical political organizations, threatened to arm workers with alternatives to the pyramidal social structure accepted as natural by most employers, civic organizations, and governments. It represented an intolerable deviation from middle-class Americanism.[103]

West Virginia joined several other states in legislative attempts to criminalize dissent, the most prominent example in the immediate postwar period being the 1919 flag bill. Within a few days after the outbreak of the February general strike in Seattle, Monongalia County delegate William S. John, author of the wartime Compulsory Work Law, sponsored a bill to promote the state's and nation's ideals, institutions, and government and "prohibit the teaching of doctrines and display of flags antagonistic to the form or spirit of their constitutions and laws." The bill proscribed "unlawful methods of terrorism" for economic or political purposes, or for "the overthrow of organized society." The act forbade the display of any red or black flag or "any other flag, emblem, device or sign of any nature whatever" that implied opposition to the government, institutions, or ideals of West Virginia or the United States. Any person violating these provisions, or speaking, printing, or communicating in any fashion sympathies antagonistic to American ideals and institutions "now or hereafter existing" under the U.S. and West Virginia constitutions, would be guilty of a misdemeanor. A first conviction could bring a fine of one hundred to five hundred dollars and/or one year in the county jail. A second offense was treated as a felony and could bring a term of one to five years in the state penitentiary.[104]

The wave of legislation to compel social and political conformity was supplementary, however, to the omnipresent public relations ventures by the specialized classes to protect their interests. John Higham accurately points out that the postwar Americanization movement, even among many of the most vigilant 100 per cent Americanizers, was primarily "a venture in persuasion," in which "the force of law was ancillary to that of propaganda." Frances Kellor understood this when she sought control of the foreign language press.[105] The Committee on Public Information had demonstrated the importance of coordinating propaganda and flooding channels of communication with facts that amounted to officially approved information, and, as Shawkey implied earlier, these lessons were not lost on policymakers.[106]

As labor-management struggles rent the West Virginia coal industry in 1919–21, many of the state's political, business, educational, and civic leaders mobilized to insure that their vision of a well-ordered industrial system in the state would prevail. The Americanization of West Virginia merged with national campaigns to disable organized labor, implement management-dominated programs of "welfare capitalism," and create a national consciousness founded on law and order, the sanctity of private property, preindustrial ideals of individual contracts, and nationalistic economic expansionism. In this struggle, just as in the wartime campaigns, the battle for hearts and minds depended on the successful manipulation of information. First in the context of industrial conflict and then with strategies for the universal application of their ideological model, West Virginia's industrial Americanizers embraced that struggle.

5

The Political Culture of the Red Scare in West Virginia, 1919–1921

The February 1919 general strike in Seattle was begun by thirty-five thousand shipyard workers over wages and cost-of-living issues. They sought and received support from the Seattle Central Labor Council. Soon more than one hundred Industrial Workers of the World and American Federation of Labor union locals joined in a citywide strike. The mayor of Seattle, Ole Hanson, described the peaceful five-day general strike as "the weapon of revolution, all the more dangerous because quiet." Hanson deputized twenty-four hundred men, and the United States government sent nearly a thousand sailors and marines to put down the strike, which was followed by raids and arrests of Seattle Socialists and IWW members.[1]

The Seattle strike was one major event in a national postwar wave of labor unrest involving more than four million American workers. Boston's police struck for union recognition. Massachusetts textile workers went out. Railroad workers promoted government ownership of the railroads under a comprehensive proposal drafted by attorney Glenn Plumb.[2] In September 1919, more than two thousand UMWA delegates met in Cleveland and, with acting president John L. Lewis's reluctant acquiescence, passed a resolution for nationalization of the coal industry. At the Cleveland convention, facing left-radical insurgents and pressure from rank-and-file miners caught between rising consumer prices and wages frozen at October 1917 levels by the Washington Agreement, Lewis authorized a strike for November 1, which was settled only with the direct intervention of Woodrow Wilson.[3] Shortly after the UMWA Cleveland convention, more than three hundred thousand AFL steelworkers went on strike to organize the steel industry. The strike was directed by twenty-four craft unions forming the National Committee for Organizing Iron and Steel Workers, guided by former IWW member and future American Communist party leader, William Z. Foster.[4]

The steel strike resumed the bitter conflict, which had been suspended during the war, between employers and workers over employees' rights to collective bargaining. Although they usually acknowledged a worker's individual right to union membership in the abstract, industrialists in coal and steel embraced the preindustrial fiction that individual contracts between worker and employer remained the natural basis for labor-management relations. Industry's nonrecognition of unions as bargaining agents, the core of the open-shop doctrine, clashed violently in the postwar era with labor's conviction that collective bargaining should be a basic guarantee of employment.[5] Alarmed by the advances toward collective bargaining under the trusteeship of the War Labor Policies Board, industrial leaders like Judge Elbert Gary of United States Steel, now free of wartime restraints, were determined to roll back the union movement. Refusing even to meet with leaders of the steelworkers union, Gary explained that "it has been my policy, and the policy of our corporation, not to deal with union labor leaders. . . . we do not believe in contracting with unions." Gary, according to labor historian David Brody, was irrevocably committed to the employer's right not to deal with unions, regardless of the wishes of his employees.[6]

Brody notes that the steel industry, beneficiary of five years of war profits, could have indefinitely withstood even a total shutdown of production. In conference with Henry Clay Frick of U.S. Steel, John D. Rockefeller learned that the corporation was prepared to close down every one of its mills if necessary to break the strike, and to follow this strategy "at any cost." The steel strikers' organizing efforts, incapable of exerting sufficient economic pressure to break down management's resolve to save the open shop, were doomed once steelmakers perfected a means to crush the strike. The major strategy hit upon by the steelmakers was to attack the patriotic loyalty of the strikers, making the steel strike a focal point of the postwar Red Scare. U.S. Steel's company publications defined the strike as one of Americanism vs. Bolshevism, and the company advised its employees to "Keep America busy, and prosperous, and American. Go back to work." Judge Gary acknowledged that U.S. Steel often employed "secret-service men to ascertain facts and conditions," and other companies also revealed their use of undercover agents. Strikers, compelled to defend their own Americanism, surely agreed with the claim of one steelworker that by industry standards, a man could not be "a loyal American unless he is a scab . . . unless you give up all the rights your country gives you and obey your employer."[7]

The influence of political radicalism on the strike organization, while far short of the darkly apocalyptic vision of some industrialists, helped Gary and other steel magnates cast mass unionism as a threat to property and order. William Z. Foster's IWW past was proof enough to many that the strikers were infested with revolutionary radicalism. Foster's prominence as a strike leader alienated much of the conservative AFL leadership, but his organizing and mobilization skills were invaluable, and the goals of the strike were consistent with AFL trade-union principles. Samuel Gompers had advised against the strike but was overruled by younger, more militant union activists. Once the strike began, Gompers and other conservatives were compelled to defend Foster or turn him out and tacitly acknowledge that charges of his un-Americanism were true. West Virginia steelmaker E.T. Weir concluded that Gompers's tolerance of Foster proved that the old leader "has lost his grip and that the AFL is in the hands of the extremely radical element."[8] Weir, president of Weirton Steel Company, told Governor John J. Cornwell that the steel strike was an attempted revolution, carried out by radical socialists who "see it as a great opportunity to overthrow law and order." Weir claimed that the strike was directed by foreigners in disregard of "all legitimate authority." It was time, Weir said, that all "law-abiding, intelligent people of this country stand together" and prove to the radical element that Americans would not tolerate any Bolshevism or anarchy.[9]

Cornwell followed developments in the steel strike with foreboding, worried as was Weir by rumors that thousands of striking steelworkers, across the Ohio River from Weirton in Steubenville, Ohio, planned to march into West Virginia and shut down the Weirton Steel works. Weir contended that the entire city of Steubenville and the sheriff of Jefferson County, Ohio, were dominated by radical strikers.[10] Cornwell was not comforted by Frank Wilson, the Steubenville district secretary of the National Committee for Organizing Iron and Steel Workers. Wilson described the committee's mission to organize Weirton Steel as peaceful in intent, but he advised Cornwell to send investigators to Weirton to apprise the conditions of workers at Weir's plants. "This company has set up a monarchy," said Wilson, "such as we believe exists in no part of the U.S. except in Hancock County, West Virginia."[11] Cornwell wired Ohio Governor James M. Cox, requesting that his Democratic neighbor look into the potential "invasion" by Ohio strikers. "Any such effort," Cornwell warned, "will be regarded as an attack on the sovereignty of West Virginia." Cox wired the West Virginia governor that he was taking precautions against foreign-dominated mob action, confidentially assuring Cornwell that he was ordering a regiment of Ohio National Guardsmen to stand at the ready.[12] Sheriff A.S. Cooper of Hancock County wired Cornwell that Weir's plants, which briefly suspended production, would go back on line in spite of "danger of interference largely by foreign elements." Cooper requested that Cornwell send at least fifteen to twenty state police to Weirton to discourage militant overtures by Steubenville radicals. Cox's intervention, through the agency of the president of the Ohio Federation of Labor, halted the planned demonstration in Weirton.[13]

Although the march to Weirton never materialized, it was for just such an exigency that Cornwell had endured a bitter struggle with organized labor to create the West Virginia Department of Public Safety, or State Police, during a special 1919 legislative session. Signed on March 31, 1919, by Cornwell after lengthy debate, the legislation authorized a state police force of three companies of sixty men each. The superintendent was to be appointed by the governor, charged with preserving the peace, protecting property, and preventing crime anywhere in the state. Troopers were given absolute authority to command the assistance of local law enforcement officials and able-bodied citizens in situations deemed by the governor to be dangerous to public safety.[14]

Supporters of the state police legislation, commonly called the Constabulary bill, warned that West Virginia would become a popular refuge for Bolshevists and anarchists without such systematic police protection. Cornwell won the approval of some pro-labor legislators by arguing that a state police would eliminate the hated private mine-guard system by insuring that coal companies would have no excuse to employ the guards. He also appealed to states' rights sentiments, claiming that a competent state police force would reduce the state's dependence on federal troops to settle industrial disputes.[15] Adopting a common middle-class theme, the governor repeatedly asserted that only those who expected to violate laws or "overthrow constituted authority" would have any reason to fear state policemen. He assured West Virginians that the state police force was created "by the people's Legislature" solely to protect life and property, and to make West Virginia "a safer and more decent place for you to live and raise a family."[16]

Business and industrial leaders throughout the state were "solidly behind" Cornwell's plans for a state police, concurring with one supporter who wrote the governor that the "very considerable element of I.W.W. and Bolsheviki" in West Virginia, "composed chiefly of foreigners who are ignorant and lawless, must be held in check" by a state police force.[17] Officials of the Rotary Club of Elkins, the Creditmen's Association, and Chamber of Commerce of Huntington; the Bluefield Chamber of Commerce; nineteen prominent Parkersburg businessmen and the Board of Commerce; the Smokeless Coal Operators' Association; the Grafton Knights of Pythias; the West Virginia Pulp and Paper Company; the Raleigh Coal and Coke Company; the Fayette Smokeless Fuel Company, and the Ephraim Creek Coal and Coke Company[18] represented "enlightened public opinion" and "the sober, decent, law abiding people who are with you."[19] Cornwell singled out an attorney for the Davis Coal and Coke Company, who sat in the West Virginia legislature, as an important legislative ally not only for the Constabulary Bill, but "in all other matters of constructive Legislation."[20] Supporters of the state police measure concluded that the character of the opposition to the bill, comprised as it was of certain organizations who reputedly denigrated law and order, proved the need for the law.[21] To the bill's supporters, then, the opposition of unprincipled groups served as one of the bill's strongest recommendations.[22]

Such broad accusations essentially labeled most of West Virginia's labor unionists and union supporters as lawless, even as pro-Constabulary stalwarts proclaimed their individual support for the rights of organized labor.[23] John L. Lewis later spoke officially for the United Mine Workers when he described state constabularies as strikebreaking institutions and constabulary laws as dangerous usurpations of municipal police authority by a centralized state body. After the West Virginia constabulary was mobilized, Lewis scorned Cornwell's "siren song," which promoted the state police as "a panacea for all ills."[24] Lewis's, however, was only the most prominent voice of labor that was futilely raised against the constabulary. W.M. Rogers, president of the West Virginia Federation of Labor, denounced the pervasive business assault against labor's loyalty that accompanied the Constabulary bill debate. "Labor is loyal to the core," Rogers said. "We expect to carry the Stars and Stripes to the very end." But local law enforcement authorities were sufficient in the state, said Rogers, and, flirting with a theme that rankled West Virginia industrialists, urged labor to elect its own representatives to the legislature to obstruct repressive legislation.[25]

A small sampling of the resolutions of labor organizations regarding the Constabulary bill suggests labor's fear of the potential marriage of state police authority to private industrial interests. The fifty members of Fairmont Local 929 of the Painters, Decorators and Paperhangers, under the slogan "Right is Might," protested the Constabulary bill "for reasons too numerous to mention."[26] One UMWA local worried that the state police force would establish a state-sponsored "Baldwin thug system."[27] Not comforted by Cornwell's insistence that the state force would run the private mine guard system out of business, mine workers declared that in states with a constabulary, "they always take sides against the laboring man. We think it would be a bad weapon to put in the hands of some employers."[28] Nearly three hundred members of Wheeling Local 20 of the International Association of Bridge, Structural and Ornamental Iron Workers unanimously opposed the Constabulary bill.[29] Some state newspapers also questioned the prudence of a permanent police force, on other grounds. The *Morgantown Post* decried the expense of a permanent state police force, advocating instead the rejuvenation of the prewar state militia for police emergencies. The *Charleston Gazette*, media outlet for Cornwell's intraparty rival W.E. Chilton, contended that the public perception of the constabulary was that of a repressive force, which had "never worked well with our stock of people."[30]

Much of the opposition to the Constabulary bill was infused with the rhetoric of class warfare, which further steeled the conviction of Cornwell and his allies, like West Virginia penitentiary Warden J.Z. Terrell, who knew "of no State in the union that needs some kind of protection worse at this particular time than West Virginia." The state was dotted with communities, said the warden, where employees openly contended that business should be run solely for the interest of the employees.[31] State police supporters bristled at suggestions that their alleged well-regulated keepers of order would be no less than a "permanent military organization of armed, uniformed and equipped soldiers" whose task was to remind West Virginia workers to "keep on grinding out dividends for the men who are the economic masters of the State." Even labor organizations conceding Cornwell's professed impartiality predicted that in the hands of a less fair-minded successor the state police would be an instrument for breaking strikes and "crushing the rights of the workers of this State."[32]

The Constabulary bill struggle also exposed fratricidal tension in West Virginia's UMWA akin to that which dogged Lewis nationally. At the peak of the public debate over the bill, more than twenty UMWA locals in the state, acting independently of district authorities, bombarded Cornwell's office with resolutions of their conviction that a corporate/state conspiracy in West Virginia sought to crush organized labor by legislative and police power. They portrayed the Constabulary bill as an instrument of harassment and intimidation, and a manifestation of class rule.[33] The model for the "incendiary proclamations" was a resolution by Ramage Local 2901 in Boone County, under the leadership of Acting Secretary C.C. Lusk, which scored the Red Flag Bill (see chapter 4) and the Constabulary bill as "un-American class legislation resurrected from the feudal days of the dim past."[34]

The Ramage resolution was replicated by many locals in District 17 and District 29, when Ramage activists urged UMWA members to resist legislation that would lead to American institutions "being Russianized by a Prussian law." If peaceful protest was ignored by the legislators and courts of West Virginia, the "ruling class" stood forewarned that "labor by the might of its arm, stands fourteen to one and that our only means of warfare either offensive or defensive is the strike." If the state persisted in using class legislation and police action to deny labor's rights of freedom of speech and assembly, "we will not for a single moment hesitate to meet our enemies upon the battlefields" and through "the crash of systems purchase again our birth right of blood and freedom."[35]

Although the UMWA leadership in West Virginia strongly opposed the Constabulary and Red Flag laws, the break with union discipline represented by the Ramage initiative prompted an angry response from District 17 President Frank Keeney and Secretary Fred Mooney. A special convention of District 17, called to protest the Constabulary bill, had adjourned on February 11 with specific instructions from Keeney and Mooney for members to "be careful what they sign or endorse." Upon the widespread adoption of the Ramage resolution, with its "open declaration of violence," Keeney and Mooney charged the renegade locals with usurpation of power by not consulting with the district leadership. Mooney and Keeney sought and received retractions of the resolution from some of the locals, assuring its drafters that they could not count on protection from the United Mine Workers of America. It was the duty of District 17 miners, said the officers, to "eliminate from their organization that element that is preaching their different 'ism's,' and forever give them to understand that they will not be permitted to destroy our organization."[36] Mineworker H.E. Peters cautioned union men to avoid actions that might be interpreted by the public or the press as disloyal. Such documents as the Ramage resolution "breathed a feeling" he was certain did not exist among most mine workers.[37]

Organizational constraints aside, from the standpoint of many workers skeptical of the good intentions of the state, the Ramage resolution invoked principles of a type of Americanism consistent with the recent omnipresent wartime calls to resist autocracy. The maverick locals' resolution announced that just as West Virginia miners had faced German militarism, they would face industrial autocracy with "righteous protest," if necessary "amid the roar of the cannon and the groans of the dying."[38] Members of Blooming Rose, West Virginia, UMWA Local 1952 informed state legislators that they had just fought for democracy, and had no intention of bowing to a law that suggested Prussianism. "We feel President Willson [sic] 14 points covers us and appeal to them."[39] Wheeling Division 103 of the American Association of Street and Electric Railway Employees took a similar stance, calling for the establishment of locally based emergency state militia rather than a permanent police force. "We are true Americans," they announced, thirty-five of whom had fought for the nation against "that with which we are now threatened: *militarism.*"[40]

These expressions of working-class Americanism, which contradicted the conformist and hierarchical tenets of industrial Americanization, articulated the belief of some workers that legislation apparently so heavily weighted in industry's favor infringed on basic democratic rights.[41] Workers militantly opposed to the Constabulary bill recalled colonial currents of resistance to illegitimate authority, which held in reserve the threat or use of violence as a tactic of social, economic, and political protest. Historian Richard Maxwell Brown identifies the late pre-Revolutionary South Carolina Regulator movement as the prototype for trans-Appalachian vigilante movements of the nineteenth and twentieth centuries, based on the preindustrial era's ideology of popular sovereignty and marked by extralegal actions, petitions to representatives, and frequently violent actions.[42] The formation of local resistance groups willing to use force against oppressive actions by distant governments was a revered American tradition.[43] During the industrial crisis in West Virginia late in 1919, Cornwell even invoked this tradition to elevate state authority, beseeching local law enforcement officials to form "Committees of Public Aid and Safety" comprised of law abiding citizens "to protect and preserve public order," and to resist radicals "of native as well as foreign birth, who will rejoice at an opportunity to plunge the country into Anarchy."[44]

Nineteenth and early twentieth-century American political insurgents of all kinds commonly promoted their causes with pleas to return to the Revolutionary principles of popular rights against state oppression.[45] The country's most powerful labor federation of the early industrial corporate era, the Knights of Labor, combined elements of antiauthoritarian libertarianism with faith in the republican possibilities of the enlightened state. The Knights' Declaration of Principles warned against the "aggressiveness of great capitalists and corporations," which, if unchecked by the voluntary organization of all workers, would render the state the primary obstacle to a humane and cooperative social order.[46] The egalitarian Americanism espoused by the Knights, and by socialists and other insurgents, however, clashed with the prevailing middle-class concept of Americanism, which exalted order and individual property rights over radical industrial democracy. Such progressive ideals of Americanism sanctified progress, science, technology, efficiency, law and order, and scientific management of work and society. These, in turn, coalesced with reactionary, or nationalistic, Americanism, which envisioned hierarchical social organization based on white, Anglo-Saxon Protestant virtue and discipline. Together, the progressive and nationalistic impulses formed a powerful alliance against noncapitalist, anti-elitist alternatives for industrial America, and cast them as disloyal.[47] As the appropriation of the state by political capitalists became more evident, it was usually those who militantly envisioned a revolutionary redistribution of social and economic power who most faithfully cleaved to fundamentally conservative "Regulator" checks against centralized police authority. Local 1808 of Elkridge, which bitterly condemned the Constabulary law, instructed Governor Cornwell that "The *posse comitatus* [has] always proven competently handling outbreak [sic] of violence, always caused directly or indirectly by the methods and tactics of the employers class."[48]

Cornwell was alarmed at the militancy sparked by the Constabulary bill, avowedly mystified by suspicions that the state police bill and the Red Flag bill were "aimed at the trade unionists." He repeatedly insisted to labor leaders that the legislation was directed at any disloyal person or any criminal, including disreputable coal operators, manufacturers, and lawyers. The governor was distressed that trade unionists would fear laws conceived only to punish lawbreakers and subversives. To Cornwell, there were but two classes of people, "those who obey the laws and those who break the laws—the good and the bad." By opposing the Constabulary bill, loyal unionists were "undertaking to put on shoes that were not meant for them."[49] Cornwell's conciliatory tone with some of labor's representatives was cast aside in his correspondence with political allies. In these instances, Cornwell designated any opposition to the state police law as an "attempt to destroy our Government and wreck the whole industrial and social system in this country."[50]

Cornwell affirmed that the state police, made up of a small, well-trained corps of officers and reserves, would be free of political pressures by virtue of their appointment by circuit court judges, whose integrity would automatically insure that the selection of the police force would not be influenced by "sinister motives." Cornwell told the legislature that "a proper force of discreet, high-class men . . . furnishing protection against law-breakers of all classes," was the duty of municipal, county, and state authority in any orderly society.[51] He desired to cooperate with union labor whenever possible but would not allow radicals to make West Virginia their headquarters.[52] Cornwell had long encouraged labor to be organized and managed according to business principles, warning that unions must never resort to "anarchic methods" when threatened by injustice, but should appeal to enlightened public opinion. Labor must never forget that an employer was entitled to the loyalty of his employees and that workers would lose the trust of the public and business if they allowed the "spirit of Bolshevism or I.W.W. 'ism" to infect their unions. To demonstrate his empathy, he often noted that "it was not so long ago that I was carrying a dinner pail, none too full, for a dollar a day."[53]

That claim was disingenuous in light of the fact that for the quarter-century before he became governor, Cornwell had been a teacher, newspaper editor, railroad investor, bank president, timber company executive, and corporate retainer in Hampshire County for the Baltimore and Ohio Railroad.[54] Cornwell's political and economic thought was thus firmly guided by the middle-class assumption, as explained by Martin Sklar, that large-scale corporate capitalism was the natural product of social evolution and that society would best be served by a legal and institutional environment favorable to the continued growth of industrial capitalism.[55] Cornwell often proclaimed that he was neither a progressive nor a reactionary, but "merely a democrat." He even claimed, apparently seriously, that his early work as a laborer made him "in no sense a capitalist."[56] He sought to protect capitalism, however, and he understood the stabilizing influence of progressive legislation. He consequently supported mine safety reforms, woman's suffrage, and eight-hour day, child labor, and workman's compensation laws. Cornwell was not, says one historian, opposed to measures that would ameliorate the hardships of labor. He simply opposed labor's exercise of political power.[57]

Legislative adjustments to modern industrial growth were consistent with Cornwell's embrace of elite bipartisanship in government, and he firmly believed in the control of industrial reform by business interests.[58]

Corporate recognition of the wisdom of pro-capitalist industrial reforms antedated the World War and later formed the basis for the 1920s practice of welfare capitalism. The alleged "organic" expansion of industrial capitalism had faced ideological and social challenges during the late nineteenth and early twentieth centuries, results of the rapid corporate reorganization of the American economy.[59] Even John J. Cornwell, acknowledging the political if not the ideological validity of socialism, had deliberately courted West Virginia Socialists to win the governor's office in 1916, offering to this active political minority a sympathetic hearing from a Democratic reform administration in Charleston. Socialist strongholds in Fayette, Tucker, and Greenbrier counties backed Cornwell, and he lobbied hard for Socialist votes in heavily industrial Ohio County. Socialist voters looking for a reasonable alternative to certain defeat for any gubernatorial Socialist party candidate delivered several thousand votes to Cornwell, who won the election over liberal Republican Ira E. Robinson by less than three thousand votes.[60]

By 1919 Cornwell had foregone even rhetorical tolerance of socialist theory, linking it inextricably with the other "strange experiment," Bolshevism.[61] Cornwell joined like-minded political, business, and intellectual leaders in a conscious movement to insure public acceptance of corporate capitalism as the inevitable form of business enterprise and allocation of wealth.[62] The governor told Wetzel County teachers that advocacy of schemes, like the nationalization of railroads, and other "Socialistic talk" was foreign to American ideals, and propagators of such heretical dogma were pushing "the Russian doctrine or even worse." By the time of the Seattle strike, Cornwell's perception of disloyalty encompassed all proponents of public ownership of industries who, he affirmed, inflicted unrest and agitation "as dangerous and threatening as any day during our war experience." Sanity and patriotism were his prescription for resisting the tendency toward communism, as found in such schemes as the Plumb Plan for government ownership of railroads. "Such un-American, revolutionary and dishonest doctrines" might lead gullible people to embark "on a campaign of pillage and murder in their effort to 'politely kick out' the owners of mills and factories and farms." He appealed to teachers to guide their pupils away from alien doctrines "promoted by the lazy and shiftless who want the benefits of someone else's labor." Teachers were engaged in a war to protect loyal citizens who owned their own homes and firesides and were "not willing to communize their little heritage" by jeopardizing the sanctity of private property. It was their duty, "dealing with young and plastic minds," to "see that the American ideas and ideals are implanted there."[63]

The plan presented by attorney Glenn E. Plumb was the focus of postwar debate over whether railroads should be retained and operated by the government or permanently returned to private management. The

Plumb Plan recommended that administration of the railroad industry be placed "in the hands of the men who have invested in that industry the great, creative human effort-labor in all its manifestations."[64] Plumb proposed a government corporation managed by a board of directors representing railroad employees, railroad officials, public consumers, and the president of the United States. Profits would be allocated equally to employees and to operators, with much of the corporate profit channeled into investment and improvement of rail properties. The plan, says David Montgomery, complemented coal miners' demands for nationalization of the coal industry and served as a model for social reformers within the American Federation of Labor.[65]

Galvanized by an address by Plumb, UMWA delegates endorsed the Plumb Plan at the union's 1919 Cleveland convention. They approved formation of an alliance with railroad workers. Describing coal resources as the birthright of the American people, the Cleveland delegates also approved a resolution to nationalize the mining industry, recommending federal administration and equal representation on boards of authority for mine workers to determine wage, hour, working-condition, and grievance policies. At Cleveland, acting UMWA president John L. Lewis, engaged in a power struggle with Frank Farrington of Illinois and radical Kansan Alex Howat, joined forces with Farrington to crush Howat's attempt to seat an insurgent "One Big Union" faction from Illinois. Despite the marginalization of Howat, Lewis still faced two thousand union militants at Cleveland who had no particular loyalty to him. Unenthusiastic about nationalization, Lewis sought to deflect the UMWA policy committee's endorsement for public ownership of the industry, but given the activist climate at the convention and the precariousness of his leadership position, Lewis could not afford to reject nationalization at that point.[66]

John J. Cornwell's renunciation of the Plumb Plan escalated after the UMWA Cleveland convention, as he combined the steel strike and the nationalization campaigns into an intricate strategy by labor leaders to "starve and choke the country into submission." In a widely reported address to the National Paint, Oil, and Varnish Association at White Sulphur Springs, West Virginia, the governor warned that labor's militant actions "strike at the very roots of our form of government and at the very foundation of organized society." Plans were in place, said Cornwell, to organize every industry so that labor unions would have absolute control of the country. The union strategy included affiliations with policemen and firemen, "so when the crucial moment comes the custodians of the public peace will no longer be the guardian of the public, but will be under orders from the labor leaders." If the "weird, fantastic, Bolshevistic theory" of nationalization was not checked, it would spread to all industries, projecting the misguided notion that the United States government represented the interests of capitalists above those of the whole people.[67] The Plumb Plan was "Socialism run mad," said the governor, and it would lead to "Russia reproduced here on American soil."[68] Cornwell denied that he implicated all of organized labor in his sweeping charges, but one labor leader asked that if this were the case, why did the governor not direct the state's police powers against unlawful acts "rather than conduct a propaganda which now needs explanation and which has been construed as a reflection on organized labor."[69]

In the view of Cornwell and his class, illegitimacy of social and economic alternatives to industrial capitalism elevated predominant values and institutional procedures that consistently favored some persons and groups at the expense of others, leaving the beneficiaries in a dominant position to promote their interests under protection of law.[70] Business and political leaders did not presume that the "rules of the game" were tilted in their favor but that natural economic laws rewarded virtue and punished vice. Successful capitalist enterprises were derived not from an imbalance of power between business and labor, but from the genius of modern entrepreneurs.[71] Cornwell embodied this middle-class view, having grown up in modest circumstances, supported and educated himself, acquired a fortune "by his own industry and ingenuity," and internalized "a philosophy of labor that was idealistic and elevating." His business and political success had freed him from physical labor, but he praised labor's "new dignity," which it had acquired by demonstrating its loyalty during the war.[72] Such unconscious condescension reflected the predisposition of successful capitalists who identified "the people" as the "better citizens," vested with "natural and patent superiority," which qualified them for leadership. Moreover, the assiduous extension of political, social, and economic control by capitalists and corporations was seen by their representatives as politically neutral.[73]

C.C. Lusk, who drew Cornwell's attention as secretary of Ramage UMWA Local 2901 during the Constabulary bill controversy, recognized the contradiction in business and political elites' claims to public-minded neutrality in the industrial struggles of 1919. While attesting to his union's desire to trust and support the state's chief executive, Lusk told Cornwell that the governor lived in "an industrial and political atmosphere" that led Cornwell and "those like you situated," to suspect as disloyal "the men and women that feed the world, clothe the world and that gives [sic] the world drink." Lusk concluded that this suspicion was "the result of class reasoning and is the cause of class hatred," meaning "the rich nor their retainers do not want a reconstruction or change." Lusk suggested that this class identity emanated from a "social, religious or even psychological standpoint."[74]

Lusk's analysis of elite class consciousness does much to clarify Cornwell's rather remarkable contention that circuit judges, in appointing state policemen, would not be influenced by political considerations. If agitated by Lusk's observations, Cornwell probably took heart from the sentiments of coal operator Justus Collins, who congratulated him when the Constabulary bill became law. "Every decent man in the state should take his hat off to you. The others don't matter," wrote Collins, who also recommended that the new state police use a pair of "French type 75s which are light field guns" for mob control. If facing "overwhelming odds, the two pieces would be more effective than several hundred trained infantrymen." Cornwell thanked Collins but was "inclined to believe that a machine gun would be more advantageous, as it could be handled more easily."[75]

Beliefs held by elites about the natural and proper organization of American society no longer accommodated the indigenous "Socialist Alternative" articulated by Eugene Debs and other prewar radicals, promoting a cooperative commonwealth rather than private enterprise, as trustee of "the sources of wealth and the means of life."[76] After the war, such doctrines were assiduously expelled from the narrowing public discourse, and anarchists and socialists were generally described as lacking the capacity for patriotism. Educator Waitman Barbe identified critics of capitalism as "men and women without a country." "Glance at the list of our most notorious Reds," Barbe said, "and you will see, I think, that here lies the secret of their strange aberrations. There are no Sons or Daughters of the American Revolution among them." The National Association of Manufacturers labeled Socialism as not only un-American but un-Christian, since "the whole appeal of the Christian religion is to individual impulse and to individual responsibility."[77]

Such attitudes permeated the volatile industrial climate in the fall of 1919. Governor Cornwell had divided the world into "the good and the bad," and it was from that perspective that he viewed the labor-management conflict that rent his state. Frank Keeney's pledge to organize miners of the Guyan field in Logan County, concurrent with the early September steel strike and the impending UMWA national strike, convinced Cornwell that West Virginia was on the verge of industrial revolution. Cornwell rushed to address some four thousand miners at Lens Creek when armed Kanawha miners shut down their own mines and mobilized near Marmet to march into Logan County, in response to reported killings and beatings of District 17 organizers by private Logan County mine guards.[78] Cornwell reportedly displayed considerable personal courage, and his own and some other accounts suggest that his eloquent and fair-minded appeal to investigate the miners' complaints changed their minds. Other reports credit District 17 President Frank Keeney with persuading the miners to return to their homes and point out that the march was only abandoned when Cornwell warned the miners that unless they disbanded, he had arranged for federal troops under General Leonard Wood to forcibly disperse them.[79]

Cornwell appointed a commission to study the alleged intimidation of UMWA organizers, but Frank Keeney refused to cooperate when the focus of the investigation was shifted to fixing blame for the aborted march.[80] Keeney's wariness was not unfounded. Justus Collins volunteered information for Cornwell's investigation, which the governor gratefully received, "concerning the miners who started the march to Logan County on the night of August 30." Collins told Cornwell he knew enough about the unions that such a demonstration had to be "ordered, financed, and directed by their officials." Collins went beyond indictments of local UMWA leaders to charge the old craft unionist Samuel Gompers, who, "in a larger way, is today undertaking to terrorize, coerce, and subdue by force and intimidation the whole country."[81]

As the steel strike and labor-management divisiveness in West Virginia widened, Cornwell was convinced that his stand against labor radicalism, especially his nationally distributed White Sulphur comments, had put him in harm's way, particularly from certain UMWA leaders who "feared I might influence the rank and file of the mine workers against the leaders and officers of the Union." Cornwell had been warned during the Constabulary fight that "some of these dinks might assassinate you in the dark"; he now dictated a letter to his secretary in which he predicted his death for refusing to "permit them to unionize the Guyan Coal Fields by force and in defiance of law." Cornwell insisted that believers in law and order must assert themselves or "not only our Government but civilization itself is doomed." He was willing to die if his sacrifice would "help stay the tide of Bolshevism and Anarchy."[82]

No assassination attempt materialized, and when the UMWA refused the Wilson administration's proposed 14 percent wage increase, a national coal strike, deemed illegal by Wilson under terms of the Lever Act and the Washington Agreement, was scheduled for November 1.[83] Cornwell appealed to Keeney, linking his hope that West Virginia miners would not go on strike to the "same loyalty and patriotism they manifested during the war." "The people," Cornwell declared, expected that loyal miners would reject the strike call. Keeney responded that the coal operators' prices had gone up 184 percent since 1916, while union wages had risen 63 percent. Because of cost of living increases and the operators' "arbitrary stand" against union recognition, miners were forced to carry out the strike policy approved at the UMWA Cleveland convention. Cornwell had already alerted Leonard Wood to have federal troops at the ready to send to West Virginia. Officers of the West Virginia Coal Association pressured the governor to secure federal troops to combat radical strikers. Cornwell complied, and some nineteen hundred federals were brought in, many in the southern open-shop fields.[84]

Cornwell also instructed West Virginia mayors and law enforcement officers to organize "A Committee of Public Safety, composed of patriotic, courageous and public spirited citizens, men who can be trusted and whose loyalty to the government and its institutions is beyond question." Cornwell feared the strike would be used by "the criminal and radical element" to foment industrial revolution. "We are not fighting a strike," the governor warned. "We are combatting an attempt at revolution, and governmental authority can only win by the moral support of the good people everywhere."[85] State police duties during the strike consisted largely of surveillance of suspected IWW agitators in the northern panhandle and protection of some northern open-shop mines. Undercover agents J.N. Crincefield and C.M. Jones reported to the state police that "5% of the men are radicals" in Whipple and Scarboro in District 29. They asked workers in the strike zone if they knew of UMW agitators who were intimidating miners who opposed the strike. Some miners signed affidavits providing the names and addresses of union activists.[86] Surveillance extended south into strongholds of the open shop and yellow-dog contract. F.S. Monahan of the Lick Fork Coal Company confidentially informed Cornwell that most of his miners were uninterested in the strike issues until "aggravated by Socialists, I.W.W., etc." The men lost "their own good judgment" when "carried away by the stormy words of the Country Wreckers. This does not exempt District Officials and National Officials."[87]

Cornwell believed that most West Virginians, unlike radical agitators, were liberty-loving and law-abiding, and would make any sacrifice to preserve public order. He was worried, however, that the state's citizens were unaware of the magnitude of the danger that radical elements posed to organized society. When Ohio County Sheriff Howard Hastings remarked that there were no revolutionaries among Wheeling's union men, Cornwell informed the sheriff that his personal investigations had revealed the presence of Bolshevik and IWW elements in Ohio County. They were engaged in "active, open propaganda in the Wheeling district," and as governor, Cornwell intended to cooperate with the federal government in breaking the unlawful strike such radicals were directing. "It is unnecessary to say," the governor said, "that I think the attitude of all public officials should be the same."[88]

In addition to soliciting federal military aid to put down the coal strike, Cornwell occasionally sought federal undercover assistance against suspected radicals to supplement his network of personal informants. Acting on a request from Cornwell, U.S. Attorney General A. Mitchell Palmer instructed agents of the Bureau of Investigation (BI) to investigate suspected radicals in Tucker County.[89] Cornwell informed Palmer of IWW locals at Grant Town in Marion County and Wendel in Taylor County, led by alien agitators who "should have been deported long ago." Palmer sent BI agents to arrest "all alien radicals."[90] Cornwell also pleaded with Postmaster General A.S. Burleson to purge from the U.S. mail all publications which, for example, carried statements by V.I. Lenin. "Can't we start a campaign to prevent the use of government machinery to articulate propaganda to overthrow the Government?"[91] The Bureau of Investigation also forwarded to Federal Marshal C.E. Smith, an officer with Consolidation Coal in Fairmont, a list of West Virginia subscribers to the Italian anarchist publication *Cronaca Soversiva*, described by the Justice Department as the country's most dangerous newspaper. The list included the name of Consolidation employee Guiseppe Cavalieri of Worthington, and the BI suggested that Consolidation's company police "keep an eye on" Cavalieri, as it was "a good idea to watch every one of this stripe."[92]

While he courted and applauded federal censorship, Cornwell also understood the value of the propaganda model employed by the wartime Committee on Public Information. He realized the importance of relying primarily on the cultivation of public opinion to attract popular support for his increasingly strident antilabor positions. He believed, for example, that organized labor in West Virginia, under the populist guise of "fighting corporations," had built an alliance of West Virginia legislators from agricultural and industrial areas to threaten the Constabulary bill. The fact that the bill became law was exceptional, Cornwell insisted, since labor leaders "have had their way absolutely in Washington as well as Charleston." The governor thus concurred with the National Association of Manufacturers, which cried that in Congress and in "every state legislature, the insidious and artful minds of the labor trust leaders are represented in bills of socialistic and dangerous character." Cornwell favored state and national industrial disputes laws to outlaw strikes and believed that public awareness of labor's resistance to the state police legislation would help "bring the American people to their senses" about such attempts to "destroy our Government."[93]

Cornwell joined many other business spokesmen in issuing dire predictions about the domination of legislation and the manipulation of public opinion by labor's radicals. The public was insufficiently organized, a writer for *Coal Age* complained, to oppose effectively labor's organized minority, who had expelled the AFL's "conservative, sane leaders" from positions of authority. Moreover, labor organizations had ignored legislation to "safeguard the public against the aggression and extortion of combinations," and they should waive the right to strike in return for the creation of proper committees of experts to determine wages and adjust disputes.[94] The industrialists' position was that workers combined in restraint of trade when they went on strike, or threatened to strike. The "labor trusts must be suppressed," then, because their actions "injure the public."[95] To expel radicalism and protect the public, Governor Cornwell recognized that industrial dispute legislation, while important, would be insufficient to recapture the national "unity of thought and purpose" that resulted in the Allied victory over German autocracy. Cornwell agreed with the National Association of Manufacturers that only a properly educated public could secure the unity needed to back up proper industrial legislation. The governor cautioned businessmen that guileless workingmen, without time to read and analyze important public issues in depth, would become ever more dependent for information and social philosophy on their union officials, many of whom had a facility for portraying industrial problems in terms of "idealistic and socialistic theories." Radicalism must be met openly, systematically, and immediately. To defeat radicalism, Cornwell declared, "Counter propaganda is imperative."[96]

Organized business efforts at counter propaganda in West Virginia took form in the context of the UMWA struggle to organize the southern West Virginia coalfields. Miners in Mingo and Logan counties refused to comply with a federal injunction prohibiting the November 1919 strike, and thirteen thousand unorganized miners in these counties continued to strike after the ambiguous federally negotiated agreement to suspend the national coal strike in December. Thousands of miners who joined the UMWA were fired and expelled from company housing, under the coal operators' authority from the *Hitchman* decision (see chapter 3), and were forced to move with their families into tent colonies. The crisis degenerated into warfare between miners and company gunmen, with the UMWA determined to organize Mingo and Logan as a wedge into the rest of southern West Virginia and eastern Kentucky. Mingo County coal operators groused that the new state police were being overly neutral in their tolerance of strike agitation, in too literal compliance with the terms of the Constabulary Act. Cornwell expressed his hope that those provisions might be changed in the future, and he later turned to federal intervention in an effort to guarantee coal production in the region. The Matewan Massacre of May 19, 1920, in which local union supporters and Baldwin-Felts agents engaged in a deadly gun battle, prompted further federal action. Cornwell dispatched state police to the Matewan strike zone, where unionists enjoyed safe haven provided by local police chief Sid Hatfield. The incongruity of a pro-union law enforcement officer in the rabidly open-shop Mingo fields infuriated the autocratic Mingo-Logan operators. The acquittal of Hatfield and eighteen codefendants, charged with murder of Baldwin-Felts guards, by a pro-union Mingo County jury further embittered the region's operators. Hatfield was assassinated by Baldwin-Felts agents on August 1, 1921, having been called to neighboring McDowell County to answer strike-related sabotage charges. His death contributed to the mobilization of thousands of West Virginia miners for the march to Blair Mountain late in August.[97]

As the coal strike had spread throughout the southern West Virginia fields, businessmen mobilized to protect their interests and generate public opinion in their favor. In February 1920, editor Wightman Roberts of the *West Virginia Mining News* called upon responsible business leaders to "resist and offset the aggressions of organized minorities—the labor unions and their false leaders." Roberts proposed forming an "American Federation of Business Men," a propaganda body to disseminate the principles of the United States Constitution and destroy closed-shop unionism. Quoting Cornwell, Roberts pledged that individual ownership and property rights "would not be sacrificed to the terrorists of organized labor." He called for an organizational meeting of the American Federation of Business Men at Charleston's Kanawha Hotel on March 4, 1920.[98]

Cornwell supported Roberts's plan and agreed to address the inaugural meeting of the organization, attended by about 150 businessmen, who bypassed Roberts's name for the group in favor of the American Constitutional Association (ACA).[99] The mission statement of the ACA included the organization's goal to "inculcate in the minds of our people, both native and foreign-born, the true spirit of Americanism." Officers and directors of the organization included Cornwell, E.W. Oglebay, Edwin M. Keatley, Robert Archer, Phil Conley, William McKell, Dr. I.C. White, and Howard M. Gore.[100]

Cornwell described the ACA as a "defensive and offensive alliance of business men" determined to crush the Plumb Plan and UMWA designs to nationalize the coal industry. The governor expressed his hope that the ACA would be an important factor not only in the interests of business "but in the interests of the whole people, and the American government." Roberts was elected assistant secretary of the ACA, with businessman Edwin Keatley, who later became speaker of the West Virginia House of Delegates, as secretary. The officers pleaded with Cornwell to be ACA president; after initially declining, Cornwell accepted the presidency, partly because of Keatley's participation.[101]

Shortly after the founding of the ACA, Mingo County coal operators restated their position not to negotiate with the UMWA concerning the organization of the Williamson field, plainly stating their belief that "no useful purpose could be served by any meeting with the miners." Instead, the operators embarked on a campaign of counter propaganda to offset UMWA activities in Mingo County. To present their case, the operators procured space in Mingo County newspapers, emphasizing their roles as owners of $30 million to $40 million in property, whose taxes supported public institutions, schools, and roads, and who provided employment for five thousand workmen.[102] The *Logan Banner* later endorsed similar public relations tactics, claiming the cure for southern West Virginia's "labor troubles" was "information from the printed page instead of from the whispered rumor."

Newspapers must do their part so that workers would no longer be fooled by agitators. "The isolation of the mountain hollows," the *Banner* intoned, would be overcome only by "the light of information through the medium of the newspapers." Only then would "the disorder of southern West Virginia be ended and the law reign in every mountain valley."[103]

Newspapers, however, were just one of many important avenues for the promulgation of anti-union propaganda by the ACA and its allies. Like the National Association of Manufacturers (NAM), the ACA defined itself primarily as an educational organization, making a studied effort to impress the public with the merit of its anti-union principles, employing various channels such as schools, churches, the press, and agencies of state and private industry.[104] The ACA insisted that America must "adopt a systematic plan of teaching love of country, through schools, churches, industries and homes. . . . in books and patriotism, loyal Americans must offset radical doctrines."[105] The ACA became an important vehicle for organizing and transmitting propaganda at the intersection of several interrelated movements, each affirming the moral and social authority of business, including welfare capitalism, the open-shop movement, and the polemical foundation underlying these movements, known as the American Plan. The ACA in West Virginia assumed the task of educating and mobilizing the public with the goal of imparting to these class-conscious business strategies the rectitude of democracy, freedom, and liberty. Committed to disseminating their particular type of Americanism by all available means, ACA activists envisioned a broad business coalition to apprise the public, most of whom "don't believe the danger of radicals." "Call me alarmist," an ACA officer wrote to Cornwell, "but . . . conditions are not what they were ten years ago; there is not the regard for law and law enforcement that prevailed when I was a boy."[106] The statewide goals of the ACA and its allies were ingredients of a broad national movement in the early 1920s, when a concerted effort was launched to destroy independent labor unionism.

6

Welfare Capitalism, the American Plan–Open-shop Movement, and the Triumph of Business Unionism

By May 1921 the American Constitutional Association claimed one thousand members and enjoyed the support of the West Virginia Manufacturers' Association and the major coal operators' associations.[1] Speakers from the organization's speakers bureau, led by the ACA's indefatigable managing director, Phil Conley, addressed meetings of the WVMA, county bar associations, Rotary Clubs, and meetings of county school superintendents.[2] Although the reputation of the National Security League had been tarnished when congressional hearings unearthed its war profiteering and authoritarian impulses, the ACA welcomed the national orientation of the NSL, and the two joined forces to sponsor patriotic demonstrations.[3] Conley informed the ACA Executive Committee that he and the American Legion's director of Americanization work in West Virginia had formulated plans to coordinate the Americanization programs of associations statewide, including the West Virginia Federation of Women's Clubs, the Daughters of the American Revolution, the Young Men's and Young Women's Christian Associations, the Chamber of Commerce, Kiwanis and Rotary clubs, and the State Federation of Labor.[4]

The ACA's occasional tepid rhetorical overtures to organized labor inevitably receded, however, since the mission of the organization fundamentally contradicted that of the United Mine Workers and other independent unions in West Virginia. The ACA was pledged to protect the competitive interests of nonunion southern West Virginia coal operators, who were determined to undersell coal produced in the unionized Central Competitive Field. The UMWA foresaw the organization of southern West Virginia as assuring wage protection for its members nationwide. The ACA picked up the anti-union gauntlet thrown down by United States Steel's successful resistance to the 1919 organizing strike and became a forceful advocate in West Virginia for the open-shop doctrine promoted by U.S. Steel President Elbert H. Gary.[5]

The determination of southern West Virginia operators to roll back union advances and prevent new inroads was reinforced by helpful judicial and legislative initiatives. The greatest of these was the 1917 U.S. Supreme

Court *Hitchman* decision, which made union membership punishable by loss of employment under terms of individually negotiated yellow-dog contracts and allowed the broad issuance of court injunctions to prohibit union activity. Open-shop advocates also benefitted from the long-established expertise of the National Association of Manufacturers, which had led the organized efforts to smash American unionism since the early twentieth century.[6] The organizing principles of these tactics were incorporated into a national coalition of businessmen and industrial capitalists under a "well-financed and militant drive to reduce the power of labor organizations," which adopted the slogan "American Plan." Formalized at a January 1921 conference of state manufacturers' associations in Chicago, the American Plan ideology argued that each worker should determine his own terms of employment with his employer, free of interference from business agencies or unions. The American Plan movement used the latest methods for shaping public opinion, says historian of American labor Philip Taft, conducting an aggressive campaign that contributed to a drastic decline in trade union membership nationally by 1923.[7]

While antiradical demagoguery, coercive labor contracts, and injunctions comprised important elements of the business assault against unionism, nationally and in West Virginia, coal operators and their supporters also embraced the doctrine of "welfare capitalism" on a wide scale. Operators' efforts to defuse working-class militance included sponsorship of mine safety programs, employment of social workers, economic support for public school systems, and support for religious, social, and fraternal activities.[8] The West Virginia Coal Operators Association, affirming that conscientious coal operators wanted "to secure good men, reliable workmen," lauded expenditures by state coal men to make their company towns attractive and comfortable, where children would learn to be good citizens of the state and nation. Some companies paid for YMCA buildings and hired their recreation directors. Companies built and maintained baseball diamonds and provided uniforms and equipment for company teams.[9] Lundale Coal Company of Lundale, West Virginia, in Logan County, provided a "dance hall for white people and one for colored and baseball teams and playgrounds for both classes."[10]

Companies spent thousands of dollars on schools, nurses, churches, Sunday Schools, "and other factors necessary to the right sort of community life."[11] Lundale Coal built three churches for its employees, including a Catholic, a Protestant, "and a church for the colored people."[12] Ministers were frequently paid in whole or in part by the companies, since the coal men believed proper religious training aided their search for the best class of workmen. It was seen as good business for a coal company to support religious and community activities.[13] E.D. Knight, chief engineer of the Cabin

Creek Consolidated Coal Company of Kayford, West Virginia, praised the "value of the 'indirect approach' to mine problems" achieved by a minister and school teacher in his community. Operators dismissed accusations that providing churches and paying ministers' salaries allowed them to control religion in company towns. Perhaps some operators were greatly concerned about "the theological views of their employees. We have not found any [such operators]."[14]

Welfare capitalism is described by a recent sympathetic account of company towns as "contentment sociology," a term used by the Stonega Coke and Coal Company of southwestern Virginia. Contentment sociology was built on the belief that a satisfied working class would be stable and productive, even if miners sacrificed much of their personal control over the job.[15] Benevolence, however, ideally would create more than contentment among the workers; it could also be a profit-making enterprise. J.G. Bradley, president of the West Virginia Coal Association, told delegates to the 1922 West Virginia Coal Mining Institute that operators providing amenities should realize a return on the additional costs, since the people of the community would be willing to pay on a per use basis.[16]

A 1920 article in *Coal Age* emphasized the importance of welfare work not only for contented workmen but for future workers, who needed education to "so train their minds that they can understand economic conditions," insuring that "their relations with this company or some other when they will go to work will be on a higher plane than that of their fathers." *Coal Age* recounted the personal arrangement of one Pennsylvania coal company president with the local board of education. Although the company did not pay teachers, the president selected the teachers, insisting primarily on their "high moral view-point."[17] An official for Consolidation Coal in Jenkins, Kentucky, explained that most mining companies tried to secure the most progressive teachers. Unless company officials took an interest in the selection of teachers, unconcerned board of education members would send their worst teachers to the mining towns.[18] Depending on business fortunes, Winding Gulf coal tycoon Justus Collins supplemented teacher salaries. Collins once loaned money to the board of education for high school construction at Winding Gulf, even though some businessmen feared that an inappropriate high school education might turn youngsters away from industrial work rather than toward it.[19] Coal company executives rejected charges of undue company influence in the classroom, however, claiming it was impossible to "put a great deal of propaganda into the teaching of the three R's." On company control over selection of teaching personnel, "it is probably true, but we do not believe that this is an undesirable situation. On the contrary, we feel that this tends toward securing more competent teachers."[20]

Welfare capitalism was a prime ingredient in the recipe for employer control over production, efforts to thwart unionism, and the creation of an obedient, content, and thrifty working class. Business leaders agreed that proper education was the primary source of worker contentment and stability, from which miners and their families could acquire appropriate "habits of industry."[21] Comprehensive education transcended the classroom, sometimes extending to management control of lending library reading material, but more pervasively infusing workers' communities with the companies' own propaganda generated by employee magazines. The first such publications appeared in 1907 and proliferated dramatically between 1915 and 1920, when over four hundred companies published monthly or bimonthly journals. Designed to convince employees that the company was concerned about their individual happiness, goals, and successes, employee magazines sought to bind worker to employer in a consciousness of cooperation, trust, and affirmation of probusiness views of industrial relations.[22] Readers learned that happy men and women knew that "work is not drudgery, it is a pleasure. We do the best work we are able to do not because we receive more pay for it, but because it is our duty and we love to do our duty." One editor frankly stated that the employee magazines represented a necessary and "continuous campaign of thought direction" waged to guarantee "the greatest degree of loyalty and efficiency."[23]

The ideological currents of industrial Americanization, scientific management, anti-unionism, and the American Plan are well-defined in one of the most prominent coal industry employee magazines, the *Consolidation Coal Company Mutual Monthly*. Consolidation's Employment Relationship Department, described in a promotional article as "particularly active as regards publicity matters," published about eleven thousand copies of the magazine monthly, featuring biographical sketches of the company's prominent men, gardening tips, baseball scores, and stories about all activities sponsored by the Employment Relationship Department.[24] Under the masthead "Employer and Employed: Our Own Interests Being Identical, We Work Together for Our Common Good," the Consolidation journal shifted its wartime focus (see chapter 1) from patriotic production to whip the Hun to patriotic production to eliminate "those who would destroy our liberties and government." Americans who stood for law and order and against anarchy and destruction would join forces to "rid our country of these menaces to civilization."[25] True Americanism demanded "expression in our work, in our recreation and in our religion," and carried an obligation of "aggressive loyalty . . . to help crush every power that opposes the principles of Americanism." Patriotic loyalty was embodied in the American Plan, where labor and capital became "brothers in reality," each working for the others' best interests, and where workers settled their individual disputes in consultation with reasonable employers, provided strikes and lockouts were abolished by law and grievances were "not instigated by outside influences."[26]

Consolidation's journal easily transferred the propaganda of wartime mobilization to postwar domestic industrial affairs. A column called "Human Relations" warned that America was engaged in a life-and-death struggle in which the American people must "furnish antidotes for the poisons that have been injected by fanatical radicals." Many seemed oblivious, however, to the magnitude of the threatened social upheaval. Society's welfare depended on "organized effort on the part of sound thinkers who have the welfare of all humanity at heart." "We must act in unison to defeat the united effort of civilization's enemy or suffer what poor deluded Russia is suffering today."[27]

As the Consolidation journal sounded the alarm against radicalism, it advised its readers as to how to prove their loyalty to the principles of true Americanism. One must obey all laws, rejecting false prophets who attacked the ideals and laws of the republic. Chiefly, any American citizen, native or foreign-born, could prove they were worthy by displaying the accepted habits of industry. "Your love for America will be measured by how true you are to your daily tasks," the magazine stated. "Busy people are invariably more contented than loafers. Industry always breeds content," and discontent vanished in the face of accomplishment "in some line of habitual endeavor."[28] The magazine was an aggressive promoter of the American Plan, describing its open-shop principle as conservator of personal freedom, liberating workers from the grasp of union agitators so they could negotiate directly with their employers, individually or in company dominated committees, with each working man free of the dictatorship of "paid hirelings to do his thinking for him." UMWA intentions to unionize all the nation's coal miners was attacked as un-American, particularly union demands for the mandatory checkoff of union dues from a worker's wages. Such practices were an insult to a workman's honesty and intelligence, and the American Plan would guarantee labor dignity and "freedom from rule of organization politics."[29] No "real man" would tolerate the checkoff or mandatory union membership. He would agree that compensation for work performed was a matter to be decided between employer and employed, free from outsiders' influence. Finally, the American Plan was firmly grounded in the belief that every man had a right to work for whomever he saw fit, and "every employer has the right to employ such men as he sees fit to employ."[30]

West Virginia coal operators expertly manipulated the pre-industrial mystique of individual contract, bolstered by their sweeping powers under *Hitchman* to require nonmembership in a labor organization as a condition of employment.[31] A boon to marginal operations in the nonunion sectors of competitive industries, *Hitchman* had demonstrated to employers how potent the combination of yellow-dog contracts and labor injunctions could be. Supreme Court Justice Mahlon Pitney's 1917 majority opinion interpreted the use of yellow-dogs as a property right, which could be defended by injunctions to block outside interference. Pitney recognized the rights of employees to form unions, but employers also had the right to run nonunion mines, a right violated by the organizational efforts of the UMWA. Broad court injunctions virtually outlawed the UMWA in parts of West Virginia and led to bitter strikes in the hosiery industry in Pennsylvania, Wisconsin, and Indiana.[32] Failure to abide by the terms of yellow-dog contracts, which were widely used in the Mingo and Logan fields, subjected the employee to dismissal. Terms usually went beyond membership in the UMWA or IWW to include any action interpreted by the employer as giving aid to any labor organization. Claiming that *Hitchman* made it impossible for the union to protect miners in unorganized fields, the UMWA sought to turn the tables on operators' flag-waving by labeling yellow-dogs as violations of workers' constitutional rights of assembly.[33]

The UMWA described the yellow-dog contract as the means used by some employers to "smash labor unions and reduce working people to the old-time level."[34] Naturally, anti-union coal operators saw this element of the American Plan differently. Individual contracts between loyal employees and benevolent companies, which recognized the business benefits of fair treatment, would reinstitute "earlier and simpler forms of industrial organization." Developments in modern industry, including the infusion of foreigners into the American industrial system, had undermined the traditional "cordial relationship," where the employee easily identified himself with the interests of the employer.[35] *Coal Age* lamented that "we have drawn away from the old habits," when the "workman called round in the evening" to talk with his boss. The modern journal of the coal industry recommended restoration of the "old personal touch."[36]

These were effective if transparent tactics. The UMWA recognized the threat to its existence posed by the American Plan, including coal operators' determination to use saturation propaganda to "disabuse" the public mind of "widespread misconceptions which have been carefully implanted in it" about the alleged avarice of coal companies.[37] (*UMWJ*) editor Ellis Searles charged that "un-American" nonunion operators in West Virginia spent millions of propaganda dollars to protect their influence on public policy and law enforcement.[38] A letter to the *UMWJ* warned that since "most of the big papers are controlled by capitalists," the public constantly heard that union workers were radical and unpatriotic.[39] Searles attributed the American Plan–open-shop movement to a "gigantic conspiracy" to reestablish archaic industrial practices, and defended union discipline as industry's great stabilizer, necessary to any organization.[40]

The systematic propaganda campaigns to paint organized labor as disloyal put unions on the defensive. John L. Lewis was obliged to announce that "Coal miners are Americans" and that the UMWA was "an American institution that believes in and upholds American ideals."[41] Lewis also courted industrialists receptive to the idea that conservative unionism was good business. Disciplined and well-paid union workers meant greater productivity and profits, and Lewis ridiculed "those old mossback employers who live in the past," lacking the vision to see that labor-industry partnership would mean "more automobiles, more general education, more modern plumbing, more gramophones and bigger real wages."[42] Lewis earlier singled out Judge Gary, contending that the steel baron regarded his corporation as more powerful than the U.S. government. Lewis concluded that he hoped Gary represented "the old-time autocratic type of employer that is rapidly passing from the scene."[43] Ironically, even as the American Plan–open-shop movement sought to destroy unionism, Lewis was able to seed alliances with many national-minded industrialists who had long steered for the broad, smooth gulf between the swirling waters of radical anticapitalist workers and radical "anarchists" in the business community who most stridently pushed the open-shop campaign.[44]

Lewis's probusiness outlook and personal antiradicalism allowed him to consolidate his authority in the early 1920s by weakening his left opposition in the UMWA, at a time when union solidarity would appear to have been most critical. As put by Lewis biographers Dubofsky and Van Tine, Lewis's personal power in the union rose in the 1920s in proportion to the UMWA's decline in strength and influence. Lewis's "anti-red hysteria," played out in the pages of the *UMWJ*, won him the confidence of many businessmen and Republican politicians and allowed him to impugn the loyalty and undermine the political power of his more radical union opponents. By 1924 Lewis had neutralized insurgency within the union, and *UMWJ* editor Searles had "closed the columns" of the journal to activists who tried to keep nationalization of the coal industry, never a desirable objective to Lewis, alive.[45] The most accomplished of these dissidents, District 2 President John Brophy, was compelled to seek out the minimally distributed journals of the battered American radical left, such as *Labor Age*, to publish his arguments. One of Brophy's articles promoted "The Miners' American Plan," based on public ownership of the industry. Brophy's American Plan also adhered to basic union principles that institutionalized the right to strike and warned that any proposal to deny this right and collective bargaining to labor "is the beginning of slavery for the mining community."[46]

Brophy's was a consistent but muted call to the UMWA rank and file to reinvigorate radical criticism of the inequities of industrial capitalism. Although Lewis faced occasional internal challenges, his power was such that he always emerged stronger rather than weaker. Lewis's successes permitted him to steadily divert the flow of union authority away from the locals to the national, and he embarked on his design for union-industry cooperation, or "business unionism," as broader social objectives for the UMWA, embraced by Brophy and other insurgents, were undercut.[47] In a curious twist, the reactionary American Plan–open-shop movement and John L. Lewis struck an unspoken bargain, and crushed the vestiges of a noncapitalist model for American industry.

As Lewis formulated capitalist-based strategies to devalue or discredit social radicalism, nationalization, and working-class consciousness, business leaders cultivated capitalist-based strategies to secure their dominance of American political, social, and economic thought. Deviating from the rhetoric of industrial partnership, *Coal Age* proudly announced the self-conscious promotion of middle-class interests. National, state, and regional engineers meeting in Washington in June 1920 developed a sense of "engineering harmony" based on "publicity, class consciousness, co-operation and public service." The engineers agreed that they should serve "two distinct national functions," welfare work and professional activity. Professional activity demanded the "development of class consciousness of a professional type among engineers," requiring them to participate in "public service and the politico-economic life of the nation."[48]

Although business and industrial leaders perpetually intoned that America's greatness rested on "the abolition of class and caste," their own class identity, resting on internal assumptions about their personal values, was strong.[49] This surface contradiction was easily reconciled. It reflected the major structural changes in American society that accompanied modern industrialization in the early twentieth century. Social relations became primarily dependent on the production and exchange of goods and services, and one's value to society was identified with his productivity and contribution to sustained economic growth. The increasing division of industrial labor heightened class distinctions based on ownership or nonownership of property. For public consumption, the class-consciousness of owners or managers who succeeded in business or property accumulation was defined in terms of values and belief systems. Antimarket, or noncompetitive, values or beliefs were defined as "irrationalism" or ideology. In this context, "business" was not simply economic activity but a system of deliberate ideas and ideals geared toward the shape of society, law, politics, and moral standards. The ascendance of business as arbiter of values constructed a social hierarchy based on capital and labor as interdependent yet separate factors of production, with some individuals as superiors and some as subordinates. In a capitalist society, since the normative beliefs of capitalists determine the purposes and goals of social and political systems, capitalists became what classical theorists called a dominant or "ruling" class. Historian Martin Sklar points out that in recent years, social scientists have cast this term aside in favor of a less direct term, "hegemonic." As many historians and contemporary analysts of the emergence of industrial capitalism have demonstrated (chapters 3, 4, and 5), national values were to be shaped by those experts deemed qualified for public leadership. When industrial policies based on accepted elite values evoked widespread opposition or resistance, the whole people were then defined in a limited sense, as the "better citizens" or the "thinking" members of society.[50]

This reasoning permitted open-shop groups like the National Association of Manufacturers (NAM) to identify employers' interests as those of all society, deserving protection from outside interference. It also permitted the NAM and its open-shop allies to promote their own class interests while attacking labor-sponsored "class legislation," such as measures prohibiting injunctions in labor disputes, protecting picketers, and shortening workdays. Such class-favoring special legislation, in the view of open-shop advocates, impeded natural liberty and threatened the property rights of employers.[51] Coal miners' demands for a six-hour day and five-day week, for instance, coupled with doubletime pay for Sundays and holidays, would amount to an "indirect wage increase" and a "limitation on production." Coal executives interpreted such measures as "un-American. We regard them as an attempt to make of the miners a favored class." Union organizers, on the other hand, invested their demands for higher wages, shorter hours, and good working conditions with the rhetoric of patriotism, speaking of an "American standard" of material and social security.[52]

Cognizant that the desired sustained industrial expansion would perpetuate a system where "only a few are naturally adapted to professional life," businessmen implemented strategies to guarantee the internalization of professional class values by the masses.[53] Former CPI strategist Roger Babson wrote that no anticapitalist "ism" would "help you or me in our own individual struggle." Disengenuously, Babson lamented that the saddest feature of unionism was "the false doctrine that labor no longer has any hope of developing into the employer class." He chastised the wage earner's attitude that he would remain a wage earner, voiced in UMWA leader John Mitchell's statement that the worker "has given up hope" of becoming a capitalist, and "asks that the reward for his work be given him as the workingman." This was simply not so, said Babson, and conscientious workers had great opportunities to advance, if only they would "develop themselves so as to assume greater responsibilities." Babson then suggested the political dimensions of working class consciousness. It would be disastrous, he maintained, if the wage worker believed "he is always going to remain just as he is with no hope of further development." If workers believe "they are doomed ever after to remain in their present position without hope of advancement, they will try to get everything possible for their class to obtain."[54]

To avoid the danger of this kind of obstructionism among their workers, employers were obliged to equip them with appropriate social and industrial attitudes. Nonunion West Virginia coal operators, for example, in order to upset the designs of "the predatory union leader" who "stands as the enemy of society in general," were advised to use their own educational advantages to educate their miners, who are "deprived of perspective." The miner's "vision is more restricted, but he is quite willing to be shown" that he and his fellows suffer "when he fails to do his allotted part" in maintaining production. When workers came to appreciate "natural forces and economic laws," labor would "give all it can for a dollar" rather than giving as "little service as it can for a dollar." When labor understood the natural processes of the market, it would "welcome a co-operative alliance with the employer's brains."[55] In such a partnership, advancement would be swift for the ambitious, responsible worker. Moreover, educational and social opportunities flourished in orderly company towns, where the "arm of the law has been strengthened." Welfare capitalism had finally brought the world to the doors of West Virginia's "mountain people, who for generations were shut off by barriers of isolation. Unlimited opportunities are afforded the native mountain men and the foreign employes to advance to responsible positions, and to become mine owners."[56]

Class conflict in the southern West Virginia coalfields erupted violently in the Miners' March (see chapter 5) of late summer 1921. The march, capping the volatile early postwar readjustment, reaffirmed businessmen's resolve to make their values universal. Foremost among the "American Ideals" promoted by the American Constitutional Association was "Adequate Reward for Labor." Appropriate compensation was determined by "the development and expansion of business interests," which would provide the new consumer goods that would afford "inexhaustible opportunities for labor."[57] Property rights were also inviolate, and Americans could be secure in the knowledge that even a wealthy man "may not acquire a cottage belonging to the poorest man except by the full consent and legal conveyance by the owner."[58] The fundamental ideal of "Equality of Opportunity" was articulated by Edwin M. Keatley, who succeeded Cornwell as president of the ACA in 1922. In America, said Keatley, even the "man without a cent who is capable, is given the opportunity to forge ahead of the procession. . . . And to attempt a goal usually means success." Success, he continued, "depends entirely upon the individual."[59] Keatley, a New York native who came to West Virginia as a young man to manage properties for the J.P. Morgan Company, likewise voiced another basic principle of orderly social organization. "Children properly reared," he wrote, "early learn submission to authority."[60]

ACA members foresaw a daunting task ahead in their goal to instill "in the minds of our people, both native and foreign-born, the true spirit of Americanism."[61] True, the American Ideals professed by the Association transcended ideology to enter the realm of "fundamental truths," each of them "a clear statement substantiated by the doctrines of Christ." Certainly, if Christ had "formed a Government while on earth," it would have anticipated the forms of American democracy.[62] The ACA warned, however, that anticapitalist radicalism was not exclusively of alien origin, but homegrown. Indeed, Bolshevism had originated on American soil, conceived by radical labor organizer William "Big Bill" Haywood of the Industrial Workers of the World.[63] The ACA charged forty-five organizations, with a million members and a central directorate, with being "either extremely radical or mildly radical." These organizations conducted secret meetings, attended by working men who often worked a full day in "factories and shops, and then spend four to six hours in the evening, without pay, distributing literature of a radical nature."[64] The American Constitutional Association stood as the "official organization" in West Virginia to oppose "all Reds, all Bolsheviks, I.W.W.'s and other Government-destroying agencies."[65] It was the duty of loyal Americans to assist in exposing the propaganda of these agents.[66] It was the mission of the ACA, as a purely patriotic organization, to use information and education "to inculcate, not to drive, in the minds—not the passions of our people" its brand of Americanism.[67] The organization promised to distribute "our propaganda in the open, above board, where everybody can see what we are doing."[68]

The ACA's melding of the open-shop campaign with antiradicalism, following the lead of steelmakers who had defeated the 1919 strike, engaged powerful corporate allies in West Virginia. Some of the country's largest coal companies—including Consolidation, Island Creek, and subsidiaries of U.S. Steel-expanded their development of southern West Virginia coal properties in the immediate postwar years, attempting to avoid high union wages and regulation of production. These tactics succeeded in capturing markets from the unionized producers of the Central Competitive Field, markets the West Virginia operators were determined to protect.[69] Cornwell personally solicited support for the ACA from Consolidation's Clarence Watson, telling him that good results could be obtained by the ACA "if the business people will cooperate in pushing it along."[70] The association's most conspicuous corporate supporter was Judge Gary of U.S. Steel, national spokesman for the American Plan–open-shop drive. In the first decade of the twentieth century, Gary and William Edenborn of U.S. Steel had entered into partnership with a Greenbrier County banker to purchase the holdings of the Flat Top Coal Land Association. They soon acquired 80 percent of the Pocahontas coalfield, leasing it to coal companies. One of Gary's most prominent lessees was

a subsidiary of U.S. Steel, the U.S. Coal and Coke Company. U.S. Steel therefore had a direct interest in keeping production costs down in the Pocahontas field, as it secured its coal and coke supplies through its southern West
Virginia operations.[71]

Gary concurred with the ACA that if the American people would
only "study the facts," they would understand that individuals could realize
the full benefits of American opportunities "only through the principles of
the open shop as distinguished from the dominance and arbitrary control
of the union labor leaders." Disregarding the fact of the yellow-dog contract, Gary proclaimed that the open shop guaranteed freedom to employees to enter into any "line of employment, at any place and time, upon
terms and conditions voluntarily agreed upon between the employee and
the employer."[72] He was convinced that the great majority of employers and
workers believed that labor unions benefitted only union leaders.[73]

Judge Gary responded generously to an appeal from Edwin M. Keatley
to support the ACA's campaign. Acting through a Wheeling intermediary,
Keatley secured a $5,000 donation from Gary to the ACA, and Gary required
all U.S. Steel subsidiaries in West Virginia to endorse the association.[74] Keatley informed Cornwell late in 1920, eight months after the founding of the
ACA, that the association had secured several thousand dollars in pledges for
its work in 1921. Most pledges came from large employers who contributed
one dollar per employee.[75]

The anti-union campaign in West Virginia, in keeping with the nationwide American Plan strategy, targeted entrenched union strongholds as well
as unorganized coal-producing regions. The *American Plan Review*, a newsletter issued from Wheeling, included in the "ten commandments of the American Plan" the obligation of employers to "protect all employes in the
American right to earn a livelihood" in exchange for maximum loyalty from
all workers. Employers would allow employees to submit grievances to their
bosses, and all complaints would be adjusted fairly by the company "without
assistance or interference from outsiders." The review invoked a declaration
from the United States Chamber of Commerce that capital represented the
will of the majority, while labor promoted the tyranny of the unionized minority over the public interest. Moreover, capital believed in the force and
right of law, while labor had "no faith in the law and advocates employing, in
its stead, force, violence, and strikes."[76] In June 1921, American Plan–open-
shop businessmen in Wheeling launched an open-shop battle between
building trades unions and construction companies, who announced their
intentions to hire and place workers without regard to union or nonunion
status. Contractors initiated the open-shop strategy to break a two-month
strike in the Wheeling construction trades by union workers who refused to
accept 20 percent wage reductions when their union contracts had expired.[77]

The United States Chamber of Commerce, lining up with the rigorously open-shop National Association of Manufacturers, drew the lines for the national open-shop drive with its announcement in the summer of 1920 that "American business men are preparing to take a definite and united stand on the labor question." The Chamber registered the votes of more than thirteen hundred trade organization representatives nationwide on principles of industrial relations, including "the right of an employer to deal with his own men without the interference of outside agents." The Chamber's directors stated their belief that the right of open-shop operation "is an essential part of the individual right of contract possessed by each of the parties."[78] Nationally, member Chambers endorsed the open-shop principles 1,665 to 4, and for good measure the Bluefield, West Virginia, Chamber of Commerce circulated a resolution deploring the efforts of John L. Lewis to unionize coalfields in the Pocahontas district.[79]

The vote by Chamber members represented the Chamber's abandonment of neutrality on industrial struggles. The Chamber's shift helped unify employers' groups throughout the nation, who swiftly joined ranks to put labor on the defensive. The *Socialist Review* interpreted the Chamber's vote as a watershed in a well-organized plot by the nation's businessmen and organizations, dating back to the 1919 actions of the Associated Industries of Seattle, whose propaganda model was imitated by other open-shop groups. The Associated Employers of Indianapolis distributed 1.5 million pieces of open-shop literature across the nation, offering tactical advice to open-shop organizers.[80] The National Association of Manufacturers, which had kept the open-shop ideals before the public since 1903, sported an Open-Shop Department, whose functions the NAM defined as purely educational. One of its most effective strategies was to publish the *Open Shop Encyclopedia for Debaters*, and to send speakers to address college assemblies on the virtues of breaking unions.[81] The moral force of the presidency was behind the NAM's open-shop principles, as Warren G. Harding announced that it was "the right of every free American to labor without any other's leave."[82]

Soon after the American Plan organizational meeting was convened by Gary in Chicago in January 1921, job printing shops in Salt Lake City announced they would operate under the plan's open-shop tenets.[83] Builders in Albany and Troy, New York, endorsed the American Plan that summer. Chicago meatpacking firms followed suit shortly after, prompting a strike by the packers' employees. Fourteen independent packers in St. Louis also adopted the American Plan, as did the Texas and Pacific Coal Company.[84] The Chicago Association of Commerce, the Illinois Manufacturers' Association, and others formed a "Citizens' Committee" to help enforce an open-shop decision by Federal Judge Kenesaw Mountain Landis, pledging to raise $3 million to import nonunion tradesmen to Chicago if necessary.[85]

The Williamson, West Virginia, Coal Operators' Association claimed the pre-rogative to operate open-shop mines "as a matter of law and right" and blasted the organizing practices and complete unionization goals of the UMWA as being inimical to "fundamental freedom and the American Government" and "contrary to public policy."[86]

Organized resistance to the American Plan–open-shop was broad but fragmentary, scattered, and poorly funded. Power struggles and a fiscal crisis within the miners' union hindered a unified oppositional front. The UMWA spent $8 million between 1920 and 1922 to organize southern West Virginia, only to be turned back by the vigilance of the operators and their business and political allies.[87] The Miners' March of August–September 1921 briefly galvanized national attention on the West Virginia miners' struggle, but the ensuing trials of nearly six hundred march participants further depleted meager union resources. Even though John L. Lewis assisted in the defense of union activist and march organizer Bill Blizzard at Blizzard's treason trial in 1922, Lewis angrily condemned the officers of District 17 for trying "to shoot the union into West Virginia."[88] In October 1922 the UMWA abandoned the Mingo County strike and desperately attempted to resist the rollback of union contracts in the Kanawha, New River, and Fairmont fields. Lewis later insisted that wage rates be maintained in these fields, despite a disastrous depression in coal sales and prices after 1923. When Frank Keeney and Fred Mooney protested this policy, Lewis removed them in favor of a more compliant subordinate, Percy Tetlow, a common Lewis tactic to undermine the independence of his officers.[89]

Such internecine battles undercut a unified front against the American Plan movement, but beleaguered unionists mustered moral support from various sources. The executive committee of the Methodist Federation of Social Service charged open-shop advocates with hypocritically mouthing the rights of workers to join unions while they maneuvered to fire or blacklist unionists. The American Plan, said the committee, denied fundamental rights of labor to organize and would lead to "chaos, anarchy, and warfare in our industrial life, and intolerably delay the development of constitutional democracy in industry." The Federal Council of Churches of Christ also rejected the American Plan, prompting angry criticism from the National Association of Manufacturers.[90] *The Nation* charged nonunion New River coal operators in West Virginia with using hunger, evictions, injunctions, and blacklists to deny their employees fundamental rights of voluntary association and collective bargaining, and union operators with attempting to divide and conquer the UMWA with district agreements for "essentially a national industry." The intellectual liberal journal predicted that if the union were crushed, the coal fields would fall into anarchy, with the miners "helpless before a despotism which in the past has dominated every department

Eligible West Virginia males from Ohio County await the results of the first draft, May 1917. West Virginia State Archives, Paula Cornett Collection.

On September 19, 1917, Wheeling citizens turned out in a farewell demonstration for 156 of their drafted men, bound for Camp Lee at Petersburg, Virginia. West Virginia State Archives, Mrs. Elmer Bibbee Collection.

West Virginia steelworkers gather for patriotic Four-Minute speeches during a 1918 Liberty Loan Drive. West Virginia State Archives, Kirk Collection.

A 1918 Liberty Loan parade in Wheeling. West Virginia State Archives, George Dockstetter Collection.

West Virginia's wartime governor, John J. Cornwell, flanked by West Virginia military officers in July 1918. West Virginia State Archives.

Jackson Arnold of Weston, West Virginia, a U.S. Army lieutenant colonel in WWI, first superintendent of West Virginia's Department of Public Safety (state police), and first commander of the state's American Legion. West Virginia State Archives, West Virginia State Police file.

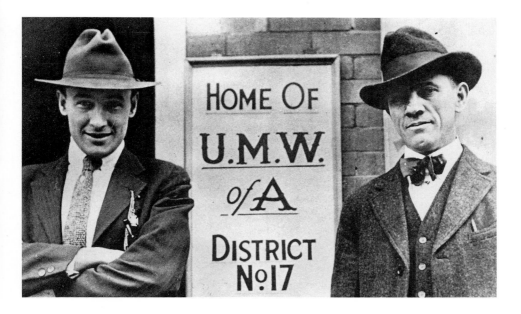

Fred Mooney (left), secretary treasurer, and Frank Keeney, president, of District 17 of the United Mine Workers of America. West Virginia State Archives.

West Virginia state troopers beside their Ford patrol car in 1922. A machine gun, which Governor Cornwell described as "advantageous" for mob control, is mounted on the passenger side. West Virginia State Archives, West Virginia State Police file.

West Virginia
miners and
company
officers in the
early 1920s.
West Virginia
State Archives.

Company housing in Coretta, West Virginia, in the late 1920s. West Virginia State Archives, Carol DeHaven Collection.

A picture of the "civic religion." Black children in Charleston, West Virginia, display the Christian flag and the American flag in 1924. West Virginia State Archives.

Philip M. Conley, school administrator, war hero, human relations officer for Consolidation Coal, managing director of the American Constitutional Association, and founder of the *West Virginia Review,* in 1923. West Virginia State Archives, from *West Virginia Illustrated* 2:7 (Aug./Sept. 1971), p. 42.

of their lives."[91] AFL President Samuel Gompers also warned of the destabilizing effects on business if collective bargaining rights were withheld, claiming that the country would careen into Sovietism and Bolshevism if unions were destroyed. Fred Mooney, while he still enjoyed Lewis's good graces, accused the "labor-hating fakers" of the National Coal Association of secretly conspiring with communists to destroy the confidence of rank-and-file workers in responsible labor leaders.[92]

One of the dreams of many open-shop advocates was to make strikes illegal and to submit disputes to industrial courts. This short-lived adjunct to the American Plan–open-shop movement flourished in Kansas, where recurrent miner walkouts directed by the charismatic Lewis rival Alex Howat fueled the region's antiradical hysteria. Kansas instituted a law, later declared unconstitutional, that effectively outlawed strikes and established compulsory arbitration of labor disputes, a development that was "an anathema to the entire American labor movement."[93] On at least one occasion the Kansas court of industrial relations turned the tables on infuriated antiunion forces in the state, ruling that employers could not inflict capricious or arbitrary layoffs on their workers with each business downturn. Delighted with this particular decision, the UMWJ pointed out, however, that the court was created to compel the state's miners to work whether they were treated fairly or not.[94]

Governor Cornwell had long advocated an industrial-court law for West Virginia, without success.[95] Cornwell left office, to become general counsel for the Baltimore and Ohio Railroad, early in 1921. He was succeeded by an equally firm supporter of business interests, Republican Ephraim F. Morgan, an opponent of labor radicalism and the League of Nations, who enjoyed a Republican majority in the legislature.[96] Nevertheless, the legislature declined to approve an industrial court law in 1921.[97] In 1923, however, Senator William J. McClaren of Welch sponsored Senate Bill 337 to create a West Virginia Court of Industrial Relations, with the judges of the court to be appointed by the governor. The West Virginia proposal, said the UMWJ, made the Kansas industrial court "look like a plugged nickel, when it comes to destroying the rights of workers." Section 14 of the McClaren bill recognized the right to collective bargaining by unions or associations of workers incorporated by state law, an allowance rendered virtually meaningless by the provisions of Section 9, which established the principle of the individual contract, and by Sections 15 and 17. Section 15 defined picketing, boycotting, advertising, and union propaganda as unlawful conspiracy, if the court decided these actions injured any corporation or business. Section 17 made strikes illegal, forbidding any person to "conspire with other persons to quit their employment or to induce others to quit their employment" for purposes of interfering with business or industrial operations.[98] By proposing to institutionalize the employer's right to negotiate individual contracts and to deny labor's right to strike, the West Virginia bill confirmed what the AFL had long stated. AFL Vice President Matthew Woll affirmed that denying the right to strike offset any right to collective bargaining. "To assert that you have the right of collective bargaining, and cannot strike," said Woll, "is simply a contradiction."[99]

Despite Governor Morgan's hopes, the industrial-court bill stalled in the legislature. It is likely that some industrialists and businessmen, regardless of their desires to cripple unionism, were wary of provisions that gave the judges jurisdiction to regulate working and living conditions, hours of labor, and even to standardize wages. Such powers vested in a state regulatory body, while in keeping with the structural changes in corporate capitalism, might very well elicit opposition from independent business anarchists who rejected the corporate liberalism of nationally oriented or progressive industrialists.[100] Perhaps some were aware that the Kansas law, although decisively favorable to industry, had still once been used to muzzle arbitrary layoffs and firings. Organized labor in West Virginia, although reeling from the southern coal strike, perhaps mobilized enough opposition generated by the state's trades assemblies to block the bill. Morgan's election, after all, had not implied a popular mandate for the governor. He had defeated a labor-supported nonpartisan candidate in the 1920 election, Samuel B. Montgomery, who probably drew most of his votes away from the Democratic candidate, Arthur B. Koontz. Together Montgomery and Koontz outpolled the victorious Morgan.[101] The failure of the industrial court plan suggests that even with the temptations of the antistrike provisions, open-shop businessmen were cool to the idea of a state body that, at least in theory, could intrude on the prerogatives of unregulated free enterprise as well as labor organizing.

Whatever the degree of tactical contentiousness between anti-unionists that can be read into the West Virginia industrial-court fizzle, however, the American Plan–open-shop crusade expanded its struggle for the hearts and minds of the public. That struggle reached beyond the mass industries and trades into other sectors. W.C. Ruediger of George Washington University wrote late in 1918 that efforts by the American Federation of Labor to organize schoolteachers would lead to "consciousness of class, and that of the Bolshevik variety." Teachers above all others must be "free from all predetermined class alliances." Otherwise, they could not shape the "wholesome mental development of all the children of all the people." Class-conscious teachers would sacrifice the trust of lawyers, doctors, ministers, and business owners and managers, who wanted their children educated in schools where impartiality prevailed. Professional consciousness among teachers was acceptable, but teacher affiliation with "labor unionism" was undemocratic.

Ruediger feared that unionized teachers would turn the public schools into "schools for labor unionists."[102]

A respondent suggested that Ruediger denigrated workers' consciousness but fully approved of class identity among owners, managers, bankers, and lawyers, the respectable elements who sought to dominate society's manners, intellectual interests, and morals through the subsidized press and class-conscious journals. To Ruediger's critic, unionization among teachers merely showed their solidarity with common people.[103] The American Federation of Labor agreed, and suggested that teachers should be independent of boards of education, which had "no proprietary right in the schools." The *UMWJ* encouraged teachers not to limit their organizations to professional meeting societies but to "learn to wield the big stick" against arbitrary bosses.[104]

Union sentiments among teachers sent shock waves through the American educational establishment. As industrialists geared up for the 1919 steel strike, local teachers' associations in nearly one hundred communities joined the American Teachers' Federation, which was affiliated with the AFL, demanding competitive wages and joining in the growing activism among workers nationwide. School boards were disturbed by the movement to organize teachers, who arguably had a legal right to unionize but not, from the elites' perspective, to put their class interest above the public good. Administrators and board members claimed that school boards were not private bosses of teachers, but representatives of the people, and coercive action against them by teachers was undemocratic.[105]

Rumblings of teachers' unions running concurrently with industrial unionism's call for nationalization of major industries prompted editor Waitman Barbe of the *West Virginia School Journal* initially to analyze the controversy in abstract terms of individual freedom. True, it was through selfless collective effort that America and the Allies had unified to defeat German autocracy. But the victory of 1918 would produce a progressive civilization only when individuals were free, unburdened by intrusive institutions, to "develop the best that is in them." Human development, said Barbe, was not a collective but an individual process. His argument took on more concrete open-shop tones when he applauded the decision of the Lancaster, Pennsylvania, school board to dismiss teachers who had joined the AFL. Teachers must understand, said Barbe, that they were public servants, with "legal and moral obligations which a day laborer does not have." Unions were special interests, and union teachers might therefore be compelled to represent only part of the public. Echoing Pennsylvania's superintendent of public instruction, Dr. Thomas E. Finegan, Barbe concurred that fundamental Americanism demanded that teachers be free to "explain, without prejudice, the philosophy of American life, government and institutions." They must not favor the interests of one group of citizens against the interests of another group or of the whole community.[106]

Shortly after Barbe's opinion appeared in the *WVSJ*, the Morgantown Board of Education adopted an anti-union policy for the district's teachers. The board issued a standing order that it opposed organized political action by teachers.[107] The issue of union representation for teachers soon disappeared from the *WVSJ*. A 1923 column by Walter Barnes praised teachers for developing a unified state education association as an expression of professional consciousness. The *WVSJ*, however, was by that time the organ of the association, whose members had abandoned, if indeed they ever seriously considered, a flirtation with the power of collective bargaining. Barnes's invocation, like Barbe's rhetoric, sanctified individual over collective action. Power rested in the personal "ideals of vigor and virility," through which the WVEA could "breed a sterner, stronger, more aggressive race of teachers."[108]

Although the American Plan–open-shop campaign never achieved the ideal of its most radical proponents, that being the complete rollback and destruction of trade unionism and collective bargaining, it did nonetheless achieve enduring results. David Montgomery suggests that the recession of labor militance in the 1920s resulted from interdependent business organization, state repression, economic depression from 1920 to 1922, and the isolation of the left wing of the workers' movement by conservative unionism. The American Plan movement might even be interpreted as only moderately successful if national union membership is the indicator. Although AFL membership declined by at least one-third between 1920 and 1923, the federation was still larger than in prewar years.[109] In West Virginia, however, the open-shop movement enjoyed a great victory. Kanawha operators refused to contract with their union employees, and between 1922 and 1925 they evicted ten thousand union miners and forty thousand family members from company housing. Northern West Virginia operators abrogated union contracts, began open-shop operations, and obtained *Hitchman* injunctions to keep UMWA organizers out of the Fairmont field. Under pressure from increased production in West Virginia's open-shop fields, many Central Competitive Field operators imposed open-shop operations as well.[110]

While the quantitative results of the American Plan–open-shop movement were mixed, it was ultimately successful in forcing organized labor from even moderately oppositional stances on such issues as nationalization of industries and an independent labor party. The trade unions of the 1920s had adapted to an undemocratic America, whose economic structure would soon collapse.[111] Much of labor's conservatism persisted even with the tumultuous and divisive resurgence of organized labor in the 1930s, and with its ascendance during World War II. Labor's renaissance and growth, though effecting a dramatic and significant adjustment of economic power, occurred within the context of the mutual rejection by victorious labor, business, and political leaders of noncapitalist, or "un-American," solutions to the nation's economic and social crises. The triumph of business unionism as the organizing principle of the UMWA and other major unions is a significant indicator of the thorough marginalization of political and economic alternatives to American industrial capitalism.[112]

The business-friendly climate of the UMWA under John L. Lewis was well established by 1923. Lewis had steered the UMWA away from nationalization in his resolve to adapt the union leadership's longstanding suspicion of government intervention in business to modern industrial relations. The *UMWJ* claimed with certainty "that neither miners nor operators desire governmental control or regulation of the coal business."[113] By late 1924 Lewis's courting of union coal operators led some of them to ask Lewis to administer a proposed owners' association. Lewis demurred, choosing instead to parlay his dominance of the UMWA into the successful promotion of a seemingly deferential William Green to the AFL presidently, succeeding Gompers, who died in December 1924. Lewis ruled the UMWA, had negotiated wage increases for union miners in the Jacksonville Agreement, and enjoyed an amiable if not especially influential relationship with the Calvin Coolidge administration. He was recognized by financiers, industrialists, and conservative politicians, according to Dubofsky and Van Tine, as the foremost American labor leader who understood the value of harmonious labor-management relations.[114] When AFL delegates refused to endorse the idea of an American labor political party, the *UMWJ* praised the decision. The interests of the working masses would presumably be served by a nonpartisan policy to make government more responsive to their needs through the "progressive enlightenment" of the existing economic and political structure.[115]

In the early 1920s, John L. Lewis and much of the business community in West Virginia differed over the rightful place of collective bargaining and organized labor in the United States. Despite this, their differences did not extend to disagreement over the fundamental soundness of consumerism, economic expansionism, and free market capitalism as the appropriate model for the organization of American society. Union policy, adjusting to determined business assaults, therefore pushed to the margins the populist currents that ran through much of the labor unrest of the early postwar era, including the nationalization debates and the 1921 southern West Virginia miners' rebellion. The growth-oriented business unionism of Lewis and the hierarchical standards of industrial Americanization promoted by groups like the ACA did not become fully integrated until decades later, after another world conflict. Not until after the Great Depression, when labor militancy forced the federal government to endorse collective bargaining as public policy, and the crisis of the Second World War, did the adversarial bureaucratization of modern labor relations mature and atrophy. The American Plan–open-shop campaign of the early 1920s, therefore, represented a formative preliminary conflict to the dominant business/union consensus of the Cold War era. The Americanization of West Virginia in the early 1920s, however, entailed a broader ideological application than the anti-union struggle. The institutionalization of the tenets of industrial Americanization, by the American Constitutional Association and allied public and private agencies in West Virginia, required mobilization on many fronts.

7

Voluntary Associations and Americanization in the 1920s

Labor historian David Corbin has written that the federal government's wartime patriotic propaganda mechanism created a demand for conformity that ignited postwar explosions of nativism, antiradicalism, and the open-shop fervor. John Higham explains the racial xenophobia and antiradicalism of the "Tribal Twenties" as a revival of prewar nativist ferment that had temporarily been refocused on the war crisis. The collapse of the wartime boom economy by 1920—together with a dramatic increase in European immigration in the spring of that year, reversing the wartime and immediate postwar trend of migration back to Europe—recast much of Americans' economic frustrations and political fears onto the foreign-born. Entrenched perceptions linking foreigners with crime and political radicalism fostered unprecedented attempts to regiment the moral and social behavior of all Americans by law, markedly with the implementation of the prohibition amendment.[1] The West Virginia Woman's Christian Temperance Union (WVWCTU), a leading advocate of middle-class Americanization, predicted that the "phenomenal progress" made in the world crusade against alcohol would be as historically prominent as "the unspeakable war itself." Whatever the long-term results of the war, it had revealed "the true relation of drink to efficiency and success."[2] One hundred percent Americanizers, grounded in quasi-scientific assumptions of Anglo-Saxon superiority and determined to alter the drinking culture of immigrant groups, set out to "usher in a purified, regenerate society." Higham contends, however, that 100 percenters reflected a national psychological letdown after the war and were fraught with uncertainty as to the ultimate defeat of "the forces of darkness." One hundred percent Americanism therefore typically assumed a defensive posture, says Higham, taking the form of retrenchment and suspicion rather than confidence in the resilience of American institutions.[3]

Viewed in the light of national policies of diplomatic withdrawal, economic protectionism, and immigration restriction of the early 1920s, postwar campaigns to resurrect the wartime goals of "unity of thought and purpose" indeed appear predominantly defensive.[4] Nevertheless, the fabrication of industrial Americanization required more than negative legislation imposed to regulate immigration and moral behavior. Conformist patterns of political and economic thought could not be guaranteed simply by reactionary outbursts against real or imagined enemies of social stability. It was necessary to mobilize sustainable support for the business and industrial sectors that emerged as the nation's most powerful arbiters of state and private activity. Business, corporate, political, and educational elites, as well as business unionists, realized the value of the engineering of consent to promote their model for American society. "Wartime propaganda accelerated the development of opinion molding," said Edward L. Bernays, and interest groups became aware that "the great public could now perhaps be harnessed to their cause."[5]

Essayist C. Wright Mills later outlined the authoritarian potential of the "opinion business," warning against the power of elite institutional authorities to manipulate cultural symbols of loyalty. The imposition of standards of thought and behavior on a powerless public could render them merely a "collectivity of individuals" rather than full participants in a democratic polity.[6] William Graebner points out that the social engineering of early twentieth-century America implied conscious efforts at control, wherein teachers, social workers, businessmen, and other avowedly democratic social engineers attempted to shape the behavior of others who were "unaware of the totality of what was happening to them." While this type of manipulation suggests questionable ethics, says Graebner, its practitioners envisioned social engineering as a democratic process designed to insure responsible and orderly social behavior. From this process would develop standards, practices, and values that had withstood the "competition of ideas in the American marketplace."[7]

The range of acceptable thought and theory, or the *boundaries* of the marketplace of ideas, thus became a central factor in state and private attempts at "Mobilizing the Mind of America."[8] Comments by some West Virginia opinion-makers suggest that the marketplace was restricted, resurrecting de Toqueville's observation that praise for their institutions was always agreeable to Americans, and offered as evidence of free speech. Should someone dare to speak negatively of the country or its institutions, however, permission to continue was "inexorably refused."[9] Governor John J. Cornwell, to illustrate, proclaimed in 1919 that there could be no compromise on "questions affecting our form of government or threatening its stability."[10] West Virginia Attorney General E.T. England warned that "free speech does not embrace disloyal utterances against our government" and designated a wide field of intolerable utterances. Criticizing official acts and conduct of public officials was permissible but "criticizing our government . . . is inexcusable." "We must have," said England, "less disloyalty and less disrespect for the laws, and the country in which we live. Let our slogan be 'America for Americans.'"[11]

Following the standards for distribution of information pioneered by the Committee on Public Information, the national government suggested guidelines for molding patriotic citizens, whether native or foreign-born. Morris P. Shawkey announced that the U.S. Bureau of Education had launched an Americanization drive to coordinate the work of agencies nationwide.[12] A War Department bulletin stressed that to guarantee the loyalty and respect necessary for social progress and stability, Americans must be educated about fundamental facts and principles leading to "sound economic, social, political and intellectual attitudes." Good citizenship was the result of each individual's understanding that "growth in productive capacity" was essential. Young men especially must be trained to be "productive citizens and intrepid soldiers," equipped for industry, commerce, and business. Civilian schools and colleges were advised to organize their courses along military lines, emphasizing common ideas and standards of judgment. Schools were the logical agencies to "train the potential soldier and citizen" to adapt his interests to society's requirements.[13]

Americanization specialist John J. Mahoney declared that the task of all teachers was the making of Americans. To Mahoney, Americanization implied the formation of proper habits through "review and drill" administered by teachers who were "American 100 per cent pure."[14] The pursuit of pure teachers led the Morgantown, West Virginia, school district to forbid teachers from dancing, which allegedly would divert their energy and intrude on their ability to put Morgantown schools "on the highest plane of efficiency." When the state superintendent of schools declared that a contractual stipulation prohibiting dancing was unenforceable, the Morgantown Board simply issued a blanket order proscribing dancing.[15]

The national government prepared citizenship texts for the nation's public schools, principally for use in Americanization classes for the foreign-born. It encouraged all states to adopt formal Americanization programs. Many states and municipalities embarked on renewed Americanization programs after the war.[16] West Virginia Superintendent of Schools George M. Ford, who succeeded Shawkey in 1921, reported that the state Department of Education had joined with the United States Bureau of Naturalization to provide Americanization programs in the state. Ford acknowledged the benefits of free text books provided by the Bureau, which would help West Virginia offset communication barriers with the state's foreign-born, which drove them "into colonies" and isolated them from influences and associations "with which they should be related."[17]

Ford solicited the assistance of private clubs and organizations to assist in the Americanization of the state's foreign-born.[18] In Wheeling, the Americanization Committee of the Chamber of Commerce secured the cooperation of local employers in establishing immigrant workers' noon meetings, which aided in "inclining the foreign-born to our way of doing and thinking." The Woman's Club of Weston planned special Americanization programs for 1922, and the Woman's Club of Thomas had joined forces with the American Legion in "reaching the foreigner."[19] West Virginia chapters of the Daughters of the American Revolution distributed thousands of copies of "The American's Creed," and combined English night schools with essay contests on Patriotic Education and programs on radicalism and "National Industries, the Outgrowth of National Freedom."[20] The chair of the West Virginia Federation of Women's Clubs (WVFWC) Americanization Division feared that "the melting pot is not melting" and pledged to devote WVFWC energies to make the United States "a nation of one people, one language, and one flag." Mrs. A.L. Lehman recommended incorporating English instruction into immigrant women's cooking, sewing, and handicraft classes, accompanied by lectures and patriotic music to illustrate America's institutions and ideals. Immigrants should be taught to salute the flag and learn the American's Creed and be discouraged from residing in segregated colonies, where lonesomeness and homesickness would breed discontent, disloyalty, and anarchy.[21]

The WVFWC acknowledged that Americanization among segregated pockets of West Virginia's immigrants should be less daunting than many areas of the country, particularly urban centers where a new immigrant was inclined to "herd among members of his own nationality."[22] Mrs. L.H. Cammack, chair of the WVFWC Department of American Citizenship, reported that West Virginia was "peculiarly fortunate" in its comparatively small number of immigrants. Indeed, only about 10 percent of the state's 1.4 million residents were foreign born, and many had "long since adopted the Stars and Stripes and are counted our very best citizens."[23]

The veiled racial content of even the most benign architects of Americanization, such as the WVFWC and the WVWCTU, reflected the nativist impulses of social engineering common to the era. American racial nationalism, to use Higham's expression, derived from long-established assumptions among American elites that Anglo-Saxon institutions were uniquely adapted to political freedom and destined to spread its blessings.[24] James Morton Callahan's convictions about the natural civilizing influences of Anglo-Saxon culture (see chapter 2) were grounded in fundamental and pervasive early nationalist sentiments, which had led Alexis de Toqueville to comment that "Nothing is more embarrassing in the ordinary intercourse of life than this irritable patriotism of the Americans."[25] The political and economic content of postwar nativism was a legacy of popular reinterpretations of traditional theories of cultural hierarchy, portrayed as scientific, which selectively borrowed from Mendelian genetics to proclaim racial purity as a social ideal under the banner of the eugenics movement. By the time of the Great War, the doctrine of Anglo-Saxonism had been formalized in tracts such as Madison Grant's influential *The Passing of the Great Race*.[26]

Unlike the architects of industrial Americanization, Grant put race consciousness above national consciousness. Postwar Americanizers left little doubt, however, about their belief in the natural aptitude of the Anglo-Saxon character to define universal values and political forms. As a corollary, states or regions with small immigrant and black populations catered to racial nativism in their campaigns for industrial development in the 1920s. Allen Tullos notes the race-based strategies used by North Carolina Piedmont businessmen to attract investment. The Piedmont's population was advertised as "marked by racial purity and unusually high character." Piedmont whites were "native-born of old pioneer stock" and "not imbued by un-American ideas or ideals."[27] Likewise, the *West Virginia Review*, a journal boosting the state's attractions and business climate, edited by ACA Managing Director Phil Conley, emphasized the racial homogeneity of West Virginia. In the journal's first issue, his "The Man from West Virginia" column boasted of the state's 89.9 percent white population, "the highest percentage of native born white citizens to be found in any State in the Union." "We are proud of our mountain people," said The Man, people who represented "the best Anglo-Saxon blood to be found in America today." Subsequently, an article by Hays Brown feted West Virginia's "Pure-Blooded Americans." "There is scarcely a trace of foreign blood to be found," said Brown. With the exception of some of the coal producing regions, West Virginia was spared the "extended invasion of foreign immigrants." Likewise, "the mountain country has been comparatively free from negroes. . . . Negroes have never been in the mountains to any extent and are not there now."[28] The Huntington Chamber of Commerce proudly cited government figures indicating that the city's population was 98 percent American born. Even if Huntington had "no other asset," manufacturers would therefore be impressed by the "sterling citizenship of its laboring population."[29]

Although the state's relatively small immigrant population reduced some obstacles, such as pervasive language barriers, to industrial Americanization, the process demanded unifying native *and* foreign born "in perfect support of American principles."[30] Americanizers should work to assimilate immigrants, but also bear in mind that the native born must be awakened to their duty and allegiance to the country.[31] Disloyalty was home-grown as well as imported. Indeed, reported a West Virginia Americanizer, American-born radicals led the movement to undermine American life and government, radicals who must learn "to live in respect and strict obedience to every law."[32] West Virginians were reminded that the 1921 Miners' March, when the state was "discredited in the eyes of the world," was "inspired by radical leaders . . . and the distressing fact is that many of them were native born West Virginians."[33] The WVFWC's director of citizenship training affirmed that whether foreign or American-born, proper citizenship was required "for all classes of Americans. . . . we want them to think as we do, live as we do, and feel as we do, and have the same hopes that we have for our country."[34]

It was partly his background in Americanization work that recommended Philip M. Conley to Edwin Keatley when the latter was looking for a manager for the American Constitutional Association. Keatley informed Cornwell that Conley had been "engaged in morale work during the war" and since had directed education, editing, and Americanization work among foreigners. When Keatley approached Conley about joining the ACA, Conley was working for Consolidation Coal Company in the company's Elkhorn mining district, based in Jenkins, Kentucky.[35] Keatley planned for Conley to work primarily among the teachers and foreign-born workmen of West Virginia.[36]

The February 1921 edition of Consolidation's employee magazine announced that Conley had left Jenkins to accept a lucrative post with the American Constitutional Association.[37] Conley became the only salaried employee of the ACA, lured from his position with Consolidation by Keatley's offer of a $6,000 annual salary, remuneration that was equal to or higher than many West Virginia state officials.[38] He began his duties with the ACA in Charleston on January 1, 1921.[39]

One of Conley's many public relations duties for the ACA was editing and distributing the organization's newsletter, *The American Citizen*, a twice-monthly publication that first appeared late in 1920.[40] Conley envisioned the newsletter as an aid for Americanization work in mining towns and for "propaganda against radicalism and bolshevism," telling Keatley *The American Citizen* could be used "to preach a doctrine of law and order and Americanism." *The American Citizen* would be invaluable in ACA efforts to "develop a national consciousness," and Keatley reported that several large factories in Wheeling and throughout West Virginia were furnishing employee lists to the ACA for shipment of the newsletter.[41] High schools also received copies of each edition, and Conley claimed that three thousand copies of each issue were distributed. The ACA also sent out thousands of "America First" placards semi-monthly. They contained Americanization messages to be tacked on bulletin boards in factories, mills, and mines.[42] The placards contained "snappy sentences" to arouse Americans to respect the law and fight "those who are opposed to our Government." Conley embarked on a whirlwind speaking campaign, addressing the Logan Coal Operators Association and the Northern West Virginia Coal Operators, who adopted unanimous resolutions of support for the ACA. He also spoke before the annual meeting of the West Virginia Manufacturers' Association, a meeting of the Kanawha County Bar Association, a meeting of the Hunting-ton Rotary Club, and a meeting of the county and district superintendents. His message was especially well-received by the manufacturers, who re-solved to support the work of the ACA.[43]

Conley was not alone in his public appearances. Committed to "a patriotic speaker for every occasion," the ACA formed a speakers bureau to provide Rotary, Kiwanis, Lions, chambers of commerce, women's clubs, coal operators' associations, and Sunday school meetings with "four minute speakers" on law, order, and patriotism themes.[44] Founding members of the ACA anticipated eventually forming a national constituency, providing for a National Executive Committee to administer national policy for ACAs in each state. In keeping with these plans, Conley attended a March 1921 meet-ing in Washington of organizations doing patriotic and civic work, which founded an advisory body called the National American Council. Conley proudly announced that the council would probably designate the ACA as "the official organization to carry on its work in West Virginia."[45]

Commenting earlier on the impending Washington meeting, Conley had solicited a testimonial from Dr. I.C. White, West Virginia's most emi-nent geologist, who praised the efforts of the ACA to "keep alive the flame of patriotism which swept over the country during the late World War and which needs constantly to be rekindled in the hearts of the immigrant and foreign population as well as the home folks." Using a tactic perfected by the CPI, White was identified only in his professional capacity as state geologist, while his status as a director of the ACA was not mentioned.[46]

Perhaps the central maxim of the ACA was that "if real patriotism and love of country is to be developed in this country, it must be done through the public schools."[47] Conley's commitment to work in the public schools had personal antecedents. Before serving in the army in France during the war, Conley had been superintendent of public schools in Marion County, West Virginia. While director of welfare work for Consolidation Coal in Jen-kins, Conley had also been superintendent of schools (white and colored) in the Elkhorn District, where his accomplishments included night Americani-zation schools, the introduction of industrial training, and the expansion of domestic science programs in the communities of Burdine, McRoberts, Dunham, and Jenkins.[48] It is likely that Conley's background in school ad-ministration served him well in his cordial association with West Virginia Superintendent of Schools George M. Ford, who appointed Conley director of Americanization work in the public schools. Ford also designated Conley "Supervisor of Citizenship and Thrift," and in March 1921 the ACA moved from its office on Hale Street in Charleston to the headquarters of the state Department of Education.[49] In exchange for office space, postage, steno-graphic help, and telephone service, the ACA organized a school banking system, arranged school essay contests on patriotic subjects, and supervised patriotic and civic instruction in the public schools.[50] The ACA's partnership with the schools therefore realized the pronouncement by Professor Robert A. Armstrong that Americanism must be taught both by the schools and "among many men in high places of trust and profit." The ACA's arrangement with the schools, Conley informed the ACA Executive Committee, would enable the organization "to reach the adults through the medium of the children."[51]

The ACA's entree to the state's educational system, however, also included direct contact with the most important of that system's adults, the teachers. Conley and Ford arranged for the ACA to provide speakers at each county teachers institute in the summer of 1921. Conley reported that the ACA's vision of "American Ideals" could potentially reach eleven thousand teachers through the institutes.[52] Institute schedules for 1921 show that practically every county institute included a weekly address on "American Ideals," emphasizing the ACA perspective on property rights, abolition of caste and class, and adequate reward for labor by "special instructors" from the open-shop organization.[53] The ACA described these ideals as "the civic and political religion of this great nation." At their 1921 institute, Mineral County teachers denounced "Bolshevistic tendencies" in the state and advised comprehensive teaching of Americanism, good citizenship, and morality to alleviate the problem.[54]

As part of its public school agenda, the ACA initiated essay contests in West Virginia high schools. With Ford's blessing, Conley secured the cooperation of high school principals for the contests, the first of which offered prizes totaling $60.00 for the four top essays observing George Washington's birthday. The ACA Executive Committee selected the topics, and Conley reported that 576 students from forty-seven high schools participated. The winner, Mabel West of Lost Creek, West Virginia, chose "Americanism: What it Means" from the list of four approved topics and impressed the judges with her declaration that "We do not want any hyphenated Americans. We want red-blooded Americans who are willing to serve."[55]

School essay contests were commonly used by business and patriotic organizations to secure a presence in the schools' daily routine. School administrators recoiled from the potential class alliances implied by labor unionism in the schools, but they usually welcomed civic-minded organizations that avowedly refrained from partisan politics and encouraged patriotism and habits of industry in the public interest above narrow concerns. The Bluefield Chamber of Commerce, which carried the banner of the American Plan–open-shop movement, could therefore deny the political content of its position and gain access to public schools through an essay contest entitled "What a Chamber of Commerce Means to Bluefield."[56]

Writing in *The Nation*, F.B. Kaye chided the apolitical presumptions inherent in an Americanism that depended on "emotional debauchery" and "mass conditioning" rather than natural, familial feelings of love for country. The "intolerant patrioteering" of middle-class Americanization sweeping the country, said Kaye, was an educational menace expressing a "bigoted objection to things unexperienced" and "hatred of the uncongenial." Americanizers were in fact doing a disservice to the children in public schools, seeking to implant actions and opinions that reinforced narrow provincialism rather than helping pupils develop independent vision. True belief in freedom of thought, said Kaye, depended on resisting intolerance, overcoming unthinking habits and fears, and abandoning "the egoism which makes us sanctify our own reactions."[57] De Toqueville wrote that an American felt obliged to defend whatever was censured in his country, "for it is not only his country that is then attacked, it is himself. The consequence is that his national pride resorts to a thousand artifices and descends to all the petty tricks of personal vanity." Similarly, Kaye identified postwar middle-class Americanism as essentially a form of conceit:

> Self-conceit, its direct gratification inhibited by civilization, finds indirect methods of indulging itself. Thus, the flattery that would embarrass a man if aimed directly at him is quite acceptable to him if given to the body of which he is a member, every man freely taking for himself the praise given to all collectively. To some extent, therefore, patriotism serves to gratify egoism; and the same bias that prevents a conceited man from remodeling himself helps to fix a nation of uneducated patriots in ultra-conservatism. Another element which enters into rendering naive patriotism the mere tool of popular prejudice is the universal resistance to breaking habits of any kind. Thus it comes that an undiscriminating campaign for patriotism may become a campaign for conceit, provincialism, and intolerance—for a state of mind of passionate self-satisfaction, to which all things American are of equal perfection and importance—Southern chivalry and Southern lynchings, Kentucky bluegrass and Massachusetts blue laws.[58]

The Nation later singled out patriotic essay contests in public schools as examples of the egoism of provincial Americanism, homing in on a favorite target, the American Legion, which described itself as "wholly altruistic." In fact, the Legion orated that never had a society or organization been formed "with a holier, more unselfish, more patriotic purpose than the American Legion." The Legion's access to public schools, *The Nation* reported, reinforced its assumption that it was an adjunct to the government of the United States. *The Nation's* editors hoped school administrators would begin to reject the essay contests, in which school children "are not invited to choose their own side of the question, as in a debate. They are simply told to argue for a bit of prearranged propaganda," such as the Legion's 1923 topic, "Why America Should Prohibit Immigration for Five Years."[59]

Despite these protestations, the American Legion was a pervasive force in public schools nationwide. One of Phil Conley's first steps as managing director of the ACA was to establish a working relationship with Dr. J.L. Coulter, director of Americanization work for the Legion in West Virginia.[60] Morris P. Shawkey praised the unflinching "crusade against disloyalty" carried on by the Legion, predicting that the veterans' group would be a "dominant influence for decades to come."[61] Waitman Barbe welcomed the Legion as a powerful ally of the public schools. National Legion Commander Alvin Owsley told delegates to the 1921 AFL convention that the Legion supported responsible and patriotic labor organizations and stood against "the autocracy of both the classes and masses." There was but one kind of acceptable loyalty, said Owsley, "and that is the loyalty that we of the Legion have adopted: undivided allegiance to the American government." The men of the Legion would tolerate no disorder. Having saved the nation in the war, they assumed the right to protect it in troubled peacetime.[62]

The American Legion was founded by a small group of American war veterans in Paris in the spring of 1919.[63] The West Virginia Legion began at a meeting in Charleston on May 3, 1919, called by Lieutenant Colonel Jackson Arnold of Weston. Arnold, who was West Virginia's first state police superintendent, had attended the founding caucus in Paris and became West Virginia's first Legion commander. The West Virginia branch was founded as part of an intensive national organizational campaign and a furious publicity drive, leading to the Legion's first national convention in Minneapolis in November 1919.[64] The five-month media campaign was directed by public relations wizard Ivy Lee, who had impressed corporate leaders with his deft crisis management for Standard Oil after the 1913 Ludlow Massacre. For $7,500 a month, Lee promoted the Legion through three hundred thousand poster displays and by advertising in every newspaper in the country with a circulation of over 150,000 or more.[65] F.B. Kaye disparagingly remarked in *The Nation* that the Legion considered itself part of the U.S. government; if so, the members were not far wrong. The War Department pledged recognition and assistance to the Legion in August 1919, and the Congress bestowed a federal charter on the organization, which sanctioned the Legion as the legitimate representative of American war veterans. Legion publications were printed by the Government Printing Office, and the War Department issued guns to Legion posts "for ceremonial purposes."[66]

During the Red Scare–steel strike period, state and national politicians courted the Legion's favor. Every Legion post was urged to protect "constituted government authorities," and preserve law and order in times of public crisis. Wellsburg, West Virginia, Legionnaires volunteered to help keep order during the 1919 coal strike, responding to Cornwell's plea for committees of public aid and safety.[67] Although Legionnaires spoke highly of patriotic union men, they sometimes served as strikebreakers. The Legion was a predominantly middle-class organization, suspicious of change, disorder, and challenges to private property. This fear often took the form of hostility to industrial unionism.[68] William Pencak, the organization's most recent historian, says the Legion adopted a worst-case scenario in assessing domestic radicalism. The Legion's definition of un-American encompassed a broad spectrum of suspected subversives, ranging well beyond actual radicals and social revolutionaries. Although the Legion preferred using legal means to fight subversion, members' willingness to encroach upon civil liberties and stifle dissent in the name of law and order was consistent with elite standards, which regarded the law mainly as guarantor of property rights and customary power relationships.[69] The concept of law as primarily a stabilizing force, rather than as mainly the defender of free expression, was at the core of one of the era's most omnipresent slogans, "Liberty is not license."[70]

The Legion was not without early challengers for the power to officially represent the rights and interests of World War veterans. Its most meaningful early rival was a radical left group, the Private Soldiers and Sailors Legion, more commonly called the World War Veterans. Allied with the Industrial Workers of the World and the Farmers' Non-Partisan League, the World War Veterans sought to place bread-and-butter veterans' rights issues within a broad context of reform and social justice.[71] The organization demanded that the government provide jobs for all veterans, distribute unused mining, agricultural, and timber lands to World War veterans, and punish incompetent military officers. The World War Veterans scorned the American Legion as the tool of "monopoly and privilege," called by one "a gang of officers and dog robbers."[72]

A West Virginia member of the World War Veterans drew the attention of the American Constitutional Association in 1922, and the statements of the open-shop organization suggest both the Americanizers' defensiveness about the country's institutions, observed by de Toqueville, and the collective conceit scorned by F.B. Kaye. Lawson McMillan of Rivesville, near Fairmont, reportedly told delegates to a World War Veterans convention in St. Paul that coal miners in some parts of West Virginia were subject to the arbitrary power of their employers and the intimidations of "gunmen and thugs." The ACA claimed that if McMillan had demonstrable evidence to back up his charges, he should present it to the appropriate authorities, not broadcast it nationally, adding that McMillan did not pass muster as a loyal citizen of "one of the greatest States in the American Union." A St. Paul businessman cautioned Governor Ephraim F. Morgan in 1923 that the World

War Veterans were active in West Virginia, based on a letter from West Virginia Veterans in an issue of the *Voice of Labor*, a radical newspaper.[73] The World War Veterans claimed seven hundred thousand members, but Pencak concludes this is a vastly inflated claim. (The American Legion had 843,013 dues-paying members by 1920.) Even if the organization initially drew large numbers, it was soon overpowered by the American Legion's government and financial support, its sophisticated "100 percent Americanism" public relations campaigns, and the Red Scare.[74]

The American Legion was welcomed into the nation's public schoolrooms on the strength of its status as a "non-partisan and non-political" patriotic organization.[75] The Legion's Americanism commission included a speaker's bureau, through which the Legion sought to instill Americanism "by creating public sentiment in our favor." The Legion identified the West Virginia Education Association and the American Constitutional Association as two of more than a hundred civic organizations that had joined the Legion annually in sponsoring "American Education Week," which began in 1921. The Legion grandly identified American Education Week as a national institution, although some other commentators were less impressed.[76] Charles H. Ambler charged that the postwar surge of patriotism, which he termed "reactionary," was marked by an increasing number of observances and holidays that actually reduced the efficiency of school systems. The *Charleston Daily Mail* complained during American Education Week that one's patriotism seemed to be determined by being "thoroughly devoted to observing every thing appointed to be observed." The AFL accused "reactionary interests" such as the American Legion, Chamber of Commerce of the United States, National Association of Manufacturers, National Security League, and National American Council of seizing control of public education to influence the public schools against workers and progressive social movements.[77]

Leading West Virginia educators either did not hear or dismissed such criticism, particularly when directed against the American Legion. The *West Virginia School Journal* called upon community newspapers, churches, chambers of commerce, and social clubs to observe American Education Week. The basic program, the *WVSJ* explained, was prepared by the American Legion, the National Education Association, and the U.S. Bureau of Education, with emphasis on topics such as "America first," "The red flag means danger," and "Stamp out revolutionary radicalism."[78] The *WVSJ* promoted the 1923 Legion essay contest, which allegedly attracted more than three hundred thousand entries nationwide and encouraged West Virginia students to participate in 1924, when the topic would be "Why Communism Is a Menace to Americanism."[79]

Waitman Barbe told readers of the *WVSJ* that educators everywhere welcomed the cooperation of the American Legion. In a revealing passage, Barbe commented:

> The American Legion is one of the most powerful organizations in the country, and it is going to be much more powerful than it is now. More truly, perhaps, than any other body of men, it will run this country for the next forty years. With this *fact* [emphasis added] in mind, it is highly gratifying to see the attitude taken by the Legion in the matter of public education; it places the school as the foundation of Americanism.

Barbe continued that, in the words of the Legion, the school "is to the nation, in peace, what the barracks are in war. In it is developed the nation's character."[80]

Barbe's statement reflects the overlay of the tenets of scientific management and public relations. The social application of scientific management combined ideology and practice that were designed to create a political economy of facts and law, under the guidance of specially trained managers.[81] Walter Lippmann's model for molding public opinion relied on the persuasive powers of trained experts, who were linked as dispensers of facts to the general public by responsible leaders in positions of organizational authority, to create consent.[82] The shibboleths of scientific management endowed facts with the aura of "objective data," free of partisanship or self-interest and therefore incontrovertible.[83] Barbe's expression of a clearly personal opinion about the American Legion—"More truly, perhaps, than any other body of men, it will run this country for the next forty years"—he immediately proclaimed as fact, endowing his claim with objectivity and effectively removing it from the realm of debate. Barbe apparently denied or ignored the idea that facts had political content and could be organized to serve particular social interests. His colleague Joseph Marsh, however, later implicitly acknowledged the social and political power of "organized facts." School children in West Virginia and across the nation, said Marsh, required "more drill on the facts needed to back up our theories and practices in government and in life."[84]

Waitman Barbe contended that the American Legion was fighting a great struggle to unite loyal Americans, striving for "as great a victory as any victory won by its members on the fields of Europe."[85] In that struggle, patriotic organizations such as the Legion and the American Constitutional Association projected a social vision drawn from diverse but overlapping dimensions of Americanism. These dimensions are outlined in historian Gary Gerstle's complex paradigm of Americanism, which he describes as nationalist, democratic, progressive, and traditionalist. The nationalist impulse focused on America's uniqueness and the mythology of American religious, military, and political heroes. The democratic dimension embraced the ideals of a just society, such as democracy and freedom. The progressive impulse praised the "ever-improving character" of American society, based on technological advances and scientific social relations, to create abundance and reduce social conflict. Finally, traditionalist Americanism rested upon the ideals of Anglo-Saxon Protestant virtue as the model for the good society. Traditionalist Americanism, says Gerstle, "infused movements of religious fundamentalism, anticommunism, racism, nativism, and imperialism with extraordinary patriotic passion."[86]

While drawing from all of these dimensions, middle-class Americanism as expressed by groups like the ACA and the American Legion were firmly rooted in the nationalist and traditionalist impulses, legitimated by subordinate rhetorical elements from the democratic and progressive dimensions to essentially preserve and strengthen established society. To the Legion and the ACA, the nation and the community were identified with the status quo. Freedom did not imply "defiance of communal norms or the right to criticize the legitimacy of established society."[87] The Legion and the ACA, therefore, naturally joined forces in West Virginia to win hearts and minds "through the medium of the children" and to expel from public discourse alien theories of Americanism espoused by competing interest groups like the American Civil Liberties Union. The Legion, the ACA, and their allies sought the national "integral unity" suggested by Woodrow Wilson's description of liberty as the freedom to be a piston in an efficient engine.[88]

Conversely, the ACLU defined freedom as the "unfettered right of disgruntled elements to offer alternative visions of America's future." To state officials, the Legion, and the ACA, then, when the ACLU launched a free speech drive in West Virginia in 1923, it did so in the interests of "engendering class hatred and fomenting civil strife and disorder."[89] The ACLU's West Virginia campaign was designed to help miners in southern West Virginia win union recognition. The campaign culminated in March 1923, when several ACLU representatives spoke on the courthouse steps in Logan. The courthouse speeches were a direct challenge to Logan County's dictatorial sheriff, Don Chafin, who had threatened to prevent the ACLU members from speaking. Chafin chose not to interfere, however, perhaps thwarting ACLU expectations of arrests, which would have further dramatized the free-speech fight.[90]

The ACLU's campaign was thoroughly assaulted by various interests in the state. The ACA identified ACLU activist Roger Baldwin as a "near-Bolshevist" and warned that the ACLU advocated such un-American ideas as a guaranteed minimum wage. Governor Morgan was receiving police reports of IWW literature being distributed in Logan County, and Baldwin's record of championing the Wobblies in earlier free-speech struggles on the West Coast no doubt contributed to the savaging he endured from West Virginia patriots.[91] Phil Conley issued a series of circulars concerning the ACLU and other "radical activities in West Virginia" to a "selected list of thinking citizens" of the state. One circular disengenuously claimed that the ACA was uninterested in the matter of "unionizing Southern West Virginia. . . . That is a controversy between the coal operators and the United Mine Workers." It further scored the ACLU for advocating resistance to a court injunction prohibiting their scheduled Logan meeting, calling it a mob of "Lenine [sic] and Trotsky types who feel the responsibility of enforcing the laws in West Virginia."[92]

Governor Morgan spearheaded the vigorous counterattack against ACLU charges that Logan County miners were denied the right to discuss unionism and were physically intimidated by Chafin's officers. Morgan, as "servant of all the people," claimed the support of "the truthful, law-supporting citizens of our great progressive state" who agreed with him that the ACLU and its sympathizers were "destructive and un-American." Newspapers carried the governor's missives, eliciting statewide praise from businessmen and other patriots.[93] An anonymous supporter congratulated Morgan for standing up to "that Red-Neck, Russian organization." The National Association of Manufacturers applauded Morgan's stance in an article in *Industrial Progress*; across Morgan's copy of the article is a handwritten note from Phil Conley, stating that "This is the kind of publicity we need." West Virginia American Legion Commander Spiller Hicks also commended Morgan for his stand against the ACLU, which was "composed of communists, anarchists, slackers and draft evaders."[94]

Morgan, the Legion, and the ACA also received support from John L. Lewis of the UMWA, whose iron-union discipline extended to severe restrictions on free speech. As the ACLU was making ready for its Logan meetings, UMW officers in Pennsylvania's District 5 refused permission to Alex Howat for a protest against UMWA international officers.[95] The AFL, with the consent of an ailing Samuel Gompers, portrayed the ACLU as procommunist and anti-American, accusing many of its leading figures—such as Baldwin, Norman Thomas, and Scott Nearing—of engaging in "parlor Bolshevik movements."[96] The *UMWJ* warned that communist propaganda was being spread among the miners of West Virginia, and attacked Lewis rival John Brophy for encouraging Bolshevik policies and principles in UMWA District 2. Working through the pen of *UMWJ* editor Ellis Searles, Lewis accused Brophy of promoting nationalization of the coal industry through an alliance with the ACLU's "Greenwich Village coal diggers."[97]

Even after the ACLU controversy died down in Logan County, West Virginians were advised to be on guard against the ACLU's "so-called

reformers, liberal thinkers, bolshevists, I.W.W.'s and other government destroying agents who live on money collected in various ways for propaganda
purposes." Phil Conley, writing in the *West Virginia Review*, warned that
radicals came in the guise not only of disenchanted bomb throwers, but as
intelligent, educated thinkers, trained in the arts of public speaking and persuasion. The *West Virginia Review* described itself as neutral in politics, religion, and other areas of controversy, and "not a cheap and flamboyant
purveyor of propaganda," but it did not contain its alarmist attacks on the
ACLU. Conley warned that Baldwin, Ward, Nearing, William Z. Foster, and
other such men were "detrimental to the best interests of this government,"
and good citizens must develop "an awakened consciousness relative to the
menace" they represented.[98]

By 1924 the vision of Americanism shared by the ACA and the American Legion was well-established, in West Virginia and nationally. The ACLU
still called the Legion "the most active agency in intolerance and repression
in the United States," but *The Nation* noted that the Legion had moderated its
early dependence on violent extralegal intimidation of alleged enemies of the
state.[99] Much of the Legion's agenda for a well-ordered America was accomplished politically, in coalition with other patriotic groups, who influenced
the adoption of loyalty and antisedition legislation to stifle the expression of
speech or action that advocated fundamental changes in American institutions. Pencak suggests that the Legion "might well have been more violent
had it not accomplished so much within the limits of American democracy."[100] In West Virginia the institutionalization of the Legion-ACA brand of
Americanism was symbolized by legislation in 1923 establishing loyalty
guidelines for teachers and patriotic instruction in the schools. The efforts of
the ACA, the Morgan administration, and the educational establishment in
West Virginia to guarantee loyalty and obedience to their model of Americanism, in the context of the anticipated expansion of industrial capitalism, endowed industrial Americanization with spiritual authority.

8

The Sanctification of Industrial Americanization

In 1918 Interior Secretary Franklin K. Lane told teachers assembled in Pittsburgh that Americanism must become a "political religion," and that every boy, factory, and dollar must be given to "the service of Christian civilization" to win the war and transmit American ideals. In 1921 Phil Conley told West Virginia teachers assembled in Huntington that "American ideals are the civic and political religion of the United States." It was the primary job of teachers to "plant in the plastic minds and hearts of the boys and girls in the public schools the impressions that make them citizens." Training for citizenship was "the ultimate end and sole justification" for the expenditure of public money on education. The foundation of America's civic and political religion, said Conley, included adequate reward for labor, property rights, and freedom of speech and press. "So long as it is not seditious," Conley affirmed, "the press has unlimited power."[1]

Conley's work with the ACA demonstrated the maxim voiced by Herbert Hoover in 1920 that only by the manipulation of propaganda could the American public be educated in the ideals of democracy. Likewise, Conley was in accord with the statement by Edward L. Bernays that the age of mass production required a technique not only for distribution of goods, but also "for the mass distribution of ideas. Public opinion can be moved, directed, and formed by such a technique." The conscious, intelligent manipulation of the people's habits and opinions, said Bernays, was an important element in democratic society.[2] The technique for sanctifying industrial Americanization rested on combining consistent training in institutional settings, primarily schools, with ritualistic expressions of the emotional dimension of the ideology. William Pencak notes that the American Legion instilled patriotism with symbols and ceremonies rather than intellectual principles. The importance of ritual in creating an atmosphere in which America's civil religion could flourish was part of the consciousness of the Legion and other civic and patriotic organizations. The devotion to manipulation of symbols allowed their vision of Americanism to thrive, even in communities "that had never seen a red or a Wobbly."[3]

As part of its campaign to match ritualistic devotion with systematic training in schools, the American Constitutional Association inaugurated

America First Day in 1921. Held annually in the early 1920s on the Sunday of or before July 4, America First Day was conceived to "develop a national consciousness" of loyalty and cooperation, to build a "greater and better nation." Each year the association approached ministers, Sunday school superintendents, and other community leaders to discuss American ideals. It provided a guidebook prepared by prominent citizens outlining topical presentations.[4] The ACA also secured the cooperation of other patriotic and civic organizations, such as the Rotary, Kiwanis, and Lions clubs.[5] The West Virginia Federation of Women's Clubs joined with the "Constitutional Association . . . to have American Ideals preached from every pulpit in the State on Sunday, July 2nd [1922]."[6]

Governor Ephraim F. Morgan also endorsed America First Day, issuing annual proclamations to be read in church and Sunday school services and special meetings across the state. Whether the nation could "overcome the storm of radicalism and other destructive movements," he declared, depended on Americans' reconsecration to "the full duties of citizenship." Morgan implored West Virginians to "hold a steady course, have faith in your government, and stand firm for order and a strict enforcement of the laws."[7] For the inaugural America First Day in 1921, the mayor of Wheeling called upon the people to "renew their pledges of patriotism and their covenants of loyalty" to defeat forces that "threaten the very existence of organized society, and law and order." A Wheeling minister decried the disloyalty and contempt in America for the law and agents of the law, contending that "obedience to the law is liberty."[8] The president of the West Virginia Sunday School Association linked God's grace with the freedom to acquire material comforts in a country that guaranteed "every liberty and every opportunity that any right thinking man can ask." Edwin M. Keatley equated good citizenship with Christianity, intoning that American Christians comprised the nation's most substantial citizens. True Christians and loyal citizens could demonstrate "pure Americanism" by obeying the laws and by insisting that others do likewise.[9]

Accurate figures on the observation of America First Day are impossible to determine. The ACA distributed postcards to Sunday school superintendents, asking them to report on their patriotic observations. It is possible, though not demonstrable, that the organization's estimates of America First Day demonstrations were influenced by the number of cards sent out as well as by the number of cards returned. Morris P. Shawkey had employed a similar tactic in estimating wartime patriotic discussions at Parent-Teacher Association meetings, simply multiplying the number of organizations statewide by the number of weekly or semimonthly meetings, to arrive at an "idea of the amount of discussion and the number of people reached."[10] By providing the state's media with information and with no countervailing agency to

challenge (or confirm) its claims, the ACA established its estimate of participation as fact. Its practice of flooding state newspapers with press releases,
particularly when the state's chief executive was involved, insured that the
celebrations became "news." The ACA claimed that over a thousand meetings
were held statewide in 1921. One ACA "news story" sent to every newspaper
in the state estimated that over three thousand meetings were held on America First Day in 1922, in nearly every section of the state.[11] In 1923, Conley
claimed, over four thousand meetings were held.[12] Many newspapers carried
the governor's annual proclamation of America First Day and reported that
the day was widely observed. An ACA press release affirmed that governors
in nine states intended to observe America First Day in 1922, with several
other chief executives considering the matter.[13]

The ACA's tactics of mobilization can be inferred from the organization's recruitment of Andrew Price of Pocahontas County as county chairman of the 1922 America First Day observations. Price was one of the
county's most respected and influential citizens. He had served as the first
mayor of Marlinton, was the lawyer for the bank of Marlinton, and a corporate land attorney for many regional and national timber, land, and resource
companies. Price was also a naturalist, historian, essayist, and poet who was
often called "the Sage of Pocahontas." In 1892 the Price family purchased
the *Pocahontas Times* and Andrew Price became its editor. His brother Calvin
succeeded him in that position in 1900, when Price turned his full-time attention to a thriving law practice. Andrew Price remained a columnist and
contributing editor until his death in 1930. Price was active in Democratic
politics and was Pocahontas County's chairman of Four-Minute Men during
the war.[14]

Edwin M. Keatley, acting as president of the American Constitutional
Association, approached Price to be Pocahontas County chairman for the
1922 America First observances. "We are passing through one of the most
critical periods of our history," Keatley wrote to Price. "Bolshevists, I.W.W.'s
and other radicals" had brought "unrest and discontent on every hand."
Keatley had no doubt that Price, a loyal American, would do his part as a
citizen, and he enclosed an ACA plan for arousing public interest in the
counties. Price accepted the responsibility, and Keatley later told him that
thirteen other states were following West Virginia's lead in the matter of
public displays of patriotism. Each minister in the state was sent a copy of
Morgan's proclamation and a copy of the ACA American Ideals bulletin.
Furthermore, each Sunday school superintendent received a suggested patriotic program from the ACA.[15]

The ACA recommended that county chairmen encourage local ministers to prepare a special sermon on American ideals or to invite a lay speaker
to preach on that subject. Churches should be decorated with American

flags, and patriotic songs should be sung. The local American Legion post, DAR chapter, Colonial Dames, Rotary, Kiwanis, and Lion's clubs should be asked to cooperate and include patriotic programs at their meetings prior to America First Day. Each citizen should be asked to wear a small American flag in his buttonhole. All local newspapers should be contacted, and chairmen should "explain the plan fully to the editors, and give them information from time to time" about the planned ceremonies.[16]

Price energetically pursued plans for Pocahontas County. He supplemented the ACA's guidelines with an address he prepared for all pastors and Sunday school superintendents in the county, requesting that "some bright boy or girl memorize it and deliver it" on America First Day. Price's memorization exercise declared that "Americans were the people chosen" to hold "aloft the light that enlightened the world." Furthermore, the American experience had proven that "it is an advantage to be born poor. . . . Nearly all successful men were born poor. It is the land of opportunity." America's greatness depended, said Price, on loyalty and truth being taught in the schools and Sunday schools. Those schools would produce the patriots and citizens who would "continue the good work."[17]

Keatley was delighted with Price's circular, and requested fifty-four copies from Price to send to each county chairman.[18] The Price family newspaper, the *Pocahontas Times*, carried Governor Morgan's proclamation of America First Day directly above an announcement by Marlinton's mayor, Norman R. Price, that the citizens of Marlinton should observe the day in an appropriate manner. The *Times* reported Price's communique to the church administrators, announcing that "every Sunday school in Pocahontas County has been requested to sound the note of patriotism in their service that day." For good measure, Price's circular was reproduced in the paper. The *Times* also noted that the Wesley Chapel in Hillsboro would observe America First Day with a sermon entitled "A Study in Patriotism," linking "certain fundamental principles in the life of Jesus" to one's national patriotic obligations.[19] On America First Day, some churches in the state displayed the American flag next to the Christian flag, whose white field represented peace and purity, and congregations recited the Christian pledge "to the Saviour for whose Kingdom it stands." The *Pocahontas Times* denigrated "loose tongued and irresponsible persons" who rejected the "plan of civilized life that has brought so much peace, prosperity, happiness and contentment" to the American people, but pointed out that the response to Morgan's America First Day proclamation revealed the minimal levels of disaffection in the country. After all, the requests by ACA organizers for public expressions of loyalty had elicited not "a doubtful word or a hostile gesture."[20]

Given the saturation of nationalistic Americanism, it is unlikely that many "discontented cranks" in Pocahontas County would venture to raise "a false clamor against our country." The *Times* announced that to the "common people," the question of national loyalty was beyond debate; to them, patriotism was "bred in the bone."[21] Faith in the common people to act independently for the well-being of the nation, however, was not often shared by the managers of industrial Americanization. Theorists of efficient social engineering saw the middle-class as the natural agency of social development, which required the coordination of national life steered in such a fashion as to "integrate, streamline, and provide efficient direction." Industry and society could be intentionally arranged to effect a unified, intelligent democracy, in which the acceptable habits of industry and cooperation would become part of the peoples' consciousness. Industrial Americanizers ignored or discounted the fact that the top-down inculcation of industrial habits, compulsory patriotism, and scientific management in all spheres of modern life imposed a hierarchical arrangement of discipline and dependence, which were "hardly the habits of a sovereign populace."[22]

Essentially, the orderly vision of efficient, hierarchical industrial Americanization amounted to the elite determination of and planning for the national interest, a process that was called "guided" or "directed democracy" in Italy in the 1920s. In fact, Commander Alvin Owsley of the American Legion identified the Legion's readiness to defend American institutions as identical to the Italian Fascisti's use of terror against leftist radicals. Owsley told Texas Legionnaires that "the Fascisti are to Italy what the American Legion is to the United States" and endorsed a Legion takeover of the government if subversives gained undue influence. Legion spokesman John McQuigg said Fascisti aims and ideals, if not their methods, were identical to those of the American Legion.[23]

Neither the Legion nor other nationalistic Americanizers fully and systematically adopted the Fascist rejection of parliamentary/representative democracy, or its embrace of centralized social and productive power in the political machinery of the national state. Practically, industrial Americanization rendered the political state secondary in power to business and industry, leaving American devotion to private property, a noninterventionist national state, and free enterprise incompatible with a Fascist model. Moreover, as Pencak demonstrates, many of the hierarchical goals of the Legion, the ACA, and their civic and political allies were achieved by the absorption of their principles into the postwar American political economy.[24] This type of elite social control is based not upon physical force but on strategies for determining the parameters of the psychological and ideological development of the public.[25] When E.D. Knight of Kayford, West Virginia, praised the "value of the indirect approach to mine problems," symbolized by welfare capitalism, he anticipated by more than four decades a U.S. government document promoting a "system of pressurized guidance," or the "American or indirect way" of accomplishing adherence to elite values, which in totalitarian countries is accomplished by force.[26]

Guided democracy and industrial Americanization depended upon the peoples' acceptance that they were bound by standardized, uniform "claims of morality and right upon conscience or conduct." William Walton told an audience at the West Virginia School for the Blind that too many Americans believed liberty meant license, and that the "principles of pure living should be so thoroughly emphasized" that "the higher life of the nation" would be promoted. Education should teach and instill loyalty, developing the moral strength of the nation. Walton feared that these qualities were lacking, because the education received by many Americans was not "the right type."[27] Phil Conley suggested the totality of the challenge to educators when he described West Virginia's greatest need as "a State consciousness." Conley identified the interests of the people with those of corporations. West Virginia would be unified only when the "manufacturing interests, the coal interests, the agricultural interests, the gas interests, the oil interests . . . join hands for the good of the whole." Conley did not include organized labor.[28]

Governor Morgan proclaimed the crucial role of educators in creating the modern industrial state when he addressed the West Virginia Education Association in 1921. Speaking on "The State and the New Education," Morgan affirmed:

> Let me say to the members of this association that, regardless of the great progress made in our system of education, the greatest field for the application of your energy is in the teaching of Americanism to the youth of this land. Americanism means respect for American laws, American ideals, and American institutions. It means respect for the constituted authorities, obedience to law and the preservation of order. I want to urge that you men and women reconsecrate yourselves to the teaching of a loftier and more exalted Americanism in the schools of this state and that your influence as citizens be extended to the adult population of your communities in striving to inculcate the gospel of Americanism among our people.
>
> There is at present throughout the country, and in West Virginia of much greater magnitude than is generally known, an insidious effort to array every man who toils with his hands as an enemy of organized government. . . . The purpose of the campaign is plain. It would create unrest and discontent and make the workman an enemy of his government, the best that has ever been devised by mankind for the protection of the weak and less fortunate.
>
> Forces of this character are what the school teacher must combat in many of our communities, but, equipped with a knowledge of the pro-

gressive achievements of this country, the manifest desire of every patriotic citizen to do equal and exact justice, I have no fear of the outcome.

It developed during the world war that there were employed in many of the public educational institutions throughout the country teachers and professors who were not in sympathy and accord with our form of government. I do not know whether West Virginia has among her teaching fraternity any of those who may be imbued with these un-American ideas or not. I want to go on record as being unalterably opposed to the employment of any teacher or instructor, male or female, in any of the educational institutions of this state who is not one hundred percent American. Only those who stand ready to combat the dangerous, deceptive, blighting, socialistic communistic bolshevistic doctrines that are being disseminated throughout the country, striking at every foundation of our free institutions, should be entrusted with training the youths of the America of tomorrow.[29]

The American Constitutional Association believed warnings of subversion among schoolteachers were overstated, estimating that there were probably less than one thousand disloyal American teachers. If citizens had information about teachers who were radical, however, they should expose them publicly, and refrain from implicating innocent teachers. In support of this position, the ACA encouraged the West Virginia legislature's efforts to ferret out the disloyal.[30] Not willing to trust to the "bred in the bone" patriotism of West Virginia teachers, Governor Morgan supported a 1923 law introduced by Senator Wright Hugus, a Wheeling Republican, to institutionalize the teaching of patriotism and citizenship in public schools. A companion bill was introduced by Delegate F. Guy Ash, a Morgantown Democrat, requiring loyalty oaths for teachers. Both bills were passed. The West Virginia laws, and those of several other states, replicated New York legislation that emerged from that state's wartime Lusk Laws against treason and sedition, compelling demonstrable loyalty and obedience to the state by teachers.[31]

Education historian Lewis Paul Todd emphasizes even earlier antecedents to the national burgeoning of patriotic legislation in the early 1920s. The Spanish-American War, says Todd, had opened Americans' eyes to imperial possibilities and stimulated the sentiment of nationalism. Nationalistic Americanism took the form of courses of study and manuals on patriotism, and in legislation establishing patriotic observances. Courses and demonstrations typically were played out "in terms of emotionalized responses to the stimulus of symbols, rather than along the lines of a critical study of the bases of American life." The First World War escalated, but did not initiate, the trend in legally mandated patriotism. Todd points out that between 1903 and 1923, 40 percent of all educational laws were designed to manufacture local, state, and national patriotism.[32]

The West Virginia patriotism and citizenship law was broad in scope, applying to all public, private, parochial, and denominational schools. The state Board of Education drafted manuals and courses of study for the public schools, to teach, foster, and perpetuate the "ideals, principles and spirit of Americanism." Boards of authority in the private institutions were required to prescribe citizenship and patriotism courses for their schools. Failure of an administrator or teacher to abide by the law's requirements constituted a misdemeanor, and, in the case of public school employees, was punishable by suspension for one year.[33] Under provisions of the loyalty oath bill, teachers were required to swear loyalty to the state and national constitutions as a condition of yearly employment contracts. By Superintendent Ford's directive, faithful observance of the oath required teachers to "use every effort" to insure adequate patriotic education for their pupils.[34] The patriotic education and loyalty oath laws thus essentially formalized a recommended voluntary practice in West Virginia classrooms, that of recitation and discussion of the "West Virginia School Creed":

> To be loyal to West Virginia and to the United States; to learn and perform intelligently my duties as a citizen and to support the American ideals and customs; to hold patriotism above any individual, social class or party; to oppose revolutionary movements such as Bolshevism, Anarchism, I.W.W.-ism and other activities detrimental to the laws and the Constitution of the United States; to play hard, study hard, work hard. This shall be my creed on the footpath leading to the highway of good dependable citizenship.[35]

State Superintendent of Schools George M. Ford welcomed the new laws, praising a legislature that had "wisely enacted a law requiring the teaching of American principles." Ford told teachers that the most effective way to teach respect for constituted law and authority was to rigorously obey all the laws of the land, and to make certain that their pupils strictly obeyed national, state, and school laws. "Your belief in such a doctrine," Ford continued, "is now to be tested."[36]

Ford advised public school teachers to cooperate at every opportunity with local civic and patriotic organizations in observances to generate patriotism. To Secretary Joseph F. Marsh of the state Board of Education, the compulsory patriotism laws must have seemed the culmination of his long efforts to rationalize Americanism campaigns in the school system. Marsh faithfully had advised teachers to invite speakers from "appropriate organizations" to teach patriotic principles to their students. Teaching Americanism, however, should not be a campaign "of temporary bombast, but rather a deliberate well organized effort to arouse our entire State to a higher sense of obligation to our Government." Marsh could report in 1924 that

> the schools have been surcharging the youth of our country with patriotism. Each year our teachers solemnly swear to support the Constitution and to teach the principles of Americanism. In West Virginia, you may imagine some 400,000 boys and girls daily lifting their eyes to the flag which floats over every schoolhouse and giving the familiar salute.[37]

To Marsh and other leaders in business and education, Americanization required finding one's proper role in industrial America and staying with it. Marsh, who directed the state's programs in vocational education, explained that while the "old-time school gave pupils the promise of escape from toil and grimy business," vocational guidance and training in "the new school" would insure that the 95 percent of American pupils needed in the "work-a-day-world" would realize the honor of their callings, just as the 5 percent who ascended to the professions.[38] It was therefore imperative to the maintenance of an orderly, law-abiding, and efficient industrial system that its people understood that that system would "deliver all people from the world of scarcity and conflict to the world of abundance and harmony."[39] Such faith must be enforced even in times of apparent hardship. Governor Morgan predicted that West Virginia's hills would some day "be stripped of their timber, our mountains will be robbed of their coal, gas, and oil." If, however, "we then have an intelligent and educated people of sturdy character and conduct, our future will remain secure and our happiness and safety will be assured."[40]

Industrial Americanizers marshalled organized facts and statistics to verify the fundamental soundness of corporate capitalism.[41] The American Constitutional Association indignantly asked who had the temerity to criticize "so noble and so inviting a political and social structure as has been erected in America?" More than twenty million Americans had been able to buy Liberty Bonds. More than twelve million persons deposited money in mutual, stock, or postal-savings banks. There were more than 266,000 miles of railways in operation. America boasted more than three thousand public libraries with seventy-five million volumes on hand. Total wealth "is not now less than $225,000,000,000," and "the distribution of that wealth is steadily becoming more equitable and more satisfactory under the operation of the forces and principles that have guided America so long and so well."[42]

The *West Virginia School Journal* also lauded American production and consumption. Although the United States had only 6 percent of the population of the world, the nations's industrial and agricultural interests produced 66 percent of the world's oil supply, 52 percent of the world's coal, 85 percent of the world's automobiles, and 75 percent of the world's corn. The

WVSJ attributed this staggering productivity to the same "brains and grit" that had delivered the "knock-out blow" in the war. "Don't you believe," the *Journal* asked, "that we can solve all of the problems of peace?" It was in part the school pupil's drill in these kinds of facts that led Marsh to conclude that modern students could easily match "grandfather with fact for fact, although the new list will contain more of modern times and less ancient lore."[43]

The *West Virginia School Journal* predicted that the state's raw materials and water power should make it one of nation's greatest manufacturing states and recommended that West Virginia establish a school of manual arts. Elsewhere, the *Journal* documented the trend in education toward national control, citing the Smith-Hughes Vocational Training Act and a War Department plan for the enlistment of boys in college, to be trained as mechanics, which would render them "efficient for public service." Complementing the expanding vocational programs in West Virginia schools were the patriotism and citizenship lessons in which students learned the appropriate fundamental laws of production and consumption. These lessons included historical study of the nation's economic revolution, emphasizing industrial, commercial, and agricultural growth. One focus of this study was the "career" of major corporations such as the Standard Oil Company. Another was an inquiry into ominous-sounding "Labor Combinations."[44]

The powerful labor combinations, however, vigorously embraced the worship of productivity and expansion that fueled industrial Americanization. The United Mine Workers of America consistently affirmed the nascent business unionism espoused by John L. Lewis, pledging its devotion to industrial peace and stability. The *UMWJ* insisted in 1923 that continuous growth under a capitalist system must be preserved. Only then could Americans have "more for every one: more automobiles, more general education, more modern plumbing, more gramophones, and bigger real wages."[45] To guarantee steady economic expansion, the *UMWJ* campaigned for additional and more stringent restrictions on immigration. Advocating a plan, later adopted, to put immigration on a "scientific basis" by 1924, the *UMWJ* favorably reported comments by a U.S. congressman that America must be protected from "defective, dependent and objectionable or surplus aliens as our other laws protect us from defective seeds, diseased plants, inferior live stock and even surplus foreign goods made by pauper labor."[46] The *Journal* warned that unless immigration were restrained, Europeans would be followed by Africans, "Hindoos, Japs and Chinese, and labor in America would again be dragged down to the lowest level."[47] Cleaving to the progressive vision of an America freed from want by progress, technology, and efficiency, the officialdom of the United Mine Workers of America agreed with a *Wall Street Journal* forecast that any labor shortage caused by stricter immigration laws would be offset by the mechanization of American industry.[48]

The UMWA hierarchy, then, by 1923–24 fully shared the capitalist faith in the potential of modern industry, with "its marvelous efficiency and productivity," to establish a world of material abundance for all. This faith in technological progress was not inconsistent with socialist or other noncapitalist visions but diverged from noncapitalist models on the fundamental questions of ownership, distribution of wealth, and political authority. Industrial Americanization, which was institutionalized in West Virginia by 1923, limited democracy to one's freedom to participate in the proscribed marketplace of American capitalism. Industrial Americanizers anticipated equality not in political or social terms but in the mass acquisition of efficiently produced consumer goods. This vision did not question the "essential decision-making power in the shop, industry, the community or the nation," which was reserved for the managers of industrial America.[49]

By 1924 West Virginia's "army of young workers" was being systematically prepared for "some work suited to their training and talents that needs to be done."[50] Efforts at scientific management of the schools extended to officially approved history notebooks for junior- and senior-high-school students, which should "adhere to a uniform plan of arrangement to be worked out by the teacher and drilled into the pupils at the beginning of the work in history." The scientific regimentation of historical training would contribute to the students' understanding of "orderly development and change" and yield "the high moral and ethical concepts of loyalty to principles and institutions by revealing the cost at which the elements of civilization have been secured for us."[51] Time-and-motion studies were employed in the school day's division of labor, with recitation and study programs fragmented into ten, twelve-, thirteen-, fourteen-, fifteen-, and twenty-minute segments. When elementary school students practiced writing from 10:16 to 10:28 each morning, ideally the teacher saw that they did so in this manner:

> *Position*: See that the desks are properly adjusted to the pupils' needs. In teaching position, always consider health and efficiency. An erect, healthful position in writing usually leads to efficient work. All through the year pupils should be trained in the essentials of good position; such training is far more important than immediately apparent results. One of the aims of each lesson in which the pupils do any writing should be the establishing of a good position habit. Right kind of training will lead to a good quality of work.
>
> The body should face the desk in a square front position and inclined slightly forward from the hips, allowing a space of about two inches between the body and the desk. The distance of the eyes from the paper should be twelve or more inches, according to the size of the pupil. The feet should be placed apart and squarely on the floor.

> Place both arms upon the desk, forming approximately right angles at the elbows. Keep both elbows near the front of the desk. The left hand, placed just above the writing line, holds and adjusts the paper. The right arm rests only on its own weight on the muscles in front of the elbow. The only other point of contact of the right arm with the desk should be the nails of the third and fourth fingers bent under the hand, forming the "gliding rest. . . ." Care must be taken that the paper be moved upward and not the right hand downward as the writing progresses down the page.[52]

Allowances for left-handed students were not included in the teacher's manual.

Standards for the course in citizenship were well developed within a few years of the passage of the patriotic education and citizenship law. Objectives included students' understanding the necessity for law and order in the community and assisting in their preservation, and awareness that "breaking the smallest law endangers the welfare of the entire nation." Students must understand that "one will be as happy in his work as in his play, if he chooses the right vocation," and "appreciate the desirability of finding one's life work early, so that he may begin training for it." Standards for courses in social science required students to learn "fundamental laws governing social and economic life, and to obey them." Students must "follow the leadership of recognized social and economic thinkers and leaders" and protect themselves from "social and economic fallacies, misrepresentations and prejudices by constant reliance on facts and principles accepted as valid."[53]

In March 1923, the Reverend J.L. Hardy of Shepherdstown's Trinity Episcopal Church addressed the Shepherdstown Women's Club. Reverend Hardy contended that while traditional religion had given people faith in the meaning of life, "such religion has often been too narrow in its vision and too formal and external to the experience of even its devotees." The progress of science and industry, said the reverend, "outran moral and religious progress," so that traditional religion was incapable of ministering to the masses through the "moral and industrial debauch of the great war," leading to "disillusionment and uncertainty" with traditional religion. Consequently, many of the "best minds and spirits of the younger generation" had lost touch with organized religion. Therefore, a "reconstruction of religion" was necessary. The reconstruction would have to be "intellectual and social" and demonstrate that "essential Christianity is in no sense irrational or incompatible with a scientific attitude toward life and nature." "This reconstruction has already made a great deal of progress among scholars and specialists," said Hardy, "but a majority of lay people are almost completely in the dark."[54]

Hardy's call for a new spiritualism, integrating faith with science and industrial progress, serving scholars and specialists, provided the spiritual foundation for the civic and political religion created by West Virginia Americanizers to lighten the way for the lay people. Joseph F. Marsh carried this middle-class view of religion further, when he announced that "the university of the future is to have a vital influence upon *religion*" [emphasis in the original], which was "the supreme force in human society." The American university, said Marsh, "through lofty teaching and holy and beautiful environments, will be less sectarian and more Christian as it grows into its fuller possibilities." Marsh recognized no incompatibility between Christianity and the main purpose of the university, which, in his view, was to "be our best producer of wealth."[55]

Institutional education, then, like its pupils, was reduced to a factor of production. It is hard not to experience a sense of loss when Marsh's purpose for the university is set against a quite different analysis of education in the *West Virginia School Journal* in 1914, before that publication was taken over by Morris P. Shawkey. "It may be excusable," reported the *Journal*, "to use our educational system to increase the production of wealth and the value of property; but surely its paramount purpose is to produce manhood, womanhood, moral citizenship, and justice in social relations."[56] Against such simple and honest prewar sentiments, the principles of the civic and political religion of the Americanization of West Virginia, though rhetorically similar, ring hollow indeed.

Conclusion

The hierarchical vision of the West Virginia Americanizers was not forged solely in the crucible of the First World War. Rather the war crisis gave new form and urgency to perceptions that influential Americans traditionally held about themselves and their obligation to steer the masses toward acceptable, dependable behavior that would profit the country as a whole. The wartime worship of productivity, to use Robert Wiebe's expression, confirmed to industrial Americanizers that their values were sanctified as guideposts for the nation and the world in the postwar struggle for order and industrial and commercial dominance.[1] When Justus Collins congratulated John J. Cornwell, and implicitly himself, for the establishment of the West Virginia state police, he remarked that every decent man in the state "should take his hat off to you. The rest don't matter."[2]

Collins articulated a twentieth-century belief that elites had traditionally held about the virtue of their access to rule, and the righteousness of excluding the unworthy from such access. Kenneth Lockridge, historian of town life and culture in Puritan New England, notes that Puritan leaders held a firm belief in the natural inequality of men, and that obedience to men of power and rank was recognized, at least by men of power and rank, as the foundation of social harmony. The Puritan vision of the perfect corporate community demanded loyalty in exchange for membership privileges, which included peace, security, and good order in a sometimes terrifying wilderness. In such a community, there was no place for dissent or independence of mind. The ideal society would be built upon a policy of consensual exclusivity.[3]

There was, of course, a fundamental contradiction in the twentieth-century industrial Americanizers' embrace of exclusivity and hierarchy in a nation that exalted the goals of political and social democracy. The Americanizers resolved this contradiction in part by endowing their particular vision of the just society with the spiritual vestments of, in their terms, the "civic and political religion of the United States."[4] States, Francis Jennings has written, have historically understood that religion is too important to be left "to the vagaries of individual choice," since it determines the social behavior of its adherents.[5] The secular religion of corporate capitalism, in the view of the industrial Americanizers, guaranteed freedom through the social behavior of obedience to recognized authority. "Obedience," they intoned, "helps make men truly great."[6]

Capitalism, says economist Robert Heilbroner, is an arrangement of social life based on the regenerative power of society's demand for new products and characterized by "distinctive hierarchies, imperatives, loyalties, and beliefs." The idea of economic growth is as central to its nature, he continues, as the divine right of kings has been for other regimes. The principles of economic expansion are "deeply embedded and widely believed" and articulated by the system's most important representatives, business leaders. "It must be conceded," Heilbroner states, "that the class of businessmen is the only group that naturally thinks of itself, and is generally thought of, as speaking for the social order as a whole." Heilbroner believes that the American "business class" is regarded, by itself and the American people, as the legitimate embodiment of the values, goals, and sentiments of the entire society. Although American capitalists do not have official authority in the political arena, "ordinarily the government endorses the aims and objectives of the business community," since "the political realm and the economic realm are both parts of a single regime." Heilbroner concludes that capitalism has triumphed over state socialism, as practiced in the former Soviet Union and China, largely because capitalism organizes the "material affairs of human kind more satisfactorily than socialism." He acknowledges that democratic socialism "at its core" has stood for social goals of moral elevation that are incompatible with or unattainable under capitalism, given that system's dependence on concentrated economic power. He suggests, however, that the praiseworthy social vision of socialism is historically doomed, as socialist experiments lead inevitably to "centralized planning."[7]

Heilbroner expresses, then, a systemic version of Justus Collins's division of America into the decent people and the people who do not matter, or John J. Cornwell's dichotomy of good people and bad people.[8] Alternatives for social and economic organization have been reduced to two, the state capitalist model, which works "well enough," and the state socialist alternative, which, while grounded in inspirational potential, offers "no plausible economic framework."[9]

This dichotomous perspective devalues or ignores other visions, some of which have American origins. Lawrence Goodwyn, in his provocative study of American Populism, observes that the triumph of industrial capitalism implies a "cultural presumption" of social progress so "thoroughly internalized within the society that it is part of the democratic culture itself." This ideal of progress places American corporate capitalism at the top of the evolutionary scale, and, says Goodwyn, condescendingly relegates historical democratic challenges to capitalist social organization to the sidelines of the field of acceptable ideas.[10] Cast out from the mainstream public discourse is any substantive acknowledgment of the indigenous anticorporate American social theories proposed by the Knights of Labor, the populist People's party, the Industrial Workers of the World, and American socialism. Doctrinal, tactical, and organizational differences aside, each of these offered an oppositional vision of a cooperative commonwealth that challenged the hierarchical corporate culture. At its heart was the premise that to neutralize the drift toward concentration of power inherent in industrial society, the social values of its people must preserve and respect the idea that labor must be vested with the value of its product, that people could work collectively to be free individually, and that, to quote William Haywood, "society can be no better than its most miserable."[11] This Jeffersonian vision of a decentralized democratic state, implying liberation through economic self-organization, was fundamentally at odds with the progressive certainty that in modern society, only "certain kinds of people had a right to rule." Progressive industrial, political, and educational elites rejected, and feared, the notion that legitimate democratic reform could challenge the prerogatives of those who ruled.[12]

The constricted boundaries of modern politics, Goodwyn concludes, dating from the emergence of corporate capitalism after the American Civil War, are reaffirmed in the ways the "reality of the American experience—the culture itself" is conveyed to new generations. These include the commercial bonding of mass society through mass communications, and the interpretation of the American past that is transmitted through private and public education. To Goodwyn, these boundaries signal a "clear retreat" from the democratic promise of the cooperative commonwealth.[13] West Virginia Governor Ephraim F. Morgan forcefully defended corporative education in 1921. Addressing a patriotic gathering in Welch, Morgan launched a verbal attack against unidentified public school teachers and professors who were instilling "socialistic, populistic, and bolshevistic doctrines," thereby engendering "the spirit of treason in the plastic minds" of unsuspecting students.[14]

The processes of conveying acceptable values and beliefs, which will not erode the standing or social power of society's molders of opinion, are defined by educator John Gaventa in terms of hegemonic processes of "breeding consensus." In describing the acquiescence of local workers in an Appalachian valley to the encroachment and eventual dominance of industrial corporatism in the first half of the twentieth century, Gaventa argues that "the answer lies in the powers of the industrial society for establishing control and breeding consensus." That power, built exponentially upon corporate influence in politics, education, and communications, results in the dominance of a set of values prescribed for the ruled by the rulers. The process is successful when the values of the dominant class are accepted and internalized by subordinates.[15]

It is this dynamic of the conscious manufacture of general public consent to elite principles of social organization that I have examined in *The Americanization of West Virginia*. I have sought to demonstrate how adherents to the hierarchical elements of industrial capitalism attempted, I believe with great success, to implant their ideology into the consciousness of a culture and turn its tenets into cultural values that are so deeply imbedded as to practically transcend debate. I have attempted throughout to follow the example of Francis Jennings, who analyzed the ideology of colonial conquest that sanctified the destruction of Native American cultures in New England. Jennings recognized in himself a "strong aversion" toward the Puritan elites who articulated the ideology and "tried to compensate for it by documenting heavily from their own writings whenever possible." Jennings studied the documents left by the Puritan gentry, extracting reliable data from "excruciating cant and masterful guile."[16]

Likewise in this study, I have relied heavily on the words of the industrial Americanizers themselves and on contemporary and recent documentation for context. It has not been my intent to pass personal judgment on the political, labor, educational, industrial, and social elites whose private and public records are woven into this work. Indeed, I am well aware and appreciative of their many positive and sincere contributions to their fields and communities. My goal has been to present a fresh examination and interpretation of a formative era in West Virginia's history that has been strangely neglected, aside from extensive work on the coal industry. I have done so in a way that offers a countervailing perspective to the generally hagiographic contemporary accounts in which the West Virginia protagonists of this study are mentioned. In the process, I have tried to apply to them their own functional view regarding the human factors of production in modern industry. I have consciously viewed their relevance to this study less in terms of their human strengths and weaknesses than in terms of their dedication to efficient social and industrial systems. Within the parameters of this study, the industrial Americanizers are treated as pistons in an engine, just as Woodrow Wilson would have it. After all, as Frederick W. Taylor explained, "In the past the man has been first; in the future, the system must be first."[17] That was both the triumph and the tragedy of the Americanization of West Virginia.

Notes

Preface

1. Henry Shapiro, *Appalachia on our Mind: The Southern Mountains and Mountaineers in the American Consciousness, 1870-1920* (Chapel Hill: University of North Carolina Press, 1978).

2. For example, see David Walls, "Whose Bicentennial? Appalachia '76," *Appalachian Journal* 4, no. 1 (Autumn 1976): 39-42; Stephen L. Fisher, "New Populist Theory and the Study of Dissent in Appalachia," in his *Fighting Back in Appalachia: Traditions of Resistance and Change* (Philadelphia: Temple University Press, 1993), 327; Walls and Dwight B. Billings, "The Sociology of Southern Appalachia," *Appalachian Journal* 5, no. 1 (Autumn 1977): 131-44; Herbert Reid, "Appalachian Studies: Class, Culture, and Politics—II," *Appalachian Journal* 10, no. 1 (Winter-Spring 1982), 141-48; Helen Lewis and Myles Horton, "The Role of Transnational Corporations and the Migration of Industries in Latin America and Appalachia," in *Proceedings of the 1980 Appalachian Studies Conference*, ed. Sommerville Wilson (Boone, N.C.: Appalachian Consortium Press, 1981); and John Gaventa, "The Poverty of Abundance Revisited," *Appalachian Journal* 15 (Fall 1987): 24-33. Also see Gaventa, Barbara E. Smith, and Alex Winningham, eds., *Communities in Economic Crisis: Appalachia and the South* (Philadelphia: Temple University Press, 1990); and Myles Horton, with Herbert Kohl and Judith Kohl, *The Long Haul: The Autobiography of Myles Horton* (New York: Anchor/Doubleday, 1990).

3. T.J. Jackson Lears, "The Concept of Cultural Hegemony: Problems and Possibilities," *American Historical Review* 90, no. 3 (June 1985), 567-71. Harold P. Schlechtweg, "Environmentalism's 'Evil Twin': The Ideological Challenge of the Wise Use Movement," paper delivered at the Conference on Communication and Our Environment 1995, Chattanooga, Tenn., Mar. 30-Apr. 2, 1995, author's possession. See also Joseph V. Femia, *Gramsci's Political Thought* (New York: Oxford, 1981); and Antonio Gramsci, *Selections from the Prison Notebooks*, ed. and trans. Q. Hoare and G.N. Smith (New York: International Publishers, 1971).

4. Ronald D Eller, *Miners, Millhands, and Mountaineers: Industrialization of the Appalachian South, 1880-1930* (Knoxville: University of Tennessee Press, 1982); John Gaventa, *Power and Powerlessness: Quiescence and Rebellion in Appalachian Valley* (Urbana: University of Illinois Press, 1980); Altina Waller, *Feud: Hatfields, McCoys, and Social Change in Appalachia, 1860-1900* (Chapel Hill: University of North Carolina Press, 1988); Ronald L. Lewis, "Appalachian Restructuring in Historical Perspective: Coal, Culture, and Social Change in West Virginia," Research Paper 9102 (Morgantown, W.V.: Regional Research Institute, 1992).

5. John A. Williams, *West Virginia: A History* (New York: Norton, 1976);

Williams, *West Virginia and the Captains of Industry* (Morgantown: West Virginia University, 1976); Williams, introduction *Thunder in the Mountains: The West Virginia Mine War, 1920-1921* by Lon Savage (Pittsburgh: University Press of Pittsburgh, 1990); Ronald L. Lewis, *Black Coal Miners in America: Race, Class, and Community Conflict, 1780-1980* (Lexington: University Press of Kentucky, 1987); Lewis, "From Peasant to Proletarian: The Migration of Southern Blacks to the Central Appalachian Coalfields," *Journal of Southern History* 55, no. 1 (1989): 77-102; Joe William Trotter, *Coal, Class, and Color: Blacks in Southern Appalachia, 1915-1932* (Urbana: University of Illinois Press, 1990); David Alan Corbin, *Life, Work, and Rebellion in the Coal Fields* (Urbana: University of Illinois Press, 1981); Alan Banks, "Labor and the Development of Industrial Capitalism in Eastern Kentucky, 1870-1930" (Ph.D. diss., McMaster University, 1980), and for example, Banks, "The Emergence of a Capitalistic Labor Market in Eastern Kentucky," *Appalachian Journal* 7 (Spring 1980): 188-99. Dwight B. Billings examined a counterhegemonic movement in "Religion as Opposition: A Gramscian Analysis," *American Journal of Sociology* 96, no. 1 (July 1990): 1-31. Good studies of cultural resistance to industrial capitalism include a short article by Paul Salstrom, "Historical and Theoretical Perspectives on Appalachia's Economic Dependency," *Journal of the Appalachian Studies Association* 3 (1991): 68-81; and Rhoda Halperin, *The Livelihood of Kin: Making Ends Meet the "Kentucky Way"* (Austin: University of Texas Press, 1990). For a comprehensive treatment of grassroots resistance, see Stephen L. Fisher, ed., *Fighting Back in Appalachia*.

6. Reid, "Class, Culture, and Politics," 141-43.

7. For a critique of contemporary corporate culture and the wave of workplace labor-management participation programs from a labor rather than a management perspective, see Mike Parker and Jane Slaughter, eds., *Working Smart: A Union Guide to Participation Programs and Reengineering* (Detroit: Labor Notes, 1994). For an analysis of the possible social costs of the information age, see Theodore Roszak, *The Cult of Information: A Neo-Luddite Treatise on High-Tech, Artificial Intelligence, and the True Art of Thinking* (Berkeley: University of California Press, 1994).

8. Reid, "Class, Culture, and Politics," 141.

Introduction

1. The phrase "engineering of consent" was often used by public relations pioneer Edward L. Bernays, who refined the skills of manipulating public opinion during his tenure with the CPI. Bernays recounts his wartime experience in several memoirs, including *Public Relations* (Norman: University of Oklahoma Press, 1952), and *Biography of an Idea* (New York: Simon and Schuster, 1965). William Graebner borrowed the phrase for his 1987 analysis of democracy and authority in twentieth-century America, *The Engineering of Consent* (Madison: University of Wisconsin Press, 1987). The influential journalist and intellectual, Walter Lippmann, used the expression "manufacture of consent" to describe elite guidance of the masses. *Public Opinion* (New York: Free Press, 1922), 195.

2. Figures on West Virginia newspapers are from the 1917 Harris, John T., ed., *West Virginia Hand Book* (Charleston, W.Va.: Tribune Printing Company, 1917), 1-196. The *Hand Book* lists each paper, with circulation figures by county.

3. Joseph F. Marsh, *Report of the West Virginia State Board of Education: Two Years Ending June 30, 1924* (Charleston, W.Va.: State Board of Education, 1924), 43; 41.

4. *West Virginia Institute Program and Song Book: All of West Virginia 100% American* (Charleston, W.Va.: Department of Schools, 1919), 65. *Course of Study for*

the Junior and Senior High Schools of West Virginia, 1919 (Charleston, W.Va.: State Board of Education, 1919), 4.

5. Mrs. Cyrus Hall, "Outline of Work in Citizenship Training for 1924," *West Virginia Clubwoman* 3, no. 2 (Jan. 5, 1924): 4.

6. Nellie J. Sullivan, "Why Laws Are Needed," *Consolidation Coal Company Mutual Magazine* 1, no. 3 (Mar. 1918): 49.

1. War Propaganda and the Mobilization of Public Opinion in West Virginia, 1916-1918

1. *Coal Age* 11, no. 19, May 12, 1917, 826.

2. *Coal Age* listed the various elements of the parade, including the Boy Scouts, Home Guards, Verhovia Aid Association No. 32, Red Men, Knights of Pythias, Tug River No. 4 Hungarian Lodge, First Catholic Slavish Union, Servian Society No. 24, National Croatian Society, Russian Society, Odd Fellows (colored), Masons (colored), and Knights of Pythias (colored). Ibid, 826. Herndon identified in John T. Harris, ed., *West Virginia Hand Book and Manual* (Charleston: Tribune Printing Company, 1917), 115.

3. *Coal Age*, May 12, 1917, 828. *St. Mary's Oracle*, Apr. 5, 1917; Apr. 6, 1917; Apr. 12, 1917. *War Work of Marshall County: The Fighting Forces and the Inner Lines* (Moundsville, W.Va.: n.p., 1919), 15-16. *Morgantown Post-Chronicle*, Apr. 5, 1917.

4. *Daily Athenaeum*, March 31, 1917.

5. *Pocahontas Times*, April 12, 1917; April 5, 1917; April 12, 1917.

6. Harold J. Tobin and Percy Bidwell, *Mobilizing Civilian America* (New York: Council on Foreign Relations, 1940), 75-76. John Higham, *Strangers in the Land: Patterns of American Nativism, 1860-1925* (New York: Atheneum, 1975; originally published by the Trustees of Rutgers University, 1955), 200. James R. Mock and Cedric Larson, *Words that Won the War: The Story of the Committee on Public Information* (Princeton: Princeton University Press, 1939), 9-10. Mock and Larson's was the first book-length study of the CPI. Four decades later, the work of the CPI was also examined by Stephen Vaughan in *Holding Fast the Inner Lines: Democracy, Nationalism, and the Committee on Public Information* (Chapel Hill: University of North Carolina Press, 1980). The preparedness groups encouraged American military involvement for over a year before April 1917. The most outspoken advocates of preparedness were Theodore Roosevelt, General Leonard Wood, the Navy League, the American Defense Society, and the National Security League (Mock and Larson, *Words*), 9.

The largest and most militant of the preparedness organizations was the National Security League (NSL), founded in 1914, which lobbied aggressively for war and compulsory military training. Avowedly nonpartisan, the NSL defined its own version of "100 percent Americanism" and sought to stifle most expressions of political dissent. (See Robert D. Ward, "The Origin and Activities of the National Security League, 1914-1919," *Mississippi Valley Historical Review* 47 [June, 1960]: 51-65).

7. David M. Kennedy, *Over Here: The First World War and American Society* (Oxford: Oxford University Press, 1980), 60. The CPI is identified as the "Creel Committee," for example, in William Graebner, *The Engineering of Consent: Democracy and Authority in Twentieth-Century America* (Madison: University of Wisconsin Press, 1987), 37-38, 42-46, 62-63, 65, 87, and 189, and in Vaughan, *Holding Fast*, ix.

8. Censorship comments in *Pocahontas Times*, Jan. 4, 1917. Kennedy explains the government's hopes for partnership in *Over Here*, 60. CPI policy and long quote by Daniels in Mock and Larson, *Words*, 11, 49-50.

9. Morgantown *Post-Chronicle*, April 4, 1917. Woodrow Wilson, "Ways to Serve the Nation: April 16, 1917," in *President Wilson's State Papers and Addresses* (New York: The Review of Reviews Company, 1917), 392.

10. Kennedy, *Over Here*, 60. William Pencak, *For God and Country: The American Legion, 1919-1941* (Boston: Northeastern University Press, 1989), 279. Tobin and Bidwell, *Mobilizing*, 76-77.

11. List of agencies taken from Mock and Larson, *Words*, 67-72. Kennedy quoted Creel in *Over Here*, 61, from Creel's *How We Advertised America* (New York: Harper and Brothers, 1920), xiv. Also see Vaughan, *Holding Fast*, 116-25.

12. *Daily Athenaeum*, May 21, 1918. Creel estimated that the CPI's weekly columns reached approximately twenty thousand newspapers, or ten thousand less than the *Daily Athenaeum* figure, nationwide (Mock and Larson, *Words*, 68).

13. Guy Stanton Ford, "The Committee on Public Information," *Historical Outlook* (formerly *History Teacher's Magazine*) 11, no. 3 (Mar. 1920): 99-100.

14. Estimates vary as to sheer numbers of CPI publications. Historian Alan Dawley uses figures provided by Creel in his *How We Advertised America*, which estimated 75,099,023 pieces of "patriotic literature," but Dawley does not say if this includes Foreign Press Bureau publications (Alan Dawley, *Struggles for Justice: Social Responsibility and the Liberal State* [Cambridge and London: The Belknap Press of Harvard University Press, 1991], 190). Mock and Larson, in *Words*, attribute circulation of seventy-five million for 105 publications for Ford's Civic and Educational Cooperation Committee alone (68). Education historian Lewis Paul Todd estimates that about seventy-five million pamphlets were produced for domestic use, but "it is impossible to estimate how many . . . ever reached the public schools" (Lewis Paul Todd, *Wartime Relations of the Federal Government and the Public Schools, 1917-1918* [New York: Teachers College of Columbia University, 1945], 36).

15. Mock and Larson, *Words*, 6-7. Long quote from Tobin and Bidwell, *Mobilizing*, 76-77.

16. Dawley, *Struggles*, 185. Mock and Larson, *Words*, 13.

17. *Daily Athenaeum*, Mar. 21, 1918. Kennedy, *Over Here*, 75-76; 79-80. Henry Steele Commager, ed. *Documents in American History*, 8th ed. (New York: Appleton-Century-Crofts, 1968), document no. 425, 2:145-46.

18. Figures and actions of the American Protective League are from Joan M. Jensen's book on the APL, *The Price of Vigilance* (New York: Rand McNally & Company, 1968), 10, 292-93. Woodrow Wilson is quoted from his "Flag Day Address: June 14, 1917," in *State Papers*, 412. Wilson's comments were incorporated into "German Plots and Conspiracies in the United States," a short article in the *West Virginia School Journal* 46, no. 10 (Jan. 1918): 288.

19. Wilson to a reporter from the *New York World*, quoted in Dawley, *Struggles*, 185. Edward L. Bernays, *Public Relations* (Norman: University of Oklahoma Press, 1952), 71-72.

20. Jensen, *Vigilance*, 293. James A.B. Scherer, "The Nation at War," *Addresses and Proceedings of the National Education Association*, 56th annual meeting, Pittsburgh, June 29-July 6, 1918 (Washington: National Education Association, 1918), 50. *Fairmont Times*, Jan. 3, 1918.

21. *Clarksburg Daily Telegram*, Aug. 14, 1917; Aug. 22, 1917; Aug. 25, 1917.

22. Harding's "Outline" was published in *History Teacher's Magazine* (*HTM*) in January 1918 and was intended as a manual for teachers and students to assist study of the war. It was reproduced either in the magazine or as a pamphlet in over eight hundred thousand copies. As propaganda, says Lewis Paul Todd, the outline was im-

pressive, but it had serious weaknesses as a historical study. At least one-third of the outline's citations directed readers to CPI propaganda leaflets (Todd, *Wartime Relations*), 48-51.

23. A.S. Hershey, from *Indiana University Alumni Quarterly*, 1917, quoted in Samuel B. Harding, "Topical Outline of the War," *History Teacher's Magazine* 9, no. 1 (Jan. 1918): 49. Vaughan, *Holding Fast*, 157, cites the inflammatory CPI poster.

24. Dana Munro, "German War Practices," from *War Cyclopedia* (Washington: Committee on Public Information), quoted in Harding's "Outline," *HTM* (Jan. 1918), 49. Munro was another prominent historian who served the NBHS. Harding, "Outline," quoting Arnold Toynbee from *War Cyclopedia*, "The German Terror in Belgium," 15-16; and Munro, "German War Practices," 49.

25. "Obtrusive hypoplasia" comments from J. Madison Taylor, professor of applied therapeutics at Temple University, in "The Slaughter of the Innocents," *Wheeling Intelligencer*, July 27, 1917.

26. "Centers of information" comment by Waitman Barbe, "The Duty of the Schools," *West Virginia School Journal*, hereafter *WVSJ*, 46, no. 9 (Dec. 1917): 244.

27. *Wheeling Intelligencer*, July 4, 1917. The report does not specify the charges against the slackers. They may have been charged with violating West Virginia's new Vagrancy Act, also known as the Compulsory Work, or work-or-fight law, which took effect on June 18, 1917. See chapter 3 below. For more on local manifestations of overreaction, see Vaughan, *Holding Fast*, 155-88.

28. Pigs' food story in *Pocahontas Times*, May 17, 1917. *Consolidation Coal Company Mutual Monthly Magazine*, hereafter *CCC*, 1, no. 5 (May 1918): 1.

29. Robert A. Armstrong, "A Pacifist on the War," *WVSJ* 46, no. 5 (Sept. 1917): 142.

30. *Our Own People* 3, no. 10 (Oct. 1918): 3.

31. Franklin K. Lane and Newton D. Baker, *The Nation in Arms*. War Information Series no. 2 (Washington: Committee on Public Information, Aug. 1917), 4. Lane, "The New Americanism" *NEA Addresses and Proceedings*, 1918, 105-8. Lane's vision of Americanism is summarized in Vaughan, *Holding Fast*, 43-44.

32. John T. Harris, in *West Virginia Legislative Hand Book*, 1918, hereafter *WV Hand Book*. The *Hand Book* was popularly and later officially called the *Blue Book*. The 1918 edition lists West Virginia's Four-Minute Men, who included about eighty women speakers, county by county on pages 916-20. Chitwood is listed on page 918. "Gospel of patriotism" comment by Oliver P. Chitwood from his summary of "West Virginia and the World War," in James Morton Callahan, *History of West Virginia Old and New* (Chicago and New York: American Historical Society, 1923), 1:707. Matthews wrote on "Four Minute Men" in 1918 *WV Hand Book*, 913.

33. Wilson, *State Papers and Addresses*, 1917, 392. The postwar penance of some pro-war preachers is noted in Tobin and Bidwell, *Mobilizing*, 78.

34. West Virginia's Four-Minute Men are listed in the 1918 *WV Hand Book*, 916-20. The *Morgantown Post*, July 5, 1918, reported on the Methodist Episcopal patriotic meeting.

35. Jesse V. Sullivan, "State Councils of Defense," in 1918 *WV Hand Book*, 798. Hastings S. Hart, *A Suggested Program for the Executive State Council of Defense of West Virginia* (Charleston: 1917), 5. PAM 993, WVRHC.

36. Sullivan, 1918 *WV Hand Book*, 779. William J. Breen, *Uncle Sam at Home: Civilian Mobilization, Wartime Federalism, and the Council of National Defense, 1917-1919* (Westport, Conn.: Greenwood Press, 1984), 18.

37. Sullivan in 1918 *WV Hand Book*, 780-81. Establishment of the state defense council, House Bill 1, chap. 4 (*Acts of the Legislature of West Virginia*, Second Extraordinary Session, May 14-26, 1917), 34. Also see 1918 *Hand Book* for a list of war measures. The organization of the state defense council will be covered more comprehensively in chapter 3 below.

38. Executive Council list in 1918 *WV Hand Book*, 781.

39. Advisory Council explained by Chitwood in Callahan, *West Virginia*, 698-700, and by Sullivan in 1918 *WV Hand Book*, 783. Details of May 29 meeting in *Minutes* of the executive board of the West Virginia Council of Defense (hereafter *SDC Minutes*), May 29, 1917, 1. State archives, Charleston.

40. Information on bureaus organized by Advisory Council from *SDC Minutes* June 22, 1917, 5. Leading members of the fifteen-person Advisory Council included C.P. Snow, president of the West Virginia Board of Trade; A.B.C. Bray, president of the West Virginia Bankers' Association; Mrs. Joseph G. Cochran, president of the West Virginia Federation of Women's Clubs; William Rogers, president of the West Virginia Federation of Labor; G.O. Nagle, president of the West Virginia Manufacturer's Association; Dr. John Lee Coulter, dean of the College of Agriculture at West Virginia University; and Howard Gore, president of the West Virginia Live Stock Association (1918 *WV Hand Book*), 783.

41. John J. Cornwell, "Our State and the War Program," in 1918 *WV Hand Book*, 777. Breen, *Uncle Sam*, 23. Comment on immigrants from Hastings H. Hart, *A Suggested Program for the Executive State Council of Defense of West Virginia* (Charleston: Aug. 1917), 4-5.

42. Snow's appointment, *SDC Minutes* June 19, 1917, 6. Shawkey's recommendation, *SDC Minutes*, June 22, 1917, 4. Salary approval, *SDC Minutes*, June 29, 1917, 8. Background on Sullivan from *West Virginia Today, for Newspaper and Library Reference* (New Orleans: James O. Jones for the West Virginia Editors Association, 1941), 215.

43. Figures on West Virginia newspapers are from the 1917 *WV Hand Book*, 1-196. The *Hand Book* lists each paper by county, with party status, and circulation figures.

44. Sullivan in 1918 *WV Hand Book*, 787, 783.

45. Chitwood in Callahan, *West Virginia*, 707.

46. Hart, *Suggested Program*, 4-5.

47. Broadside, in broadside collection folder for 1917-19, West Virginia and Regional History Collection (WVRHC), West Virginia University, Morgantown.

48. Stevens-Shawkey meeting detailed in *Records of the State Defense Council* (hereafter *SDC Records*), July 19, 1917, box 1, folder 1. A&M 2142, state archives, Charleston.

49. Pageant itinerary in *Wheeling Intelligencer* July 17 and July 24-27, 1917. Educational and artistic value of pageant, *Wheeling Intelligencer*, July 24, 1917. Comments on draftees, *Wheeling Intelligencer*, July 26, 1917.

50. Comments on the Knights of Pythias demonstration, *Wheeling Intelligencer*, July 28 and July 30, 1917.

51. *War Bulletin* authorized, *SDC Minutes* Mar. 21, 1918, 44. Matthews appointment, 1918 *WV Hand Book*, 787. "Militant message" comment in Matthews's summary of Four-Minute campaigns in 1918 *WV Hand Book*, 912.

52. "Mouthpiece" comment and list of topics, from 1918 *WV Hand Book*, 913-14. Chitwood on distribution of bulletins from Washington, in Callahan, *West Virginia*, 707.

53. Creel's strategy is outlined in Mock and Larson, *Words*, 6-8. Chitwood's comment on "snappy speeches" in Callahan, *West Virginia*, 708. "Vacant minds" statement in Vaughan, *Holding Fast*, quoting Bertram G. Nelson, 116.

54. Chitwood in Callahan, *West Virginia*, 699.

55. "West Virginia Will Meet Third Liberty Loan Quota," *West Virginia War Bulletin*, April 20, 1918, 1. PAM 2418, WVRHC.

56. Expansion of Four-Minute network, *SDC Minutes*, Apr. 9, 1918, 47, and in 1918 *WV Hand Book*, 796. MacCorkle's "dark times" statement in William Alexander MacCorkle, *The Recollections of Fifty Years of West Virginia* (New York: G.P. Putnam's Sons, 1928), 556, 546-47.

57. "Third Liberty Loan Quota," *War Bulletin*, Apr. 20, 1918, 1.

58. "Reaching the Rurals," *WV War Bulletin*, Apr. 20, 1918, 1.

59. *Minutes* of the Elizabeth Ludington Hagans Chapter of the Daughters of the American Revolution. Box 4, Minute Book 2, Apr. 24, 1918, 17, WVRHC.

60. Morris P. Shawkey, *West Virginia in History, Life, Literature and Industry* (Chicago: Lewis Publishing Company, 1928), 2:99.

61. War Convention, *SDC Minutes*, Sept. 3, 1918, 53. Liberty Loan cancellation, Chitwood in Callahan, *West Virginia*, 702, and 1918 *WV Hand Book*, 789.

62. MacCorkle, *Recollections*, 546-50. Statement by Cornwell, Oct. 6, 1918, *John J. Cornwell papers*, hereafter *JJC*, box 122, folder 1, A&M 952, WVRHC.

63. Bernays, *Public Relations*, 75.

64. W.B. Matthews on "German propaganda," 1918 *WV Hand Book*, 914.

65. "Engineering of consent," Bernays, *Public Relations*, 71-78. Hatred statement, Harold D. Lasswell, *Propaganda Technique in World War I* (Cambridge: MIT Press), 1971, 195. Originally published as *Propaganda Techniques in the World War* (London: Kegan Paul, Trench, Trubner & Co., 1928), 195.

66. Bernays, *Public Opinion*, 77-78.

67. "Intelligent minority" quote in Stephen Schlesinger and Stephen Kinzer, *Bitter Fruit: The Untold Story of the American Coup in Guatemala* (Garden City, N.Y.: Doubleday & Company, 1982), 80. Bernays was retained by the United Fruit Company to mobilize popular opinion against the Arévalo and Arbenz governments in Guatemala, which had nationalized United Fruit land, determining compensation on the basis of the company's property assessments. Bernays's task was to soften public resistance to United Fruit's ultimately successful secret campaign to prod the United States government into the 1954 overthrow of Arbenz. Bernays's actions are discussed in *Bitter Fruit*, especially chap. 6, "Advertisements for Myself," 79-97.

68. Ford, "The Committee on Public Information," *Historical Outlook* 11, no. 3 (Mar. 1920): 97.

69. 1918 *WV Hand Book*, 900.

70. Chitwood in Callahan, *West Virginia*, 706-7.

71. Center of war work, Waitman Barbe, "The Duty of the Schools," *WVSJ* 46, no. 9 (Dec. 1917): 244.

72. "Yellow streaks" comment by Barbe, "The New Year," *WVSJ* 46, no. 7 (Oct. 1917): 178. "Army of reserves," Joseph F. Marsh, "The Teacher and the War," *WVSJ* 46, no. 8 (Nov. 1917), 203.

73. The role-defining status of the nation-state and its position as the object of ethical commitment are addressed in Dawley, *Struggles for Justice*, chap. 5, "The Dynamics of Total War," 172-217. Also see R. Jeffrey Lustig, *Corporate Liberalism: The Origins of Modern Political Theory, 1890-1920* (Berkeley: University of California Press,

1982), 225, in chap. 7, "The New Nationalism: Lineaments of Corporate Capitalism," 195-226.

74. The ascendant nationalism of educators can be discerned in speeches at the NEA convention in 1918, printed in the *Addresses and Proceedings*. West Virginia delegates to the convention mentioned by L.L. Friend in a letter to West Virginia University president Frank Trotter, Aug. 15, 1918, West Virginia University Archives, mic 91, WVRHC. Guy Stanton Ford is quoted from the 1918 NEA *Proceedings*, 208.

75. Ford, NEA *Proceedings*, 1918, 208. L.B. Hill, "Teaching as a Factor in an Ideal State System," West Virginia Education Association (WVEA) *Annual Proceedings*, June 13-15, 1917 (Keyser, W.V.: Mountain Echo, 1917), 25-27.

76. "Colleges and the War," *School and Society* 5, no. 128 (June 9, 1917): 685-86.

77. Sarah B. Fahey, "How the Public School Can Foster the American Ideal of Patriotism," NEA *Addresses and Proceedings*, 55th Annual Meeting, Portland, Oregon, July 7-14, 1917 (Washington: National Education Association, 1917), 48.

78. On national fulfillment, see James Weinstein, *The Corporate Ideal in the Liberal State: 1900-1918* (Boston: Beacon Press, 1968), 214-54. "Training camp" comment by Fahey, NEA *Proceedings* 1917, 56. On patriotic demonstrations in the schools, Margaret S. McNaught, "The Elementary School during the War," NEA *Proceedings* 1917, 166, 168.

79. To cite two examples, the *Morgantown Post* ran a short article on the city's "Review of Nations" pageant for children on July 1, 1918, and on a pageant at the Methodist Episcopal Church in the July 19, 1918, paper. Matthews commented on the Junior Four-Minute Men in the 1918 *WV Hand Book*, 914. Robert A. Armstrong, "Patriotism in Songs," *WVSJ* 46, no. 12 (Mar. 1918): 344-45.

80. Shawkey's injection of patriotism in schools was reported by Jesse Sullivan in the 1918 *WV Hand Book*, 789. The war's effect on organizations' meetings and course work was summarized by Shawkey in *Biennial Report of the State Superintendent of Free Schools of West Virginia for the Two Years Ending June 30, 1918* (Charleston: Department of Free Schools, 1918), 36-37.

81. "Our School Teachers," *WVSJ* 47, no. 6 (Aug-Sept. 1918), 493. The war question was question no. 8 of the teacher examination administered June 6-7, 1918, from *WVSJ* 47, no. 4 (July 1918): 466.

82. The 1918 *WV Hand Book*, 900, noted the time spent on the war at teacher institutes. Charles H. Ambler, *A History of Education in West Virginia, from Early Colonial Times to 1949* (Huntington: Standard Printing and Publishing, 1951), 431, on reinvigoration of the county institutes. Shawkey on institutes' value in his *Biennial Report* 1918, 67.

83. Todd, *Wartime Relations*, 72-73. The specific hatred charge is from the California Board of Education.

84. German abolished in Morgantown schools, from *Minutes of the Morgantown Independent District Board of Education* (Minute book VI, April 25, 1918), 1, WVRHC.

85. Armstrong quoted in *WVSJ* 47, no. 3 (June 1918), 440-41. The specific resolution Armstrong approved was an NEA resolution at the 1917 convention, *Proceedings*, 381. Shawkey, "To Teach or Not to teach—German," *WVSJ* 46, no. 6 (Oct. 1917), 178. Chitwood in Callahan, *West Virginia*, 707.

86. Friend to Trotter, Oct. 8, 1918, *WVU Archives*, WVRHC. "German Out," *WVSJ* 47, no. 4 (July 1918): 469. 1918 *WV Hand Book*, 900.

87. Ford, *Historical Outlook* 11, no. 3, 100. E.L. Bernays, "Manipulating Public Opinion: The Why and the How," *American Journal of Sociology* 33, no. 6 (May 1928): 959.

2. National and West Virginia Perspectives on Higher Education and the Delivery of War Propaganda

1. Carol S. Gruber, *Mars and Minerva: World War I and the Uses of Higher Learning in America* (Baton Rouge: Louisiana State University Press, 1975), 95.

2. J.H. Ackerman, "The Normal School as an Agency for Teaching Patriotism," NEA *Proceedings* 1917, 59.

3. L.R. Alderman, "The Public School and the Nation in 1917," NEA *Proceedings* 1917, 234.

4. Gruber, *Mars and Minerva*, 95.

5. G. Stanley Hall, "Some Educational Values of War," NEA *Proceedings* 1918, 99.

6. Ambler, *Education in West Virginia*, 563-64.

7. Florence A. Kellogg, "War-time Changes in the Schools," *WVSJ* 47, no. 7 (Oct. 1918): 528, quoting WVU librarian L.D. Arnett.

8. Barbe cited in *Daily Athenaeum*, Sept. 27, 1918.

9. SDC *Minutes*, Feb. 7-8, 1918, 37.

10. Joseph F. Marsh, in Superintendent Morris P. Shawkey's *Biennial Report for 1916-1918*, 1918, 39.

11. Ambler, *Education in West Virginia*, 564.

12. "War Aims" reference in *Daily Athenaeum*, Sept. 27, 1918. Chitwood's book was *The Immediate Causes of the Great War*, 2d ed. (New York: Thomas Y. Crowell, 1918). He cited the *War Cyclopedia* in footnote 10, 248, and footnotes 21 and 23, 262. He cited the National Security League in footnote 16, 253.

13. *Daily Athenaeum*, Mar. 12, 1918.

14. "Salem Pledge," *WVSJ* 47, no. 1 (Apr. 1918): 380.

15. Bernays, *Public Relations*, 74.

16. "Teachers and Patriotism," *WVSJ* 47, no. 3 (June 1918): 434.

17. *Daily Athenaeum*, Feb. 26, 1918.

18. Callahan wrote of his institute and civic addresses to his brother, Alva, in a letter dated July 19, 1917. James Morton Callahan papers (hereafter JMC), 1917 box 3, folder 2. WVRHC A&M 839.

19. Institute topics taken from letter from Morris P. Shawkey to Callahan, June 1, 1918, JMC 1918 box 3, folder 4, May-December. Also see correspondence from Shawkey to Callahan Sept. 8, 1917, on Lewis and Jefferson County institutes, JMC 1917 box 3, folder 2.

20. WVU faculty as Four-Minute Men listed in *Daily Athenaeum*, Mar. 12, 1918.

21. Creel quoted in George Creel, *How We Advertised America* (New York: Harper & Row, 1920), 3-14. Excerpted in Stanley Coben, ed., *Reform, War, and Reaction: 1912-1932* Columbia: University of South Carolina Press, 1972, 94. Recommendations for history teachers in "What Can the History Teacher Do Now?" *History Teacher's Magazine* (hereafter HTM) 8, no. 5 (May 1917): 175.

22. George T. Blakey documented some historians' worries about manipulation in *Historians on the Home Front: American Propagandists for the Great War* (Lexington: University Press of Kentucky, 1970), 31.

23. Ames cautioned historians in Herman V. Ames, "How Far Should the Teaching of History and Civics Be Used as a Means of Encouraging Patriotism?" HTM 8, no. 6 (June 1917): 188.

24. Peter Novick, *That Noble Dream: The "Objectivity Question" and the American Historical Profession* (Cambridge: Cambridge University Press, 1988), 111.

25. Gruber, *Mars and Minerva*, 119-20, 136.

26. Ames, "How Far," *HTM* 8, no. 6 (June 1917): 189.

27. Gruber, *Mars and Minerva*, 120, quoting Andrew C. McLaughlin in *Dial* 62 (May 17, 1917): 427. The original National Board for Historical Service, or NBHS, included Victor S. Clark, Robert D.W. Connor, Carl Russell Fish, Charles D. Hazen, Charles H. Hull, Gaillard Hunt, Waldo G. Leland, James T. Shotwell, and Frederick Jackson Turner. Later additions included Carl Becker and Dana C. Munro. Guy Stanton Ford represented the Committee on Public Information at the founding meeting of the NBHS in Washington (ibid., 120-21, n. 4).

28. Blakey, *Home Front*, 20.

29. James T. Shotwell, "The National Board for Historical Service," *HTM* 8, no. 6 (June 1917): 199.

30. Creel, *How We Advertised*, in Coben, *Reform, War, and Reaction*, 94.

31. NBHS leadership and contributors to *War Cyclopedia* noted in *HTM* 9, no. 2 (Feb. 1918), 69.

32. AHA office space donated, in Novick, *Noble Dream*, 121. Free publicity in *American Historical Review*, see Blakey, *Home Front*, 19.

33. *HTM* financing by AHA, and masthead, in Novick, *Noble Dream*, 121, and *HTM*, all issues, 1917-1918.

34. Shotwell, "NBHS," *HTM* 8, no. 6 (June 1917): 199.

35. The "facts" from "To Those Who Remain at Home," *HTM* 8, no. 7 (September 1917), 213. The "desired result" from Shotwell, "NBHS," *HTM* 8, no. 6 (June 1917): 199.

36. Novick, *Noble Dream*, 118, quoting Andrew McLaughlin, "Historians and the War," in *The Dial* 62 (1917): 428.

37. Harding on "historical truth," in Novick, *Noble Dream*, 118, and Gruber, *Mars and Minerva*, 141.

38. Harding on neutrality and objectivity, Gruber, *Mars and Minerva*, 137, from NBHS papers, Dana C. Munro to Evarts B. Greene, July 17, 1917.

39. Gruber, *Mars and Minerva*, 136.

40. "Anti-British Sentiment in America," *WVSJ* 47, no. 6 (Aug.-Sept. 1918): 502.

41. Novick on Anglo-Saxonism in *Noble Dream*, 82. Alliance of British and American Revolutionary-era leaders in "Anti-British Sentiment," *WVSJ* 47, no. 6 (Aug.-Sept. 1918), 502.

42. "Anti-British Sentiment," *WVSJ* 47, no. 6 (Aug.-Sept. 1918): 491.

43. Sullivan statement June 10, 1918, in *JJC*, box 122, folder 1. A.B. Hart quoted in Novick, *Noble Dream*, 82-83. "Imperial heritage" statement by Mary Byrd Fontaine, "National Council of Teachers of English," *WVSJ* 46, no. 10 (Jan. 1918), 279.

44. Broadwater's participation in wartime teacher institutes is noted in Superintendent Morris P. Shawkey's *Report* for 1916-18, 68-69. Broadwater's comments taken from C.L. Broadwater, "How Can the Teaching of History Be Adapted to Present Conditions?" *WVSJ* 47, no. 6 (Aug.-Sept. 1918), 490.

45. Biographical material on J.M. Callahan from Cletis Pride, "History of the West Virginia University History Department" (M.A. thesis, West Virginia University, 1963), 27, 19-20. Peter Novick notes that Woodrow Wilson was Herbert Baxter Adams's first doctoral student in *Noble Dream*, 129-30. Callahan taught a seminar at Johns Hopkins in 1916 (J.M. Callahan to Alva Callahan, Mar. 2, 1917, JMC, box 3, folder 2).

46. James Morton Callahan, *Cuba and International Relations: A Historical Study in American Diplomacy* (Baltimore: Johns Hopkins University Press, 1899), 32, 495-96.

47. James Morton Callahan, *An Introduction to American Expansion Policy* (Morgantown: West Virginia University Studies in American History, Department of History and Political Science, 1908), 3.

48. Expressions of Anglo-Saxonism among historians from Novick, *Noble Dream*, 74-82.

49. Alan Dawley identifies U.S. elites as "Anglophilic" in *Struggles for Justice*, 181.

50. A.B. Hart quoted in Novick, *Noble Dream*, 75, from James McPherson, *The Abolitionist Legacy: From Reconstruction to the NAACP* (Princeton: Princeton University Press, 1975), 337-38.

51. Madison Grant, *The Passing of the Great Race* (New York: 1916), 3-36, these quotes in Coben, *Reform, War, and Reaction: 1912-1932*, 154.

52. Grant, in Coben, *Reform, War, and Reaction*, 147, 149.

53. Callahan, *Expansion Policy*, 5-6, 34-36.

54. Positivism and Social Darwinism are summarized by Peter F. Klarén, "Lost Promise," in *Promise of Development: Theories of Change in Latin America*, by Peter F. Klarén and Thomas J. Bossert (Boulder and London: Westview Press, 1986), 9. The state's role under Positivism is defined in E. Bradford Burns, *Latin America: A Concise Interpretive History*, 2d ed. (Englewood Cliffs, N.J.: Prentice-Hall, 1977), 133-34. Stages of modernization in Klarén, "Lost Promise," 9. Grant, *Great Race*, in Coben, *Reform, War, and Reaction*, 149.

55. Peter Novick describes Adams's Teutonic Germ idea in *Noble Dream*, 87-88, as does Richard Hofstadter in *The Progressive Historians* (New York: Alfred A. Knopf, 1968), 43-50. The Americanization quote is from Frederick Jackson Turner, "The Significance of the Frontier in American History," *The Frontier in American History* (Huntington, N.Y.: Robert E. Krieger, 1976), 4. Turner's essay first appeared in 1893.

56. Historians' attitude toward rebellion noted in Novick, *Noble Dream*, 87-88, 82.

57. Ibid., 98-129, especially 98, 99, 118, and 129, where Novick quotes Carl Becker on "real democratization." He identifies James Harvey Robinson, Charles Beard, Lynn Thorndike, James T. Shotwell, and Carl Becker as leading New Historians.

58. Callahan to Alva Callahan, Oct. 31, 1917, JMC 1917, box 3, folder 2.

59. Callahan to Roosevelt Non-Partisan League's Guy Emerson, May 3, 1916. JMC 1916, box 3, folder 1.

60. Dawley, *Struggles for Justice*, 175-76.

61. "Straight Americanism" quote is in a letter from Guy Emerson of the Roosevelt Non-Partisan League to Callahan, Apr. 24, 1916, JMC 1916, box 3, folder 1. Callahan regretted that his age kept him from fighting in a letter to L.J. Forman, July 25, 1917, JMC 1917, box 3, folder 2.

62. Callahan to the directors of the Foreign Press Bureau of the CPI, June 11, 1918, JMC 1918, box 3, folder 4.

63. Bernays had written to Callahan for articles on May 31, 1918, JMC 1918, box 3, folder 4. He identified Paul Kennaday in Bernays, *Biography of an Idea*, 155. The long quote on the Foreign Press Bureau's policy was included in a letter from Kennaday to Callahan, Mar. 30, 1918, JMC 1918, box 3, folder 3.

64. Paul Kennaday acknowledged receipt of Callahan's manuscript in a June 27, 1918, telegram, JMC 1918, box 3, folder 4. The articles drawn from the manuscript were reproduced as "American Foreign Policy in the World War" in *WVSJ* 47, no. 11 (Feb. 1919), 651-52.

65. Novick identifies the National Security League (NSL) as "extreme and vitriolic" in *Noble Dream*, 116. Alan Dawley notes that NSL literature demanded "Ab-

solute and Unquestioned Loyalty to the State" (*Struggles for Justice*, 176-77). Carol Gruber describes the League as "superpatriotic" (*Mars and Minerva*), 137. John Higham cites the NSL for "nationalistic agitation" (*Strangers in the Land*), 257.

66. The founding and short history of the NSL is covered by Robert D. Ward, "The Origin and Activities of the National Security League, 1914-1919," *Mississippi Valley Historical Review (MVHR)* 47 (June 1960): 51-65. The league's claim of financial disinterestedness was reported in "The Security League Conference," *The Outlook* 111 (Dec. 8, 1915): 853. Ward, "Origin," 64, summarizes the 1919 congressional hearings. For more complete details, see Congressional Record of the 3d sess. of the 65th Congress, *Proceedings and Debates* regarding the National Security League. Hearings of Dec. 4, 1918, are in volume 57 (Washington: Government Printing Office, 1919), 97-103. See especially the testimony of Mar. 3, 1919, in ibid, Appendix and Index to parts 1-5, 4922-4925.

67. List of prominent contributors in ibid., 4922, and Ward, "Origin," 64. Honorary officers of the league noted in Blakey, *Home Front*, 27.

68. Ward, "Origin," 52-53, 56.

69. League connections to CPI and NBHS are explored in Blakey, *Home Front*, 35-36. National Security League Committee on Patriotism through Education to Callahan, Dec. 26, 1916, JMC 1916, box 3, folder 1.

70. Ward, "Origin," 58, on loyalty investigations. The *Daily Athenaeum* addressed the subject on many occasions (see, for example, Mar. 21, 1918).

71. Blakey, *Home Front*, 26, (n. 28), 28. Ward, "Origin," 58. Each comments on the league's interchangeability of loyalty and capitalist ideology, as confirmed in the record of the 1919 National Security League Congressional hearings.

72. Blakey, *Home Front*, 27.

73. Ibid., 28. Novick, *Noble Dream*, 116, and quoting William Stearns on "moral equivalent," 117.

74. Blakey summarizes the arrangements for the Speakers Training Camp in *Home Front*, 29. The West Virginia delegation is named, and Shawkey's discussions with Thomas Wood Stevens documented, in *State Defense Council Papers (SDC)*, box 1, folder 1, July 14, 1917, 9.

75. Hart is quoted in Blakey, *Home Front*, 29-30.

76. Hart's academic background is summarized in Blakey, *Home Front*, 28.

77. Cletis Pride's "History of the West Virginia University History Department" notes Hart's summer visits to WVU, 29-30.

78. President Trotter informed Callahan of his appointment as delegate to the NSL Congress in a Dec. 5, 1916, letter, JMC 1916, box 3, folder 1. Callahan's service on the Patriotic Education Committee is mentioned in Henry L. West, Executive Sec. of the NSL, to Callahan, Jan. 4, 1917, JMC 1917, box 3, folder 2, and in H. Stanwood Menken, Chairman of the NSL Executive Committee, to Callahan, JMC 1917, box 3, folder 2.

79. The WVU delegation is listed in *Proceedings of the Congress of Constructive Patriotism, January 25-27, 1917* (New York: National Security League, 1917), 411. A.B. Hart's Dec. 22, 1916, letter to Callahan, and a NSL flyer sent to Callahan by Henry West, dated Dec. 8, 1916, outlined the goals of the Congress and the NSL, JMC 1916, box 3, folder 1.

80. Frederick Windsor, "Educational Preparedness," NSL *Proceedings*, 1917, 251-52.

81. *Daily Athenaeum*, May 21, 1918. Todd, *Wartime Relations*, 71-72.

82. Blakey, *Home Front*, 107-9, 116.

83. Callahan to A.B. Hart, May 7, 1917, JMC 1917, box 3, folder 2.

84. Callahan to Henry West of the NSL, Aug. 8, 1918, JMC 1918, box 3, folder 4. Hart edited this volume, subtitled *A Handbook of Patriotic Education References*, for the Committee on Patriotism through Education. The work was suggested at the July 1917 Chautauqua conference, and "intended to aid speakers, writers, readers and thinking people in general to visualize the present situation." The handbook contained nearly four hundred pages of reference books, magazine articles, and pamphlets. See Albert Bushnell Hart, ed., *America at War* (New York: George H. Doran for the National Security League, 1918), quoted from introduction.

85. Callahan to W.G. Leland, May 12, 1917, JMC 1917, box 3, folder 2.

86. Blakey, *Home Front*, 120-21.

87. H.D. Thompson of the NSL to Callahan, Apr. 25, 1918, responding to letter from Callahan to Robert McElroy, NSL Educational Director, Apr. 14, 1918, JMC 1918, box 3, folder 3.

88. The objects of the course were outlined in the *Daily Athenaeum*, May 21, 1918. My search in the university archives, the Morgantown newspapers (the *DA* did not publish in the summer months), the WVU *Monticola*, the *WVSJ*, summer school catalogues, Barbe's papers, Callahan's papers, and Trotter's correspondence uncovered no indication either that the NSL course was presented as scheduled or that it was *not* held in the 1918 summer session.

89. "A Great Undertaking," *WVSJ* 47, no. 2 (May 1918): 405. League contacts with state and local superintendents noted in ibid., 396. Reaching parents and children through teachers also in ibid., 405. The "impregnable bulwark" comment is from a short article on the "National Security League Course" in *WVSJ* 47, no. 3 (June 1918): 434.

90. McElroy's scheduled appearance at the WVEA convention was announced in "The State Education Association," *WVSJ* 47, no. 7 (October 1918), 522.

91. Robert McElroy, "The World Mission of American Ideals," NEA *Proceedings* 1918, 94-95.

92. Stanley Hall, "Some Educational Values of War," NEA *Proceedings* 1918, 98.

93. The melding of patriotism and religion was included in an address by L.R. Alderman, "The Public School and the Nation in 1917," in NEA *Proceedings* 1917, 230.

94. Florence Kellogg, "War-time Changes," *WVSJ* 47, no. 7 (Oct. 1918): 526.

95. B.T. Leland, at the Sixteenth Educational Conference at the summer school of West Virginia University, July 5, 1918, "Summer School Educational Conference," *WVSJ* 47, no. 6 (Aug.-Sept. 1918), 492.

96. J.A. Linke, Federal Board of Vocational Education, ibid., 492.

97. "Obedience to recognized authority" from Kellogg, "War-time Changes," *WVSJ* (Oct. 1918), 526. The voice of absolute finality comment is from Sarah B. Fahey, "How the Public School Can Foster the American Ideal of Patriotism," NEA *Proceedings* 1917, 53.

98. John F. Sims spoke of the plastic mold of youth in an address called "Patriotism in the Schools," NEA *Proceedings* 1917, 170.

99. L.B. Hill, "German 'Kultur,'" *WVSJ* 47, no. 9 (Dec. 1918), 586.

100. W.A. Chamberlin, "Germany's Grip on Public Opinion," *Historical Outlook* 9, no. 8 (Nov. 1918), 433.

101. Ibid., 433-34.

102. Novick, *Noble Dream*, 117.

103. Dewey expressed his vision of the war's possibilities in several articles, including "The Future of Pacifism," *New Republic*, July 28, 1917, 359-61.

104. Gruber, *Mars and Minerva*, 89-92.

105. Ibid., 89; Gruber notes the accusation of "philosophical sellout" by Dewey's critics. Dewey tempered his embrace of the war by acknowledging its authoritarian possibilities in "The Future of Pacifism," *New Republic*, July 28, 1917, 360. He concluded by war's end that the progressive promise of the conflict was endangered by the war's "cult of irrationality" (Kennedy, *Over Here*, 90). The poles of extremism comment is from Dawley, *Struggles for Justice*, 169.

106. Dawley, *Struggles for Justice*, 170. Quoting Herbert Croly, ibid., 169. "American Bismarck," ibid., 176.

107. "The Administrative Aspect of Government," *School and Society* 4, no. 83 (July 29, 1916), 164.

108. *Wheeling Intelligencer*, July 24, 1917.

109. Dawley, *Struggles for Justice*, 176-77, 170-71.

3. National and State War Bureaucracies and the American Regulatory Consensus

1. Martin Sklar, "Studying American Political Development in the Progressive Era, 1890s-1916," in his *The United States as a Developing Country: Studies in U.S. History in the Progressive Era and the 1920s* (Cambridge: Cambridge University Press, 1992), 37-77, especially 37-39. Sklar offers a concise summary of these major structural changes. Other helpful works include Melvyn Dubofsky, *Labor and the State in Modern America* (Chapel Hill: University of North Carolina Press, 1994); Ellis Hawley, *The Great War and the Search for Modern Order: A History of the American People and Their Institutions* (2d ed. New York: St. Martin's Press, 1979); Gabriel Kolko, *The Triumph of Conservatism: A Reinterpretation of American History, 1900-1916* (New York: Free Press, 1963); R. Jeffrey Lustig, *Corporate Capitalism: The Origins of Modern American Political Theory, 1890-1920* (Berkeley: University of California Press, 1982); Martin Sklar, *The Corporate Reconstruction of American Capitalism: The Market, Law, and Politics* (Cambridge: Cambridge University Press, 1988); James Weinstein, *The Corporate Ideal in the Liberal State; 1900-1918* (Boston: Beacon Press, 1968); Christopher L. Tomlins, *The State and the Unions: Labor Relations, Law, and the Organized Labor Movement in America, 1880-1960* (New York: Cambridge University Press, 1986); Robert H. Wiebe, *The Search for Order* (New York: Hill and Wang, 1967); and Olivier Zunz, *Making America Corporate, 1870-1920* (Chicago: University of Chicago Press, 1990).

2. Sklar, "Studying American Political Development," 38-39. David Kennedy, *Over Here: The First World War and American Society* (Oxford: Oxford University Press, 1980), 51.

3. Herbert Croly, from *The Promise of American Life*, 1909, in "An Intellectual Formulates the New Nationalism," in *Progressives and Postwar Disillusionment: 1898-1928*, ed. David A. Shannon (New York: McGraw-Hill, 1966), 102. R. Jeffrey Lustig, *Corporate Liberalism: The Origins of Modern American Political Theory, 1890-1920* (Berkeley: University of California Press, 1982), 196.

4. Shannon, "Intellectual," 101-2.

5. Kennedy, *Over Here*, 50. John Dewey, "The Future of Pacifism," *New Republic*, July 28, 1917, 358-60. Kennedy, *Over Here*, 39, quoting Lippmann's "The World Conflict in Relation to American Democracy," *Annals* 72 (1917): 1-10.

6. Sarah H. Fahey, "How the Public School Can Foster the American Ideal of Patriotism," National Education Association (NEA) *Addresses and Proceedings*, 1917, 54. G. Stanley Hall, "Some Educational Values of the War," NEA *Addresses and Proceedings*, 1918, 96-100. James Morton Callahan, "American Foreign Policy in the World War," prepared for the Committee on Public Information and reprinted in *West Virginia School Journal* 47, no. 11 (February 1919), 651.

7. Kennedy, *Over Here*, 51.

8. Randolph Bourne, "The State," in *The Radical Will: Randolph Bourne, Selected Writings: 1911-1918*, ed. Olaf Hansen (New York: Urizen Books, 1977), 359, 375, 357-58.

9. Bourne in Hansen, *Radical Will*, 356-59, 367, 360. Bourne was not an after-the-fact critic of the war mobilization, and its danger to democracy as he saw it. His fragmentary essay, "The State," from which the above comments are extracted, was never completed. Bourne died of influenza in December 1918 at age 34, prematurely ending a prolific career. "The State" was first published in 1919 (ibid., 548, 395). Bourne's essay covers 354-81 in *The Radical Will*).

10. Creel, *How We Advertised America*, excerpted in Coben, *Reform, War, and Reaction*, 93.

11. Grosvenor B. Clarkson, *Industrial America in the World War: The Strategy behind the Line, 1917-1918* (Boston and New York: Houghton-Mifflin, 1923), 2.

12. Samuel Harding's "Topical Outline of the War," *HTM* 9, no. 1 (January 1918), 48.

13. Clarkson, *Industrial America*, frontispiece.

14. Original members of the Civilian Advisory Council included Daniel Willard, president of the Baltimore and Ohio Railroad; Samuel Gompers, president of the American Federation of Labor; Wall Street financier Bernard Baruch; Julius Rosenwald, president of Sears, Roebuck; and Franklin Martin, secretary-general of the American College of Surgeons. Kennedy, *Over Here*, 114-15. Wilson's Americanism statement from ibid., 115. Clarkson's comments on engineers and professional men is from *Industrial America*, 4, 21.

15. Robert H. Wiebe, *Businessmen and Reform: A Study of the Progressive Movement* (Cambridge: Harvard University Press, 1962), 221. On the regulation of food and fuel, see Ronald Schaffer, *America in the Great War: The Rise of the War Welfare State* (New York and Oxford: Oxford University Press, 1991), 35. Schaffer's chap. 3, "The Managed Economy," 31-46, and chap. 4, "The War Economy," 47-63, are very helpful in sorting through a complex bureaucracy.

16. Schaffer, *Great War*, 40. Kennedy, *Over Here*, 129-31.

17. This paragraph based on Martin Sklar, "Woodrow Wilson and the Developmental Imperatives of Modern U.S. Liberalism," in his *The United States as a Developing Country*, 101-42, especially 109-10. Sklar originally published this essay as "Woodrow Wilson and the Political Economy of Modern United States Liberalism," in *Studies on the Left* 1, no. 3 (1960).

18. Clarkson, *Industrial America*, 8-9.

19. Dawley, *Struggles for Justice*, 195. The government guaranteed a 6 percent profit and gave back control to the private owners shortly after the war ended, although the debate on the nationalization of railroads survived into the 1920s (ibid.). Also see chapters 5 and 6 below. Comment on McAdoo's thoroughness and efficiency from Schaffer, *Great War*, 37-39.

20. Schaffer, *Great War*, 46-47, 55.

21. Clarkson, *Industrial America*, 9.

22. Dawley, *Struggles for Justice*, 202, 196, 170, 196.

23. McElroy's comments on "Patriotism—Past, Present, and Future" are reproduced in the NEA *Proceedings* 1918, 95. Cornwell remarked on the closeness with which American entry into the war followed his inauguration in "Our State and the War Program," 1918 *WV Hand Book*, 775. Shawkey praised the governor in Morris P. Shawkey, *West Virginia in History, Life, Literature and Industry* (Chicago: Lewis, 1928), 2:60-61.

24. Biographical material on Cornwell taken from Lucy Fisher, "John J. Cornwell, Governor of West Virginia, 1917-1921," a laudatory article published in *West Virginia History* (*WVH*) when that journal was a quarterly rather than an annual publication. Part 1 appeared in *WVH* 24, no. 3 (Apr. 1963), 258-88, Part 2 in *WVH* 24, no. 4 (July 1963): 370-89. General background on Cornwell's early political career is also found in Otis Rice, *West Virginia: A History* (Lexington: University of Kentucky Press, 1985), 217.

25. Cornwell to T.G. Pownall of Cumberland, Md., Jan. 26, 1916. Cornwell to Pownall, Jan. 31, 1916. *JJC*, box 37, folder 1.

26. Cornwell quoted from his summary of the "War Program," 1918 *WV Hand Book*, 775.

27. *Pocahontas Times*, Apr. 12, 1917.

28. Fisher, "Cornwell," part 1, 278. Governor Cornwell's Message to the 2nd Extraordinary Session of the West Virginia Legislature, May 14, 1917, in *Journal of the House of Delegates*, Second Extraordinary Session (Charleston, 1917), 39.

29. Sullivan, "Council of Defense," 1918 *WV Hand Book*, 781.

30. The importance of West Virginia products is referred to in Hastings Hart's *Program* for the WV State Defense Council, 6. Cornwell's comments on production and the postwar demand for West Virginia coal from *Proceedings of the West Virginia Coal Mining Institute*, Nineteenth Semi-Annual Session, Charleston, June 5-6, 1917, 103.

31. Senate Bill 7, chap. 12 (*Acts of the Legislature*, Second Extraordinary Session, May 14-26, 1917), 51. William S. John quoted by Chitwood in Callahan, *West Virginia*, 701, and by Sullivan in 1918 *WV Hand Book*, 790.

32. NSL *Proceedings*, 1917, 227.

33. Cornwell quoted by Sullivan in 1918 *WV Hand Book*, 790.

34. Cornwell to Rollin C. Bortle, July 20, 1917. JJC, box 54, folder 3.

35. The adoption by other states of compulsory work statutes was noted by Jesse Sullivan in his *Report of the Secretary on the Operation of the Compulsory Work Law for the Year Ending June 19, 1918* (Charleston: State Council of Defense, Sept. 20, 1918), 7. PAM 2902, WVRHC.

36. *St. Mary's Oracle*, Mar. 14, 1918, July 4, 1918.

37. "Work of Fight," *Our Own People* 3, no. 10 (Oct. 1918), 5.

38. Cornwell's "loafer" statement is in his message to the Second Extraordinary Session, May 14, 1917, *House Journal*, 12. His request for liberal newspaper space is in Sullivan's *Report . . . Compulsory Work Law*, 5-6.

39. *Wheeling Intelligencer*, June 19, 1917. Sullivan commented on the desire of many authorities to retain the law in the 1918 *WV Hand Book*, 791.

40. West Virginia Education Association (WVEA), *Annual Proceedings* of meeting in Huntington, June 13-15, 1917 (Keyser, W.Va.: Mountain Echo Press, 1917), 24.

41. The creation of the Boys' Working Reserve in "Governor's Proclamation, March 15, 1918." *JJC* box 122, folder 1. "Colored boys" comment in *West Virginia War Bulletin* 1, no. 1 (Apr. 1, 1918), 3. *JJC* box 122, folder 5.

42. Chitwood in Callahan, *West Virginia*, 701. The law's penalties are enumerated in Senate Bill 7, chap. 12 (*Acts of the Legislature*, Second Extraordinary Session, May 14-26, 1917), 52-53.

43. Sullivan, *Report . . . Compulsory Work Law*, 5-6. England's opinion is summarized in *West Virginia War Bulletin* 1, no. 2 (Apr. 20, 1918): 5. PAM 2418, WVRHC.

44. State Council of Defense resolution in SDC *Minutes*, July 2, 1918, 55. Cornwell's directive that coal operators post weekly productivity reports is in a letter he sent, for the West Virginia Council of Defense, to Mingo County coal operators, June 12, 1918. JJC box 122, folder 1. Sullivan's comments on increased production in his *Report . . . Compulsory Work Law*, 6-7.

45. Ronald L. Lewis, *Black Coal Miners in America: Race, Class, and Community Conflict, 1780-1980* (Lexington: University Press of Kentucky, 1987), 152. The black population in West Virginia in 1920 was 86,218, of whom all but 127 were U.S.-born. Less than 40 percent, or 33,347, were born in the state. Blacks comprised about 6 percent of the total West Virginia population of 1.4 million, but in southern coal counties percentages were much higher. Blacks represented more than 26 percent of the population of McDowell County, or 18,157 of 68,571. The black percentage in Logan County was 11.6 percent, in Mingo, 8.3 percent, and in Raleigh, 15.0 percent. (Department of Commerce, Bureau of the Census, *Fourteenth Census of the United States, State Compendium for West Virginia* [Washington: GPO, 1925], tables 9 and 16).

46. Joe William Trotter, *Coal, Class, and Color: Blacks in Southern West Virginia, 1915-1932* (Urbana: University of Illinois Press, 1990), 165.

47. Trotter, *Coal, Class, and Color*, 165, 125. See chap. 5, "Race Relations, Housing, and Social Conditions," 125-44, and chap. 6, "The Expansion of the Black Bourgeoisie," 145-73. Also Lewis, *Black Coal Miners*, 152. See chap. 7, "Judicious Mixture in Central Appalachia, 1880-1920," 121-42, and chap. 8, "The Fruits of Judicious Mixture, 1910-1932," 143-64.

48. Trotter, *Coal, Class, and Color*, 230-33.

49. Kennedy, *Over Here*, 29.

50. Concerns about blacks' "credulity" documented in Alfred E. Cornebise, *War as Advertised: The Four Minute Men and America's Crusade, 1917-1918* (Philadelphia: American Philosophical Society, 1984), 22, 121-22. Black lack of appreciation for Americanism in Emory S. Bogardus, *Essentials of Americanization* (Los Angeles: University of Southern California Press, 1919), 17-18.

51. Kennedy, *Over Here*, 29. William M. Tuttle, Jr., *Race Riot: Chicago in the Red Summer of 1919* (New York: Atheneum, 1970), 216.

52. Tuttle, *Race Riot*, 230. "History written with lightning" quoted in Kennedy, *Over Here*, 281.

53. Swing toward Wilson in 1912 in Tuttle, *Race Riot*, 229. Segregation of federal buildings, East St. Louis incident in Kennedy, *Over Here*, 281. Wilson's response to criticism in Tuttle, *Race Riot*, 230.

54. The "potent factor" expression is in the 1918 *WV Hand Book*, 815. Blacks' roles as soldiers, workers, etc., mentioned in Tuttle, *Race Riot*, 210. Formation and mechanics of the Auxiliary Council outlined in SDC *Minutes*, Jan. 16, 1918, 33, and Mar. 5, 1918, 39.

55. *WV War Bulletin* 1, no. 2 (Apr. 20, 1918): 2. SDC *Minutes*, Mar. 21, 1918, 43.

56. J.C. Gilmer described the composition of the Auxiliary Councils in "The Auxiliary Advisory Council of Defense," 1919 *WV Hand Book*, 488. The Auxiliary Council's stand against idleness is reported in the *WV War Bulletin* 1, no. 2 (Apr. 20,

1918), 2. Mission and loyalty of the Auxiliary Council in Gilmer, "Advisory Council," 1919 *WV Hand Book*, 488-90.

57. The leadership of the McDowell County Auxiliary is listed in the *WV War Bulletin* 1, no. 2 (Apr. 20, 1918), 2. The West Virginia State Civic League (WVSCL), described as "militant" by Joe W. Trotter, was formed by Rev. I.V. Bryant of Huntington, attorney Brown W. Payne of Raleigh County, and Dr. F.M. Gamble of Charleston. The *Birth of a Nation* protest culminated in the formation of the Charleston National Association for the Advancement of Colored People, which replaced the WVSCL as the state's leading civil rights organization (Trotter, *Coal, Class, and Color*), 246.

58. SDC *Minutes*, June 18, 1918, 53. In 1919 McDowell County state senator J.W. Luther, under pressure from black Republican constituents, introduced legislation barring "forever" plays and movies "tending to create race friction." The bill was approved, and upheld by the West Virginia Supreme Court in 1925 (Trotter, *Coal, Class, and Color*), 249.

59. Gilmer in 1919 *WV Hand Book*, 490. Nearly 18,000 of the state's 92,132 coal miners were black, according to "Nationalities of Persons Employed at the Mines and Coke Ovens by Counties of the Year Ending June 30, 1918" (W.Va. Department of Mines, *Annual Report* [Charleston, 1918], 234-35). Thirty-one nationalities are listed in the report, with whites designated as "Americans." Italians (6,869), Hungarians (4,321), and Austrians (2,192) were the largest immigrant groups represented in the coalfields.

60. David Alan Corbin, *Life, Work, and Rebellion in the Coal Fields: The Southern West Virginia Miners* (Urbana: University of Illinois Press, 1981), 177.

61. West Virginia production grew from 64,118,677 long tons in 1915 to 79,612,298 long tons in 1916 ("Table Showing Production of Coal and Coke for the Years 1883 to 1918 Inclusive," W.Va. Dept. of Mines *Annual Report*, 1918, 105).

62. Corbin, *Life, Work, and Rebellion*, 177-78, 181.

63. Ibid., 180.

64. "Labor's Task," *United Mine Workers Journal (UMWJ)* 29, no. 20 (Nov. 1, 1918): 6-7.

65. Barkey, "The Socialist Party in West Virginia," 206. The *Charleston Gazette*, Apr. 6 and 7, 1918, reported that the parade reached a length of three miles.

66. Comment on postwar employer-employee compatibility in "War Has Brought Out the Best Side of American Manhood in Efforts to Excel," *UMWJ* 29, no. 22 (Dec. 1, 1918), 10. Cornwell on workers' loyalty in 1918 *WV Hand Book*, 778.

67. Schaffer, *Great War*, 31, 33.

68. The Special Deputies Law, House Bill 34 (*Acts of the Legislature*, Second Extraordinary Session, May 14-26, 1917), 46-47. Use of special deputies is recorded in SDC *Records*, box 1, folder 1 (Gilmer County events); box 1, folder 2 (Raleigh County events); and in SDC *Minutes*, July 2, 1918, 56 (locating slackers).

69. Request by C.H. Workman, *Clarksburg Daily Telegram*, Aug. 15, 1917. Power to carry unlicensed firearms in House Bill 34, the Special Deputies Act (*Acts of the Legislature*, Second Extraordinary Session, May 14-26, 1917), 47. Quartering of special deputies in coal company buildings recorded in SDC *Records*, box 1, folder 2.

70. SDC *Minutes*, July 2, 1918, 56. Home Guards formed in Cabell, Mason, Greenbrier (SDC *Minutes*, Mar. 26, 1918, 46, June 4, 1918, 51, and Sept. 3, 1918), 60-61, and Monongalia counties. The Monongalia detachment made its public debut on July 16, 1918, marching "100 strong" with a degree of efficiency that "agreeably surprised" onlookers (*Morgantown Post*, July 17, 1918). Other Home Guard volunteers carried out more serious action. In August 1918, a group of Cabell County

Home Guards joined a sheriff's posse in Mingo County to apprehend a party of suspected deserters or draft evaders who killed two law enforcement officers. The fugitives, reported to be "dead shots," barricaded themselves in a cabin. "They are mostly supposed to be natives from away back in the woods," said the *McDowell Recorder*, "where ideas of freedom are badly warped and who will rather die than ever give up" (*McDowell Recorder*, Aug. 23, 1918). Such nonconformist principles were inappropriate in the war emergency, when "the people must realize the country is at war and citizens must obey the regulations laid down for their guidance" (*Pocahontas Times*, May 5, 1917. This statement was in reference to the killing of a civilian by National Guardsmen in Princeton, W.Va.) It was imperative that all citizens "regulate their habits of living and their conduct of business so they will conform to the national idea . . . and add their weight to the protest against domination of the world by Prussian autocracy" (*Fairmont Times*, Jan. 8, 1918).

71. Fred Mooney's fears about use of the compulsory work law against the union are noted in Richard D. Lunt, *Law and Order vs. the Miners: West Virginia, 1907-1933* (Hamden, Conn.: Archon Books, 1979), 62-63. This book was reissued in 1991 by Trans-Allegheny Books, Parkersburg and Charleston, W.Va. Cornwell's indictment of industrial slackers is in his letter, for the state defense council, to Mingo County coal operators, June 12, 1918. JJC, box 122, folder 1.

72. Mooney's complaint is in Lunt, *Law and Order*, 63. Threat to miners' draft exemption in Corbin, *Life, Work, and Rebellion*, 186.

73. George Wolfe to Justus Collins, July 6, 1918. Justus Collins papers (hereafter Collins), A&M 1824, WVRHC, box 16, folder 109. Wolfe's letter read in part "I enclose herewith a digest of slackers for three weeks, Winding Gulf, and would be glad for you to write a letter to the following: "One of the alleged slackers on Wolfe's list was Charles Akers, the miner whom Collins advised to "go to Germany." Justus Collins to Charles Akers, n.d., but probably July 7, 1918. Collins, box 16, folder 109.

74. Collins on humor of the legislature, and chance to get union to "back off," in Justus Collins to George Wolfe, May 16, 1917. Collins, box 16, folder 109. His order to "keep a sharp eye" and "discharge summarily" is in a message to E.C. Berkeley, May 17, 1917. Collins, box 15, folder 103.

75. George Wolfe, Manager and Treasurer of the Winding Gulf Colliery, to Collins, July 11, 1917. Collins, box 15, folder 105. Collins on driving the union out, Collins to Isaac T. Mann, May 25, 1917. Collins, box 15, folder 103.

76. Simeon Larson, *Labor and Foreign Policy: Gompers, the AFL, and the First World War, 1914-1918* (Rutherford, N.J.: Farleigh Dickenson University Press, 1975), 94. Frank L. Grubbs, Jr., *The Struggle for Labor Loyalty: Gompers, the A.F. of L., and the Pacifists, 1917-1920* (Durham: Duke University Press, 1968), 44.

77. Grubbs, *Labor Loyalty*, 27-28, 39-40. For the wartime actions of the IWW, see Melvyn Dubofsky, *We Shall Be All: A History of the IWW, the Industrial Workers of the World* (New York: Quadrangle, the New York Times Book Company, 1969), especially chaps. 14-17, 349-444. The Wobblies' militance in the spring of 1917 forced lumbermen to institute the eight-hour day in the West Coast forests. The Wilson government, terrified of growing IWW power, then used military police to close the woods to labor organizers and formed a "practically compulsory" company union, with a no-strike policy, called the Loyal Legion of Loggers and Lumbermen. Dubofsky, *We Shall Be All*, 412-14.

78. For the entry of pro-war Socialists into the alliance, see Grubbs, *Labor Loyalty*, 40. Holt's address is noted in Barkey, "Socialist Party in West Virginia," 201.

79. For Hilton's shift from his antiwar position, see Barkey, "The Socialist Party in West Virginia," 202. Grubbs documents involvement of the alliance with the CPI in *Labor Loyalty*, 43-45.

80. Larson, *Labor and Foreign Policy*, 127, 114-16. Larson includes a concise summary of the open-shop–closed-shop issue, wherein the closed shop provided that all workers hired in an industrial unit be members of the union, subject to its discipline, and insured of solidarity in direct action. In the open shop, workers in the unit were not required to join the union and, as practiced by many employers, nonmembership was required for employment. In an open shop, employers had the ability to "play off union members against nonunion workers, thereby blocking the union from taking any concerted measures," leading inevitably to the destruction of the union "and the flowering of the open shop" (see 115-16).

81. Clarkson, *Industrial America*, 283, 276.

82. Gompers's integration into War Labor Administration in Larson, *Labor Loyalty*, 101-2. Formation of National War Labor Board in Schaffer, *Great War*, 360. Lack of NWLB statutory power, Larson, *Labor Loyalty*, 102.

83. Frank P. Walsh, "agreement for no strikes or lockouts during the war," Mar. 30, 1918. *Collins*, box 16, folder 108. The history of the NWLB is recorded in Valerie Jean Conner, *The National War Labor Board: Stability, Social Justice, and the Voluntary State in World War I* (Chapel Hill: University of North Carolina Press, 1983).

84. The Washington Agreement is summarized in David Montgomery, *The Fall of the House of Labor: The Workplace, the State, and Labor Activism, 1865-1925* (Cambridge: Cambridge University Press, 1987), 387. Consent of West Virginia operators to the agreement interpreted by Corbin in *Life, Work, and Rebellion*, 183.

85. Montgomery, *House of Labor*, 387.

86. Corbin, *Life, Work, and Rebellion*, 183-84. Corbin says District 17 membership grew from seven thousand on Jan. 1, 1917, to more than fifty thousand by war's end. District 29 grew from nine hundred to six thousand.

87. William D. Ord to W.M. Ritter, Aug. 8, 1918 ("Miscellaneous documents of the Smokeless Coal Operators"), A&M 1830, WVRHC.

88. Corbin, *Life, Work, and Rebellion*, 184-85. Some West Virginia operators were later indicted by the U.S. Department of Justice for profiteering (ibid.), 185. Copies of the indictments are found in JJC, box 94, folder 5.

89. *Hitchman Coal and Coke Company* v. *Mitchell, individually, et al.*, 245 U.S. 1917, 229-74. In Ronald L. Lewis and John C. Hennen, Jr., eds., *West Virginia: Documents in the History of a Rural-Industrial State* (Dubuque, Iowa: Kendall-Hunt, 1991), 181.

90. Summary of Hitchman case, Dayton's role, and his impeachment in Lunt, *Law and Order*, 58. Language on working man's freedom and "allegiance or obligation" in Lewis and Hennen, *West Virginia: Documents*, 181.

91. The formation of the Fairmont Coal Club was featured in the *Fairmont Times*, Jan. 4, 1918, and in "Fairmont, W.Va.," *Coal Age* 13, no. 1 (Jan. 5, 1918): 39.

92. "Dire need" quote in *Fairmont Times*, Jan. 4, 1918; note on Fleming in *Coal Age* 13, no. 1 (Jan. 5, 1918), 39.

93. Fleming's business credentials are listed in John W. Kirk, *Progressive West Virginians, 1923* (Wheeling: Wheeling Intelligencer, 1923), 127. His duties are summarized in J. Walter Barnes, Fuel Administrator for West Virginia, "Federal Fuel Administration," in "West Virginia in the War," 1918 *WV Hand Book*, 624. Miners' charges against fuel administrators noted in Corbin, *Life, Work, and Rebellion*, 185.

94. Barnes quoted in 1918 *WV Hand Book*, 626.

95. Sklar, "American Political Development," in *Developing Country*, 49. Corporate capitalism's dominance in Dawley, *Struggles for Justice*, 170. Dawley also addresses the modern functions of the American family in the new state system. "The corporate-regulatory complex pointed the way toward a new governing system in which corporate property and a new form of the nuclear family oriented toward consumption instead of production might be better secured than in the increasingly outmoded shell of laissez-faire liberalism." (Ibid., 171)

96. Montgomery, *House of Labor*, 331, citing Creel in *How We Advertised America*, 105. Montgomery also cites remarks by General Enoch Crowder, director of the national draft, who praised the "mental revolution" implicit in the universal appeals to efficiency, 331.

97. "Charleston, W.Va.," *Coal Age* 13, no. 15 (Apr. 13, 1918), 715.

98. SDC *Minutes*, Feb. 27, 1918, 41. The major contributions were from Pocahontas, Kanawha, Guyan, Winding Gulf, New River, and Cabin Creek Operators' Associations, according to a memo of the Gentry Film Company, July 29, 1918, in *SDC* papers, box 2, folder 2. Major individual contributors included J.H. Wheelwright of Consolidation Coal, a member of the State Fuel Administration, $1,000, and W.K. Field, also of the State Fuel Administration, $1,000.

99. SDC *Minutes*, Feb. 27, 1918, 41.

100. Hugh Isaac Shott papers, A&M 908, WVRHC. Box 74, unnumbered speeches folder marked "Industrial/agriculture/crime/ law enforcement."

4. Postwar Strategies for Promoting Industrial Americanization, Antiradicalism, and Habits of Industry

1. Cornwell's comments about expansion into South American markets is from *Coal Age* 13, no. 15 (Apr. 13, 1918), 715. His plea to avoid partisan schemes is in 1918 *WV Hand Book*, 775, 779.

2. Helen E. Purcell, "Wartime Teaching of Latin American Geography," *WVSJ* 46, no. 12 (March 1918): 330-31.

3. U.S. to "guide the footsteps," from *War Work of Marshall County*, 114-15. Comments on survival of the fittest, shiftlessness, training youth to market products overseas from Mortimer L. Schiff, "Educational Preparedness," *School and Society* 4, no. 100 (Nov. 25, 1916), 799-800.

4. Higham, *Strangers in the Land*, 206.

5. Lustig, *Corporate Liberalism*, quoting Woodrow Wilson, 163.

6. Higham, *Strangers in the Land*, 207.

7. Godfrey Hodgson, "The Ideology of the Liberal Consensus," in *A History of Our Time: Readings on Postwar America*, ed. William H. Chafe and Harvard Sitkoff (New York and Oxford: Oxford University Press, 1987), 102-25, especially 110. Excerpted from Hodgson, *America in Our Time* (New York: Doubleday, 1976).

8. David McCullough, *Truman* (New York: Simon and Schuster, 1992), 547. Truman's speech outlined the Truman Doctrine, a commitment by the United States to resist economically, politically, and militarily communist and noncommunist left insurgencies around the world. His address is reprinted in ed., *Documents of American History*, 8th ed., ed. Henry Steele Commager (New York: Appleton-Century-Crofts, 1968), doc. nos. 574, 524.

9. Lane and Baker, "The Nation in Arms" (CPI War Information Series, August 1917), 8-9.

10. George Strayer, "The National Emergency in Education," NEA *Proceedings*

1918, 130, 129.

11. James P. Munroe, "Education after the War," NEA *Proceedings*, 1918, 197.

12. Address by Albert Bushnell Hart to NSL Congress on Constructive Patriotism, *Proceedings*, 1917, 279, 283, 279.

13. Dawley, *Struggles for Justice*, 170, 200. Nellie J. Sullivan, "Why Laws Are Needed," *CCC* 1, no. 3 (March 1918): 49.

14. Albion Guilford Taylor, *Labor Policies of the National Association of Manufacturers* (New York: Arno Press, 1973), 62. Originally published in Urbana by the University of Illinois, Studies in the Social Sciences, 1927.

15. John Gaventa, *Power and Powerlessness: Quiescence and Rebellion in an Appalachian Valley* (Urbana: University of Illinois Press, 1980), 14. Gaventa draws upon Peter Bachrach and Morton S. Baratz, *Power and Poverty: Theory and Practice* (New York: Oxford University Press, 1970), 43, to paraphrase "mobilization of bias."

16. Gary Gerstle, *Working-class Americanism: The Politics of Labor in a Textile City, 1914-1960* (Cambridge: Cambridge University Press, 1989), 8.

17. "The Public School," *CCC* 1, no. 3 (Mar. 1918): 37.

18. *CCC* admonished teachers to inform on "disturbers of industrial peace," and promote law and order, in a column in 2, no. 10 (Nov. 1919): 6. *School and Society* warned against incipient disloyalty in 8, no. 205 (Nov. 30, 1918): 652. The *WVSJ* commented on "true patriots" in 47, no. 11 (Feb. 1919), 631.

19. Kennedy, *Over Here*, 287-88. Also see chapter 5, below.

20. Bernadotte E. Schmitt and Harold C. Vedeler, *The World in the Crucible, 1914-1919* (New York: Harper & Row, 1984), 413. Tuttle, *Race Riot*, 15. Historian Richard Pipes rejects the early containment thesis, affirming that the sole reason for the Siberian incursion was to reopen the Eastern Front against Germany. (Richard Pipes, *The Russian Revolution* [New York: Vintage Books of Random House, 1991], 656-58).

21. Tuttle remarks on the revolutionary aura of "innocuous events" in *Race Riot*, 15. The pervasive intolerance of the era is described in Otis L. Graham, Jr., *The Great Campaigns: Reform and War in America, 1900-1928* (Englewood Cliffs, N.J.: Prentice-Hall, 1971), 112-13. The interlocked anti-German and antiradical threads are noted in Higham, *Strangers in the Land*, 223.

22. Higham describes the "clamor for absolute loyalty" in *Strangers in the Land*, 222. Tuttle comments on the cult of patriotism, demobilization, and the fear of proletarian uprising in *Race Riot*, 16-19. The labor-management conflicts of the postwar era, including the antiradicalism and open-shop drives, and the southern West Virginia coal strike of 1919-1922, will be addressed in the context of "industrial Americanization" in chapters 5 and 6.

23. *Wheeling Intelligencer*, June 23, 1917.

24. "War Has Brought Out the Best Side of American Manhood in Efforts to Excel," *UMWJ* 29, no. 22 (Dec. 1, 1918), 10.

25. "Don't Rock the Boat," *UMWJ* 29, no. 21 (Nov. 15, 1918): 6.

26. "War Has Brought Out," *UMWJ* 29, no. 22 (Dec. 1, 1918): 10.

27. Corbin, *Life, Work, and Rebellion*, 177.

28. Lewis, *Black Coal Miners*, 164. The march ended at Blair Mountain in Logan County when Federal troops intervened.

29. Corbin, *Life, Work, and Rebellion*, 176.

30. *UMWJ* 33, no. 18 (Sept. 15, 1922): 15.

31. Josiah Keeley, "After the War," *Coal Age* 14, no. 19 (Nov. 7, 1918): 868-69.

32. Robert A. Armstrong, "Democracy," *WVSJ* 48, no. 5 (Sept. 1919): 111.

33. George S. Wallace to Guy D. Goff, Jan. 23, 1919. George Selden Wallace papers, A&M 1710 WVRHC, box 3, folder 3.

34. Guy D. Goff to George S. Wallace, Oct. 5, 1919. Wallace papers, box 3, folder 3.

35. Address by H.H. Wheaton, NSL *Proceedings* 1917, 95-100.

36. *WV War Bulletin* 1, no. 2 (Apr. 20, 1918): 3. Howard Hill, "The Americanization Movement," *American Journal of Sociology* 24, no. 6 (May 1919): 625.

37. Wheaton, NSL *Proceedings* 1917, 96, 98.

38. Frederick Winslow Taylor, introduction to *Principles of Scientific Management* (Westport, Conn.: Greenwood Press, 1972), 7. Originally published New York: 1911. Greenwood reprinted a volume of Taylor's work that appeared in 1911, entitled *Scientific Management,* which included "Shop Management," "The Principles of Scientific Management," and Taylor's "Testimony before the Special House Committee." "Shop Management" first appeared in 1903, published by the American Society of Mechanical Engineers.

39. Montgomery, *House of Labor*, 229, 241.

40. Taylor, *Principles of Scientific Management*, 8.

41. Taylor spoke of "all social activities" in ibid., 8; Jeffry Lustig of "external variables" in *Corporate Liberalism*, 186. The comment on scientific social order by Bogardus, *Essentials of Americanization*, 75.

42. Daniel Nelson, *Frederick W. Taylor and the Rise of Scientific Management* (Madison: University of Wisconsin Press, 1980), 173-74.

43. Frederick W. Taylor, "Shop Management," in his *Scientific Management*, 52, 130-42.

44. Montgomery, *House of Labor*, 230, quoting Samuel Haber, *Efficiency and Uplift* (Chicago: 1964), 89.

45. Nelson, *Frederick W. Taylor*, 173.

46. Lustig, *Corporate Liberalism*, 186, 189.

47. Taylor, *Shop Management*, 57. Walter Lippmann, *Public Opinion* (New York: Free Press, 1922), 195, 197.

48. Grant, "Passing of the Great Race," in Coben, *Reform, War, and Reaction*, 150.

49. Lippmann, *Public Opinion*, 195.

50. William Graebner, *The Engineering of Consent: Democracy and Authority in Twentieth-Century America* (Madison: University of Wisconsin Press, 1987), 63-64.

51. Bernays wrote of "intelligent minorities" directing the public affairs of the country, quoted in Schlesinger and Kinzer, *Bitter Fruit*, 80. He wrote of the "active energy of the intelligent few" in a 1927 essay, excerpted in *Public Relations, Edward L. Bernays, and the American Scene* (Concord, N.H.: Rumford Press for F.W. Faxon, 1951), 16. This is a bibliography of Bernays's writing 1917-51, with no editor attributed.

52. Graebner, *Engineering Consent*, 65, quoting Bernays in *Crystallizing Public Opinion* (New York, 1923), 212.

53. Lustig, *Corporate Liberalism*, 189-90.

54. The "habits of industry" and development of the child along the lines of "its special capacity" is from NSL *Proceedings* 1917, 227. The "future skilled producer" comment is from Caroline Hedger, "The Kindergarten as a Factor in Americanization," an address to the 1918 National Education Association convention, NEA *Proceedings* 1918, 167.

55. Marsh spoke to West Virginia teachers on the "ninety-six percent" at the 1919 WVEA meeting in Fairmont, WVEA *Proceedings* 1919 (Keyser: Mountain Echo, 1920), 76. Marsh's comments on suitable training and "our army of young workers"

are in the *Report of the State Board of Education: Two Years Ending June 30, 1924* (Charleston, 1924) 41, 43.

56. West Virginia Board of Education, *Course of Study for the Junior and Senior High Schools of West Virginia, 1919* (Charleston: Tribune Printing Co., 1919), 4.

57. Shawkey, "Teaching Americanism," *WVSJ* 48, no. 7 (Nov. 1919), 172.

58. Olivier Zunz, *Making America Corporate, 1870-1920* (Chicago and London: University of Chicago Press, 1990), 4, 202.

59. Burton Bledstein, *The Culture of Professionalism: The Middle Class and the Development of Higher Education in America* (New York: W.W. Norton and Company, 1976), 4-7, 7-32.

60. Zunz, *Making America Corporate*, 4.

61. Sklar, "Wilson and the Developmental Imperatives," in *United States as a Developing Country*, 114, 132-37.

62. Shawkey's statement on "educational progress" is from "The Schools and the War," in *Biennial Report of the State Superintendent*, 1918, 13. Hanifan's comment is found in the same report, 29.

63. Ambler, *History of Education*, 389-90. Shawkey, *West Virginia in History, Life*, etc., 351.

64. Shawkey in Callahan, *West Virginia*, (1923), 633. Ambler, *History of Education*, mentions the state board's teacher training authority, 390, 394. Callahan's praise of Shawkey is in his *West Virginia*, 636.

65. Marshall Lee Buckalew, "The Life and Times of Dr. Morris Purdy Shawkey" (M.A. thesis, West Virginia University, 1941), 64.

66. William J. Reese, *Power and the Promise of School Reform: Grassroots Movements during the Progressive Era* (Boston and London: Routledge and Kegan Paul, 1986), 113, 242-47. See chap. 5, "An age of centralization and grassroots reform," and chap. 9, "World War I and the contradictions of school reform."

67. Reese summarizes the class basis of school centralization in *Power and the Promise*, 251.

68. Shawkey reported on centralization in West Virginia in *West Virginia in Life, History*, etc., 350-51.

69. Ambler, *History of Education*, 402-3.

70. Background material on Barbe is from Ambler, *History of Education*, 403, and John Kirk, *Progressive West Virginians*, 427. The *West Virginia Review* (WVR) printed a tribute to Barbe in 2, no. 3 (Dec. 1924): 85.

71. Barbe's presidential address to the WVEA, *Annual Proceedings* 1919, 22.

72. Ibid., 22-23.

73. Barbe, "The Future," *WVSJ* 48, no. 3 (June 1919): 62

74. Conley's best known work on coal is *History of the West Virginia Coal Industry* (Charleston: Education Foundation, 1960). His analogy of schoolchildren to automobiles is found in "The Teacher's Responsibility," *WVSJ* 48, no. 2 (May 1919): 28.

75. "Are We Forgetting?," *WVSJ* 50, no. 2 (May 1921): 37.

76. NEA *Proceedings*, 57th annual meeting, Milwaukee, June 28-July 5, 1919, 22.

77. Phil Conley spoke of fitting children to their industrial environment in "The Teacher's Responsibility," *WVSJ* 48, no. 2 (May 1919): 28. His words echoed those of Louis L. Park, who spoke of "certain mental traits," adjustment to one's work, and "quick thinking" in "Preparing the Boy for Industry," an address published in NEA *Proceedings* 1918, 258-59.

78. P.P. Claxton of the U.S. Bureau of Education, "The Kindergarten and the Present Crisis," featured in *WVSJ* 49, no. 4 (July 1920): 86.

79. Norman Schlicter, "New Standards in Industrial Leadership" (West Virginia Coal Mining Institute *Proceedings*, 25th semi-annual session, Dec. 6-7, 1921 (Charleston, 1921), 72-73, 74, 77.

80. Clarence J. Karier, introductory remarks to "Immigration Restriction and Americanization," in his *Shaping the American Educational State, 1900 to the Present* (New York: Free Press, 1975), 255.

81. Marsh spoke of appropriate avenues of service in the *Report of the State Board of Education* for 1922-24, 41. He wrote of "more drill" in "Our New Citizen in the Making—The Schools' Aims," *WVSJ* 53, no. 1 (Sept. 1924): 11.

82. G.F. Arps, "National Supremacy, Industrial Education and Cooperation," *School and Society* 10, no. 253 (Nov. 1, 1919), 502-3. Arps's article runs from 501-9.

83. Higham, *Strangers in the Land*, 254-56.

84. Yoke's comments on the army of schoolchildren, law and order, and Bolshevism are found in "The New World Front," WVEA *Annual Proceedings* 1919, 91. E.F. Scaggs spoke on "Americanization," quoted from ibid., 61.

85. Ibid., 62. West Virginia had a relatively small and diverse ethnic population. Census figures list 61,906 foreign-born whites in 1920, or 4.2 percent of the state's population, an increase in numbers but a decline in percentage of the population of 0.03 percent from 1910 (Figures from Fourteenth Census, *State Compendium*, 25). Foreign-born West Virginians, while engaging in a wide range of occupations, were concentrated in the coal industry, comprising 22,835 of 92,132, or 24.7 percent, of the industry employees in 1918, and 22,122 of 97,426, or 22.7 percent, in 1920, based on figures from the West Virginia Department of Mines (*Annual Report*, 1918, 234-35; 1920, 259-60). Illiterate foreign-born whites comprised 24.0 percent of the foreign-born white population over ten years old in 1920. Significant foreign-born populations resided in the counties of Brooke, 14.9 percent; Fayette, 5.3 percent; Hancock, 30.7 percent: Harrison, 8.8 percent; Logan, 6.6 percent; McDowell, 7.9 percent; Marion, 9.4 percent: Marshall, 9.1 percent; Monongalia, 9.8 percent; Ohio, 10.0 percent; Raleigh, 5.3 percent: and Tucker, 8.9 percent. (Fourteenth Census, *State Compendium*, 25-29).

86. Introductory summary of prewar Americanization from Glenn C. Altschuler, *Race, Ethnicity, and Class in American Social Thought, 1865-1919* (Arlington Heights, Ill.: Harlan-Davidson, 1982), 64-66. The references to patriotic and voluntary associations and Americanization are in Otis L. Graham, *The Great Campaigns*, 99-100.

87. The mission of women in domestic and industrial Americanization is outlined in the West Virginia Women's Christian Temperance Union's *Minutes, Addresses, Reports* of the 1919 state convention (Wheeling, 1919), 18. Comments on powerful social forces, and the declaration of Frances Kellor, are from Graham, *Great Campaigns*, 99-100.

88. "Remarks of Mr. Thomas Nelson Page," *Proceedings* of the West Virginia Mining Association Annual Meeting, Dec. 16, 1910, 26-28.

89. The statement on amalgamation into the "American race" was by educator Ellwood Cubby in 1919, quoted in Bernard J. Weiss, *American Education and the European Immigrant, 1880-1940* (Urbana: University of Illinois Press, 1982), xiii. Blue's remarks about immigrants are from Frederick O. Blue, *When a State Goes Dry* (Westerville, Ohio: American Issue, 1916), 98, 103-5. Blue's belief that the IWW was primarily comprised of foreign immigrants, while common, was not completely accurate. Melvyn Dubofsky explains that the ranks of the Wobblies were filled both by European and internal American immigrants, who shared "deep grievances against the essential institutions of the ruling classes: police, government, and church" (Dubof-

sky, *We Shall Be All*, 149-50). West Virginia historian Charles H. McCormick adds, however, that the greatest Wobbly strikes were heavily influenced by foreign-born workers ("The Death of Constable Riggs: Ethnic Conflict in Marion County in the World War I Era," *WVH* 52 [1993]: 40). Cubberly also spoke of Anglo-Saxon ideals of righteousness, law, order, and politics in Weiss, *American Education*, xiii.

90. Graham, *Great Campaigns*, 109-10.

91. John Higham describes the "frontal assault" against foreign influence, and the campaign for "unquestioning reverence," in *Strangers in the Land*, 242-47. Altschuler mentions the institutionalization of these forms of nativism, signaled by the restrictive immigration laws, in *Race, Class, and Ethnicity*, 70-71. Also see chapters 5-7, below.

92. Higham, *Strangers in the Land*, 219. Blue, *When a State Goes Dry*, 102. The warning to Hungarian miners appeared in *CCC* 1, no. 3 (March 1918): 20.

93. The perceived dangers of divided allegiance are noted in NSL *Proceedings* 1917, 249-50. The NSL's forecast for Americanization as the business of citizenship from Edward George Hartmann, *The Movement to Americanize the Immigrant* (New York: AMS Press, 1967), 220-21.

94. Hartmann outlines the growth of postwar community Americanization programs in *Movement to Americanize the Immigrant*, 223-35.

95. Higham, *Strangers in the Land*, 258.

96. Kellor's statements on the manipulation of the foreign-language press are from her address to the National Association of Manufacturers, in *Proceedings of the National Association of Manufacturers*, 24th Convention, May 19-21, 1919 (New York: 1919), 364-68. In 1922 Robert E. Park published *The Immigrant Press and its Control*, in which he portrayed the ethnic press as a "transitional phenomenon," which ideally eased the process of assimilation, but, "in its radical manifestation . . . struggled against the current in American life, misleading and slowing down the natural tendency toward acculturation." More recent scholarship, based on hundreds of ethnic radical papers, especially German-American radical papers, has revealed greater complexity in the foreign-language press than the "march to the melting pot" prescriptive approach of earlier historians of the press. For a recent survey of the diversity of the American foreign-language press, see Elliot Shore, Ken Fones-Wolf, and James P. Danky, eds., *The German-American Radical Press: The Shaping of a Left Political Culture, 1850-1940* (Urbana: University of Illinois Press), 1992. Observations herein are from 4-7

97. Inundation with antiradical propaganda in Higham, *Strangers in the Land*, 258, and Hartmann, *Movement to Americanize the Immigrant*, 221-23. America First Publicity Association advertisements appeared regularly in the Huntington *Herald-Dispatch*, including the examples here from the Mar. 14 and Mar. 7, 1920, editions.

98. West Virginia Coal Institute, *Addresses and Proceedings*, 25th semi-annual session, June 3-4, 1919, 53-54.

99. Shawkey, "Teaching Americanism," *WVSJ* 48, no. 7 (Nov. 1919), 172. Shawkey in *West Virginia Institute Program and Song Book: All of West Virginia 100% American* (Charleston: Dept. of Schools, 1919), 80, 65.

100. Higham, *Strangers in the Land*, 257.

101. Graham, *Great Campaigns*, 113.

102. See Howard Zinn, *People's History*, 355-56.

103. James R. Barrett, "Americanization from the Bottom Up: Immigration and the Remaking of the Working Class in the United States, 1880-1930," *The Journal of American History* 79:3 (December 1992), 998-99.

104. Bessie L. Pierce includes a summary of "Flag Legislation and Observance Days" in her *Public Opinion and the Teaching of History* (New York: Alfred A. Knopf, 1926), 93-98. Excerpts from the West Virginia flag law, House Bill 104, chap. 24 (*Acts of the Legislature*, Regular Session 1919), 153. Delegate John introduced the flag bill at Cornwell's urging. The governor claimed credit for the legislation in an address to the New England Society at its 114th festival, New York, Dec. 22, 1919. PAM 11493, WVRHC, 8.

105. Higham, *Strangers in the Land*, 259.

106. Vaughan, *Holding Fast*, 194.

5. The Political Culture of the Red Scare in West Virginia, 1919-1921

1. Howard Zinn, *A People's History of the United States* (New York: Harper-Collins, 1990), 368-70.

2. Melvyn Dubofsky, *Industrialism and the American Worker, 1865-1920* (Arlington Heights, Ill.: Harlan-Davidson), 126-28.

3. Melvyn Dubofsky and Warren Van Tine, *John L. Lewis: A Biography* (New York: Quadrangle/New York Times, 1977), 47-49.

4. Dubofsky, *Industrialism and the American Worker*, 129. William Serrin, *Homestead: The Glory and Tragedy of an American Steel Town* (New York: Vintage, 1992), 149-56.

5. David Brody, *Labor in Crisis; The Steel Strike of 1919* (Philadelphia and New York: J.B. Lipincott, 1965), 52-56.

6. Dubofsky mentions Gary's determination to roll back unionism in *Industrialism and the American Worker*, 130. Gary's intransigence regarding union contracting in Brody, *Labor in Crisis*, 57, 124-26.

7. Brody, *Labor in Crisis*, 147, 158-59.

8. Ibid., 142-43. Brody quotes Weir on Samuel Gompers, 141.

9. E.T. Weir to John J. Cornwell, Sept. 34, 1919, JJC box 110, folder 5.

10. Weir to Cornwell, Oct. 3, 1919, JJC box 110, folder 5.

11. Frank Wilson to Cornwell, Sept. 29, 1919, JJC box 110, folder 5.

12. Governor Cornwell wired Governor Cox with his reservations on Sept. 25, 1919, and Cox replied with a wire to Cornwell on Sept. 28, JJC box 110, folder 5.

13. A.S. Cooper to Cornwell, Sept. 30, 1919. Weir to Cornwell, Sept. 29, 1919, and Oct. 3, 1919. JJC box 110, folder 5.

14. House Bill 4, chap. 12 (*Acts of the Legislature of West Virginia*. Extraordinary session, 1919), 30-36. Barkey notes the size of the state police force in "Socialist Party in West Virginia," 212.

15. Richard Lunt repeats the supporters' common contention on the state as a Bolshevik refuge and the approval of some prolabor lawmakers in *Law and Order vs. the Miners*, 63-64. Cornwell wrote to John Summers that the force would eliminate private guards, n.d., JJC box 94, folder 6.

16. Circular letter issued by Cornwell after passage of the Constabulary Bill, n.d., JJC box 94, folder 7.

17. E.J. McVann of the Smokeless Coal Operators' Association made the "solidly behind" comment in a letter to Cornwell on Mar. 15, 1919. The need to hold foreigners and Bolsheviks in check with state police was addressed by F.M. Reynolds to Cornwell, Mar. 12, 1919, JJC box 94, folder 7.

18. Resolutions and letters of support to Cornwell on the Constabulary Bill are mostly found in box 94, folder 7, of the Cornwell papers. The dates of the commendations listed in this paragraph are:

Elkins Rotary and Huntington Creditmen and Chamber of Commerce resolutions, Mar. 12, 1919.

Bluefield Chamber of Commerce, Mar. 14, 1919. Also, the Chamber's Annual Report for the Fiscal Year Ending July 1, 1920, PAM 1501, WVRHC, 4.

Parkersburg Business Men and Board of Commerce, Mar. 23, 1919.

Smokeless Coal Operators' Assoc., E.J. McVann to Cornwell, Mar. 15, 1919.

Grafton Knights of Pythias, officers, Mar. 21, 1919.

WV Pulp and Paper, Geo. T. Mills to Cornwell, Mar. 13, 1919.

Raleigh Coal and Coke, officers, Mar. 1, 1919.

Fayette Smokeless Fuel, officers, Mar. 31, 1919 (the date of passage of the Constabulary Bill).

Ephraim Creek Coal, Supt. Wm. Warner to Cornwell, Mar. 15, 1919.

19. The comment about "enlightened public opinion" is from W.A. Wilson of Wilson and Sons Builders, Wheeling, to Cornwell, Apr. 2, 1919. The reference to the "sober, decent" people is from F.N. Sycafoose to Cornwell, Mar. 13, 1919, JJC box 94, folder 7.

20. Cornwell to R.P. Maloney, Vice President and General Manager of Davis Coal and Coke in Cumberland, Md., Apr. 12, 1919, JJC box 94, folder 6.

21. W.G. Peterson, Pres. of the Home Security Co., to Cornwell, Mar. 26, 1919. Organizations who "denigrated law and order" were scored by George T. Mills in his note to Cornwell, Mar. 13, 1919, *JJC* box 94, folder 7.

22. Peterson to Cornwell, Mar. 26, 1919, JJC box 94, folder 7.

23. William Warner to Cornwell, Mar. 18, 1919, JJC box 94, folder 7.

24. "What President Lewis Said about Proposed [Indiana] State Constabulary," *UMWJ* 32, no. 5 (Mar. 1, 1921): 3, 4.

25. *Fairmont Times*, Mar. 3, 1919.

26. Fairmont Local 929 of the Painters, Decorators and Paperhangers to Cornwell, Mar. 7, 1919, JJC box 94, folder 6.

27. Laurel Creek Local 3549 Resolution to Cornwell, Mar. 7, 1919, JJC box 94, folder 6.

28. John Summers, Sec. of Local 1741, Leewood, Va., to Cornwell, Mar. 5, 1919, *JJC* box 94, folder 6.

29. Resolution of Wheeling Bridge, Structural and Ornamental Iron Workers to Cornwell, Mar. 8, 1919, JJC box 94, folder 6.

30. *Morgantown Post*, Mar. 5, 1919. *Charleston Gazette*, Feb. 26, 1919.

31. J.Z. Terrell to E.E. Hood, editor of the Keyser, W.Va. *Mountain Echo*, Mar. 10, 1919, *JJC* box 94, folder 7.

32. "Position of the Kanawha Valley General Labor Union on the Proposed State Constabulary," addressed to the members of the West Virginia legislature, n.d., *JJC* box 94, folder 7.

33. Fisher, "John J. Cornwell," *WVH*, July 1963, 371.

34. Fisher labeled the Ramage resolution "incendiary" in ibid., 373. Description of the Constabulary Bill as "un-American class legislation" from Resolution of UMWA Local 2999, Wendel, W.Va., Feb. 25, 1919. The Wendel resolution, identical in content to the original Ramage resolution, was printed under the headings "Workers of the World Unite," and "United We Stand, Divided We Fall." *JJC* box 94, folder 6. See next paragraph for details of the resolution.

35. *JJC* box 94, folder 6.

36. Keeney and Mooney, "To the Officers and Members of District 17, United Mine Workers of America," Mar. 17, 1919, *JJC* box 94, folder 7.

37. *Fairmont Times–West Virginian*, Mar. 3, 1919.

38. Wendel Local 2999 res., Feb. 25, 1919, JJC box 94, folder 6.

39. Resolution of Blooming Rose, W.Va. UMWA Local 1952, Sept. 9, 1919, *JJC* box 94, folder 6.

40. Wheeling officers of the American Assoc. of Street and Electric Railway Employees, Mar. 1, 1919, JJC box 94, folder 6.

41. Corbin, *Life, Work, and Rebellion*, 241-43.

42. Richard Maxwell Brown, "Violence and the American Revolution," in *Essays on the American Revolution*, ed. Stephen S. Kurtz and James H. Hutson (New York: Norton, 1973), 86-88. Brown's essay is found on 81-116 of the volume. Brown cites Gordon Wood, 108-9, on the popular sovereignty impulse, from *The Creation of the American Republic, 1776-1787* (Chapel Hill: University of North Carolina Press, 1969), 319-21, 383.

43. Altina Waller, *Feud: Hatfields, McCoys, and Social Change in Appalachia, 1860-1900* (Chapel Hill: University of North Carolina Press, 1988), 169.

44. Lunt, *Law and Order vs. the Miners*, 82. Governor Cornwell's "Message to the Sheriffs of the Respective Counties and Mayors of the Various Municipalities," Oct. 30, 1919, JJC box 108, folder 3. Cornwell's call for this state-directed hybridization of vigilante justice will be covered below.

45. Gerstle, *Working-class Americanism*, 9, quoting John L. Lewis in *The Miners' Fight for American Standards* (Indianapolis: UMWA, 1935), 179-80.

46. Leon Fink, *Workingmen's Democracy: The Knights of Labor and American Politics* (Urbana: University of Illinois Press, 1985), see chap. 1, "Working-Class Radicalism in the Gilded Age: Defining a Political Culture," 3-17, and chap. 2, "The Uses of Political Power: The Knights of Labor and the State," 18-37, especially 21-23.

47. Gary Gerstle outlines the disparate elements invoked by Progressives and nationalists to realize a stable social order in *Working-class Americanism*, 10-11.

48. Resolution of UMWA Local 1808, Elkridge, W.Va., to Cornwell, n.d. but probably March 1919, JJC box 94, folder 6.

49. Cornwell to C.C. Lusk, officer in the Ramage Local, Mar. 13, 1919, *JJC* box 94, folder 6.

50. Cornwell to L.J. Foreman, Nov. 5, 1919, *JJC* box 107, folder 3.

51. Fisher recounts Cornwell's belief about the impartiality of circuit judges in "Cornwell," *WVH*, July 1963, 372. Cornwell spoke of the absence of sinister motives and the class of men for state police positions in his *Message to the Legislature*, Jan. 8, 1919, *JJC* box 122, folder 7.

52. Statement by Cornwell to the Executive Committee of the State Federation of Labor, n.d., 3, *JJC* box 94, folder 7.

53. Fisher quoted the Governor on Bolshevism in "Cornwell," *WVH*, July 1963, 373-74. Cornwell's oft-spoken dinner pail story was here used in an address to Wetzel County teachers, reported in the *Martinsburg World*, Aug. 28, 1919.

54. Rice, *West Virginia*, 217. Fisher, "Cornwell," *WVH*, July 1963, 387.

55. Sklar, "Wilson and Developmental Liberalism," in *U.S. as a Developing Country*, 137, 135.

56. Cornwell's claim to being a democrat, *Hampshire Review*, Mar. 17, 1919. His contention that he was in "no sense a capitalist," to C.M. Watkins, Nov. 19, 1919, *JJC* box 107, folder 7.

57. Fisher listed Cornwell's legislative achievements in "Cornwell," *WVH*, July 1963, 371-72, 376. Richard Lunt acknowledged Cornwell's belief in the stabilizing effects of reform, and that he opposed the power of labor, in *Law and Order*

vs. the Miners, 63-64.

58. Fisher pointed to Cornwell's bipartisanship in "Cornwell," *WVH*, July 1963, 370.

59. Sklar, "Wilson and Developmental Liberalism," in *U.S. as a Developing Country*, 134.

60. Barkey, "Socialist Party in West Virginia," 216-17, 189-94.

61. *Hampshire Review*, Mar. 17, 1919.

62. Sklar, "Wilson and Developmental Liberalism," in *U.S. as a Developing Country*, 134.

63. The thoughts in this paragraph were from an address Cornwell delivered before a Wetzel County teachers institute, reported in the *Martinsburg World* on Aug. 28, 1919. Cornwell's paper, the *Hampshire Review*, reprinted most of the text of the speech from the *World* on Sept. 3, 1919.

64. Philip Taft introduces the Plumb Plan in *Organized Labor in American History* (New York: Harper & Row, 1964), 372-73. Plumb's comment on "creative human effort" can be found in *Report of Proceedings* of the fortieth annual convention of the American Federation of Labor, held in Montreal June 7-19, 1920 (Washington: Law Reporter, 1920), 323. Plumb addressed the delegates on June 11.

65. Taft summarizes the Plumb Plan in *Organized Labor*, 373. For Plumb's own summary, see his address to the AFL, *Proceedings* 1920, 318-25. Montgomery, *House of Labor*, 401.

66. The UMWA action on the Plumb Plan at Cleveland is covered in "Convention Indorses [sic] the Plumb Railroad Plan and Votes for Alliance with Railroad Workers," *UMWJ* 30, no. 19 (Oct. 1, 1919): 12-13. The AFL withheld an endorsement of the Plumb Plan in 1919, but delegates to the 1920 Montreal convention overruled Samuel Gompers by approving the plan by a vote of 29,159 to 8,349, reacting to Plumb's "rousing" speech (Montgomery, *House of Labor*), 401. The *UMWJ* article, "Convention Indorses," also recounts the Cleveland "One Big Union" insurgency and the defeat of Howat. John L. Lewis's unsuccessful efforts to avert the UMWA's favorable vote on nationalization is covered in Dubofsky and Van Tine, *John L. Lewis*, [1977 unabridged Quadrangle ed.], 50-51.

67. *St. Mary's Oracle*, Oct. 2, 1919.

68. Cornwell to W.C. Cumberlidge, July 29, 1919, JJC box 107, folder 3. *St. Mary's Oracle*, Oct. 2, 1919.

69. Frank Morrison, Secretary of AFL, to Cornwell, Aug. 15, 1919, JJC box 107, folder 3.

70. Steven Lukes, *Power: A Radical View* (New York: Macmillan, 1974), 17, quoting Peter Bachrach and Morton S. Baratz, *Power and Poverty: Theory and Practice* (New York: Oxford, 1970), 43-44.

71. "Rules of the game" quote in ibid. Lustig, *Corporate Liberalism*, 81, on the genius of entrepreneurs and its rewards.

72. Fisher, "Cornwell," *WVH*, July 1963, 375, quoting *Charleston Gazette*, Dec. 2, 1917.

73. Robert Wiebe quotes a 1914 statement by business aristocrat Irving Bush on the "better citizens" qualified for leadership in *Businessmen and Reform*, 181. The perceived neutrality of business control is from Lustig, *Corporate Capitalism*, 82.

74. C.C. Lusk, for Ramage Local 2901, to Cornwell, n.d. but probably March 1919, JJC box 94, folder 6.

75. Fisher, "Cornwell," WVH, July 1963, 372, on political neutrality of circuit judges. Collins spoke of "decent" men in a note to Cornwell, Apr. 1, 1919, and rec-

ommended the French weapons on Apr. 7, 1919. Cornwell expressed his preference for machine guns in a short letter to Collins on Apr. 12, 1919. All in JJC box 94, folder 7.

76. Eugene Debs, speech accepting the Socialist presidential nomination in 1912, in Coben, *Reform, War, and Reaction*, 13. Leon Fink notes that the Knights of Labor often spoke of the "cooperative commonwealth," in *Workingmen's Democracy*, 12.

77. Waitman Barbe, "Historical Memories," *West Virginia Review* (WVR) 2, no. 3 (Dec. 1924), 85. National Association of Manufacturers (NAM), *Proceedings* of the 24th Convention (New York, 1919), 354.

78. Cornwell divided the world into good and bad in a letter to Ramage activist C.C. Lusk, dated Mar. 13, 1919, JJC box 94, folder 6. Background to Cornwell's Lens Creek address in Lewis, *Black Coal Miners*, 161.

79. Fisher, in "Cornwell," *WVH*, July 1963, 377-78, credits the governor with virtually standing off the miners with his appeal to reason. Cornwell's casual memoir, *A Mountain Trail* (Philadelphia: Dorrance and Company, 1939), 57-59, supports this accounting of the incident. Ronald L. Lewis notes that Frank Keeney probably played a role in turning back the 1919 march, *Black Coal Miners*, 161. Richard Lunt points to the coercive threat of federal troops as Cornwell's trump card in halting the march, *Law and Order vs. the Miners*, 78.

80. Lunt, *Law and Order vs. the Miners*, 78. Provision 7, "Scope of Investigation," JJC box 108, folder 6.

81. Collins to Cornwell, Sept. 16, 1919, JJC box 108, folder 6.

82. The warning of possible assassination during the Constabulary fight came from "J.G." to Cornwell, Mar. 13, 1919, JJC box 94, folder 6. Cornwell's concerns for his life and his confidence that rank and file miners supported him are voiced in the letter dictated to Margaret I. Kellor on Sept. 26, 1919, JJC box 107, folder 3.

83. Lunt, *Law and Order vs. the Miners*, 80.

84. Cornwell to Keeney, Oct. 26, 1919. Keeney to Cornwell, Oct. 27, 1919, *JJC* box 107, folder 7. Lunt details the governor's and coal association's plans for federal intervention, *Law and Order vs. the Miners*, 81-82.

85. Cornwell's call for patriotic committees and his reference to criminals and radicals in the strike, from his message "To the Sheriffs of the Respective Counties and the Mayors of the Various Municipalities," Oct. 30, 1919, JJC box 107, folder 7; box 108, folder 3. He invoked the moral support of the "good people" in a letter to J.E. Baugham, Mayor of Sutton, W.Va., on Oct. 31, 1919, *JJC* box 108, folder 3.

86. Lunt reports the actions of state police during the strike in *Law and Order vs. the Miners*, 87-88. Report from Crincefield and Jones on Whipple and Scarboro, in "Confidential Report on Strike Conditions in District 29," n.d. but probably Dec. 3, 1919. Affidavits from "Wickham" and "Mabscott," in Scarboro, W.Va., Dec. 4, 1919, are just two among dozens, JJC box 107, folder 8.

87. F.S. Monahan to Cornwell, Dec. 9, 1919, JJC box 107, folder 8.

88. Cornwell expressed his concern that most citizens were unaware of the magnitude of the crisis in his message "To the Sheriffs . . . and the Mayors," Oct. 30, 1919. Sheriff Hastings took a moderate tone in a letter to the governor on Nov. 1, 1919; Cornwell lectured Hastings in his reply of Nov. 3, 1919, JJC box 108, folder 3.

89. Palmer to Cornwell, Nov. 24, 1919, JJC box 107, folder 4.

90. Cornwell to Palmer, Nov. 13, 1919. Palmer to Cornwell, Nov. 13, 1919. JJC box 107, folder 7.

91. Cornwell to Burleson, Oct. 11, 1919, JJC box 107, folder 3.

92. Justice Department opinions about *Cronaca Soversiva* are documented by Paul Avrich in *Sacco and Vanzetti: The Anarchist Background* (Princeton: Princeton University Press, 1991), 127. Material on Cavalieri in Clarence Edwin Smith papers, A&M 1604, WVRHC, box 1, folder 1.

93. Cornwell wrote to L.J. Foreman that labor leaders "had their way absolutely," and mentioned the desirability of industrial court laws, in his letter of Nov. 5, 1919. JJC box 107, folder 3. The perspective of the NAM is from Albion Guilford Taylor, *Labor Policies of the National Association of Manufacturers* (New York: Arno Press, 1973), 59-60. Reprint of 1927 edition by University of Illinois.

94. Charles Piez, "Labor and its Responsibilities," *Coal Age* 16, no. 22 (Dec. 11 and 18, 1919): 882-83.

95. Untitled, *Coal Age* 16, no. 19 (Nov. 6, 1919): 754.

96. Cornwell spoke of the "unity of thought and purpose" of wartime in his biennial message to the legislature, reported in the *Hampshire Review*, Jan. 8, 1919. NAM view on public opinion from Taylor, *Labor Policies*, 63. Cornwell's statement on "counter propaganda" from his White Sulphur address to the Paint and Varnish assembly, reported in *St. Mary's Oracle*, Oct. 2, 1919.

97. Lewis, *Black Coal Miners*, 157-58. Lunt, *Law and Order vs. the Miners*, 103-11. The most thorough treatment of the Matewan Massacre is in Lon Savage's *Thunder in the Mountains: The West Virginia Coal War, 1920-1921* (Pittsburgh: University of Pittsburgh Press, 1990).

98. Wightman Roberts, *West Virginia Mining News*, Feb. 21, 1920, JJC box 107, folder 1.

99. Cornwell to Roberts, n.d. JJC box 107, folder 1. The number at the inaugural meeting is from the *Charleston Daily Mail*, Mar. 4, 1920.

100. Mission statement of ACA from its "Declaration of Purposes," adopted at the founding meeting on Mar. 4, 1920. Officers' identified in an ACA flyer of July 14, 1921. Conley joined the organization on Jan. 1, 1921. Conley to Cornwell, Feb. 19, 1921, JJC box 107, folder 1.

101. Cornwell's comments on the "defensive and offensive alliance" and the interests of "the whole people" from his address to the founding meeting of the ACA, Mar. 4, 1920, 4-5. Cornwell's acceptance of the presidency, from letter to Roberts, Mar. 22, 1920, JJC box 107, folder 1.

102. "Williamson, W.Va.," *Coal Age* 17, no. 24 (June 10, 1920): 1216.

103. *Hampshire Review*, July 15, 1922, quoting the *Logan Banner*.

104. Taylor, *Labor Policies of the NAM*, 63-67.

105. Statement by the ACA, June 22, 1920. E.M. Showalter, "American Ideals," prepared for the ACA, n.d., JJC box 107, folder 1. "American Ideals" also in the Ephraim F. Morgan (hereafter Morgan) papers, A&M 203, 1660, WVRHC, box 19, folder 3.

106. Phil Conley to Cornwell, Jan. 31, 1922, JJC box 107, folder 1.

6. Welfare Capitalism, the American Plan–Open-shop Movement, and the Triumph of Business Unionism

1. Lunt, *Law and Order vs. the Miners*, 157. "The Work of the American Constitutional Association," flyer, n.d., JJC box 107, folder 1.

2. Phil Conley to ACA Executive Committee, Mar. 31, 1921. *JJC* box 107, folder 1.

3. Ward, "The Origin . . . of the National Security League," *MVHR*, June 1960, 63-65. Also see hearings of the 65th Congress on the National Security League.

4. Conley to Executive Committee of the ACA, Mar. 31, 1921, JJC box 107, folder 1.

5. Lunt, *Law and Order vs. the Miners*, 92, 157.

6. Lunt refers to several uses of broad injunctions in ibid., especially 92-97. Albion Taylor analyzes the open-shop ideology of the NAM in *Labor Policies of the NAM*, especially 40-71, 82-85.

7. Taft, *The AFL in the Time of Gompers*, 401. Lunt mentions the Chicago conference where the American Plan was formalized in *Law and Order vs. the Miners*, 156. David Montgomery says AFL membership dropped by one-third by 1923, *Fall of the House of Labor*, 6-7. Lunt quotes a figure of 24 percent, 157. In southern West Virginia, of course, the American Plan movement was less one of rolling back an entrenched UMWA than of blocking its formation in the first place. See below for more on the tenets of the American Plan.

8. Trotter, *Coal, Class, and Color*, 65.

9. Advertisement for West Virginia Coal Operators Association, *West Virginia Review* (*WVR*) 1, no. 10 (June, 1923): inside cover. For a concise summary of welfare work by a major coal company, see "Sociological Work Accomplished by the Consolidation Coal Company," *Coal Age* 15, no. 2 (Jan. 9, 1919): 54-58.

10. "Company Provides Churches and Dance Halls," *Coal Age* 17, no. 24 (June 10, 1920): 1218.

11. West Virginia Coal Operators Association ad, *WVR* 2, no. 10 (July 1924): inside cover.

12. "Company Provides," *Coal Age* 17, no. 24 (June 10, 1920): 1218.

13. Ad for WV Coal Operators Association, *WVR* 2, no. 5 (Feb. 1925): inside cover.

14. E.D. Knight quoted in *Coal Age* 17, no. 24 (June 10, 1920): 1218. Operators shunned the notion that they exercised any control over religion in *Proposed Findings as to Certain Aspects of the Bituminous Coal Mining Industry* (hereafter *1923 Coal Commission*) (submitted by the Bituminous Operators' Special Committee to the United States Coal Commission for its Consideration and Determination, July 30, 1923, vol. III, sec. D, "Living Costs"), 25. Also see Stuart Brandes, *American Welfare Capitalism, 1880-1940* (Chicago and London: University of Chicago Press, 1976), 52-65.

15. Crandall A. Shifflet, *Coal Towns: Life, Work, and Culture in Company Towns of Southern Appalachia, 1880-1960* (Knoxville: University of Tennessee Press, 1991), 54, 191, xv.

16. J.G. Bradley, "The Coal Operator and the Coal Miner, a Partnership," *Proceedings of the West Virginia Coal Mining Institute*, 26th semi-annual session, Dec. 5-6, 1922, 31.

17. Deaver C. Ashmeal, "Welfare Work in an Anthracite Colliery," *Coal Age* 17, no. 9 (Feb. 26, 1920): 382.

18. "The Mining Town School Problem, *CCC* 3, no. 5 June 1920, 1. The dispatch was submitted by "our Elkhorn Division Correspondent," and it is highly likely that correspondent was Phil Conley. Conley worked for Consolidation in Jenkins, Kentucky, and served as superintendent of schools in the Elkhorn district before joining the American Constitutional Association.

19. Justus Collins to L. Epperly, Mar. 27, 1922. Collins, box 18, folder 128. L. Epperly to George R. Collins, July 26, 1923, Collins, box 19, folder 137. Brandes

affirms the suspicions that some industrialists harbored toward high-school training in *American Welfare Capitalism*, 58.

20. *1923 Coal Commission*, Bituminous Operators Report, vol. II, sec. D, "Living Costs," 24.

21. Brandes, *American Welfare Capitalism*, quoting the Man, W.Va. school year-book of the Tridelphia District Schools, *The Hillbilly*, on "habits of industry," 52.

22. Ibid., 61-65.

23. Quote on love of duty is from "Love of Your Job," *CCC* 8, no. 3 (June 1925): 11. Comment by editor on thought direction is in Brandes, *American Welfare Capitalism*, 65.

24. "Sociological Work . . . Consolidation Coal Company," *Coal Age* 15, no. 2 (Jan. 9, 1919): 56.

25. Ibid., 54, highlights the *CCC* masthead slogan. Comments are from "Patriotism," *CCC* 5, no. 9 (Nov. 1922): 1, and "Law and Order," *CCC* 2, no. 2 (Dec. 1919-Jan. 1920), 8.

26. Invocation to "crush every power" from "True Americanism," *CCC* 3, no. 6 (July-Aug. 1920), 4. Labor and capital as brothers, from J. C. Kinney, "A Workman's Remedy," *CCC* 5, no. 2 (Feb. 1922): 2. "Outside influences," editorial in *CCC* 5, no. 5 (June 1922): 2.

27. "Human Relations," *CCC* 8, no. 3 (June 1925): 11.

28. *CCC* 8, no. 4 (July-Aug. 1925), 3.

29. "The American Plan," *CCC* 8, no. 5 (Sept.-Oct. 1925): 1-2.

30. "For Men Must Work," *CCC* (July-Aug. 1925): 22.

31. "Standard Employment Contract of the Red Jacket Consolidated Coal and Coke Company." Presented to U.S. Senate Committee on Interstate Commerce, *Conditions in the Coal Fields of Pennsylvania, West Virginia, and Ohio*. Hearing of the 70th Congress, 1st sess., Washington, D.C., 1928, 1846. In Lewis and Hennen, *West Virginia: Documents . . .* , 187.

32. Daniel Ernst, "The Yellow-Dog Contract and Liberal Reform, 1917-1932," *Labor History* 30, no. 2 (Spring 1989): 251-55. Ernst's article covers 251-74.

33. "John Doe" and "Richard Doe," employees of the Stone Mountain Coal Company in Mingo County, W.Va., wrote of employers' broad and arbitrary interpretation of the nonunion provision of yellow-dog contracts in "Another 'Yellow Dog,'" *UMWJ* 32, no. 4 (Feb. 15, 1921): 17. Yellow-dogs as violations of basic rights mentioned in "Yellow Dog," *UMWJ* 32, no. 5 (Mar. 1, 1921), 6.

34. Ibid.

35. *1923 Coal Commission*. Findings of Bituminous Operators, submitted July 30, 1923, vol. III, sec. D, "Living costs," 5-6.

36. R. Dawson Hall, "Our Time-Honored Industrial Democracy," *Coal Age* 17, no. 9 (Feb. 26, 1920): n.p.

37. *1923 Coal Commission*, findings of Bituminous Operators, vol. III, sec. D, 5-6.

38. "Those Awful Coal Miners," *UMWJ* 35, no. 14 (July 15, 1924): 8.

39. Charles E. Lanning to *UMWJ* 35, no. 16 (Aug. 15, 1924): 11.

40. "Union Busters," *UMWJ* 33, no. 5 (Mar. 1, 1922): 6.

41. "Coal Miners Are Americans," *UMWJ* 31, no. 2 (Jan. 15, 1920): 1.

42. "Days That Are Gone," *UMWJ* 34, no. 1 (Jan. 1, 1923): 6.

43. "Gary Shows His Hand," *UMWJ* 30, no. 20 (Oct. 15, 1919): 6.

44. Discussion of the destabilizing tendencies of highly individualistic, or anarchic businessmen, in James Weinstein, *The Corporate Ideal in the Liberal State* (Boston: Beacon Press, 1968), 6.

45. Dubofsky and Van Tine, *John L. Lewis* (abridgement of 1977 biography; Urbana: University of Illinois Press, 1986), 86-87, 96-97.

46. John Brophy, "The Miners' American Plan," *Labor Age* 11, no. 10 (Nov. 1922): 4-5.

47. Brophy's and others' efforts to preserve a radical voice in the UMWA is covered in Alan J. Singer, "Class-Conscious Coal Miners: Nanty-Glo versus the Open Shop in the Post–World War I Era," *Labor History* 29, no. 1 (Winter 1988): 56-65. Dubofsky and Van Tine point out Lewis's ability to emerge stronger from union in-fighting in the 1986 University of Illinois abridgement of their 1977 *John L. Lewis*, 95. Singer, in "Nanty-Glo," outlines Lewis's 1920s refinement of traditional business unionism in the UMWA, 64-65. For Lewis's often brilliant strategies with left radicals in later years, *see* Robert H. Zieger *American Workers, American Unions* (2d ed., Baltimore: Johns Hopkins, 1994), esp. 29-30; 54-55; 72-74; 128-34.

48. "Federated American Engineering Societies Formally Organized," *Coal Age* 17, no. 24 (June 10, 1920): 1221.

49. W.H.S. White, "Abolition of Class and Caste," in *American Ideals* (a pamphlet issued by the American Constitutional Association, Charleston, 1924), 10. Morgan, box 19, folder 3.

50. This summary analysis of structural developments in the age of industrial capitalism depends on Martin Sklar, "Studying American Political Development in the Progressive Era, 1890-1916," in *The United States as a Developing Country*, 37-77 (see especially 49-61). The comment on society's "better citizens" is from Wiebe, *Businessmen and Reform*, 181. For references to others who have analyzed these developments, see chapter 3, n. 1 above.

51. Taylor, *Labor Policies of the NAM*, 59-62.

52. "Miners' Demands Un-American," *Coal Age* 17, no. 6 (Feb. 5, 1920), 275. Barnett, "Americanization from the Bottom Up," 1009.

53. This comment on the natural gifts of the few is from Judge E.M. Showalter's manuscript outline prepared for the ACA, entitled "American Ideals" (n.d., 5), which became the outline used by ACA speakers throughout West Virginia, JJC box 107, folder 1, *Morgan* box 19, folder 3.

54. Roger Babson, "Millionaires Everywhere," column featured in the *Morgantown New Dominion*, July 2, 1921.

55. These comments are from an address by J.G. Bradley, president of the West Virginia Coal Mining Institute. *Proceedings* of the 26th semi-annual meeting, December 1922, 31-33.

56. The American Constitutional Association, *Life in a West Virginia Coal Field* (Charleston: ACA, 1923), 55, 57-58.

57. Governor E.F. Morgan, "Adequate Reward for Labor," in *American Ideals* (Charleston: ACA, 1924), 3. *Morgan* box 19, folder 3.

58. J.R. Laird, president of the Bluefield Trust Company, "Property Rights Respected," in ibid., 11.

59. Edwin M. Keatley, "Equality of Opportunity," ibid., 11-12.

60. Keatley's work as agent for the Morgan company is from a profile in *WVR* 2, no. 6 (Mar. 1925): 192. He wrote of submission to authority in "Reverence for Law and Order," *WVSJ* 50, no. 11 (Mar. 1922), 259-60.

61. "Declaration of Purposes" of the ACA, adopted Mar. 4, 1920, JJC box 107, folder 1. Also see Constitution of the Association, Article II, in 1922 *WV Hand Book*, 696.

62. "American Ideals; Suggested Notes," n.d., similar to Showalter's draft, 1, JJC box 107, folder 1.

63. "The Enemy within Our Gates," *American Citizen* 1, no. 8 (June 1, 1921): 1 (ACA newsletter, hereafter *AC*). JJC box 107, folder 1. Higham refers to this particular warning in a short passage on the ACA in *Strangers in the Land*, 232.

64. "Enemy Within," *AC* 1, no. 8 (June 1921): 1.

65. "Where We Stand," *AC* 1, no. 3 (Mar. 1, 1921): 2, JJC box 107, folder 1.

66. "Enemy Within," *AC* 1, no. 8 (June 1, 1921): 1.

67. Governor Cornwell told West Virginia mayors that the ACA was "purely patriotic" in a letter dated Mar. 27, 1920, JJC box 107, folder 1. Wightman Roberts wrote of the ACA's desire to "inculcate" ACA doctrines in "To Members and Friends," June 22, 1920, 1-2, JJC box 107, folder 1.

68. "Where We Stand," *AC* 1, no. 3 (Mar. 1, 1921): 2.

69. Dubofsky and Van Tine, *John L. Lewis*, 1986 abr. ed., 59-60.

70. Cornwell to Watson, May 7, 1920, JJC box 107, folder 1.

71. Trotter, *Coal, Class, and Color*, 14.

72. Gary's comments are from a speech he delivered in Syracuse, N.Y., reported in the *Wheeling Intelligencer*, June 13, 1921.

73. "Through Judge Gary's Hat," *UMWJ* 32, no. 10 (May 15, 1921): 6.

74. Keatley reported Gary's donation in a letter to William B. Schiller, Dec. 7, 1920, JJC box 107, folder 1. The Wheeling intermediary was John W. Kirk, who received, after extended negotiations with the ACA, a 25 percent commission on Gary's donation, according to a letter from Charleston attorney Claude Smith to the ACA, Feb. 8, 1922, JJC box 107, folder 1. In 1923 Kirk compiled for the *Wheeling Intelligencer* a reference volume entitled *Progressive West Virginians*, a guidebook to the state's political, industrial, and educational power brokers. Richard Lunt reports that Gary required his subsidiaries to support the ACA in *Law and Order vs. the Miners*, 157.

75. Keatley to Cornwell, Nov. 12, 1920, JJC box 107, folder 1.

76. "The American Plan Review," subheading "Let's Wheel Wheeling, W.Va. to Industrial Sanity!" Sept. 15, 1920, 1-2, JJC box 107, folder 1.

77. *Huntington Herald-Dispatch*, June 5, 1921.

78. "Business to Take Stand on Labor," *Nation's Business* 8, no. 7 (July 1920): 20.

79. The Chamber of Commerce vote total is from "Open Shop," *Socialist Review* 9, 4 (Sept. 1920): 119. The Bluefield Chamber's resolution on John L. Lewis is summarized in Carroll Woods, *Annual Report of the Secretary-Manager* of the Bluefield Chamber of Commerce for the Fiscal Year Ending July 1, 1920, 17, PAM 1501, WVRHC.

80. William E. Bohn, "Labor's Answer to the Open-Shop Drive," *Socialist Review* 10, no. 4 (Apr.-May 1921): 41.

81. Albion Taylor, *Labor Policies of the NAM*, Open-Shop Department, 82-83. *Open Shop Encyclopedia* noted, 68.

82. H.H. Lewis, editor of *Industrial Progress*, the NAM journal, to West Virginia Governor E.F. Morgan, Apr. 2, 1923. *Morgan*, box 19, folder 3.

83. Lunt, *Law and Order vs. the Miners*, on the American Plan convention, 156. Salt Lake job printing announcement in *New York Times*, Mar. 25, 1921, 17, no. 5.

84. These indicators of the spread of the American Plan are documented in the *New York Times* as follows: Albany and Troy builders, July 6, 1921, 17, no. 7; Chicago meatpackers and employees' response, Sept. 15, 1921, 15, no. 3, and Oct. 2,

1921, 1, no. 2; St. Louis packers, Dec. 24, 1921, 12, no. 5; Texas and Pacific Coal Company, Oct. 21, 1921, 19, no. 3.

85. Robert M. Buck, "Kenesaw Mountain Landis Decides," *Labor Age* 11, 1 (January 1922): 12-13.

86. Statement made by the Operators' Association of the Williamson Field, subcommittee of the Committee on Education and Labor of the United States Senate, Appointed to Investigate Conditions in the Coal Fields of West Virginia in the Territory Adjacent to Kentucky, July 14, 1921 (Washington: GPO, 1921), 54, 53.

87. Figures on UMWA expenses from Lewis, *Black Coal Miners*, 163.

88. Lunt notes John L. Lewis's presence at Blizzard's defense table in *Law and Order vs. the Miners*, 158-59. The UMWA president's charge of shooting the union into the state reported in Lewis, *Black Coal Miners*, 163, from Fred Mooney, *Struggle in the Coalfields* ed. James W. Hess (Morgantown: West Virginia University Library, 1967), 116-28.

89. Williams, *West Virginia*, 148. Lunt, *Law and Order vs. the Miners*, 165-66.

90. "Methodist Church Declaration on the Open Shop," *UMWJ* 32, no. 7 (Apr. 1, 1921): 10. Federal Council of Churches of Christ/NAM exchange reported in *NYT*, Jan. 31, 1921, 24, no. 7.

91. *The Nation* 115, no. 2975 (July 12, 1922): 39, 11.

92. Gompers was quoted in *NYT*, Aug. 26, 1921, 8, no. 3, and *NYT*, Feb. 15, 1921, 10, no. 1. Mooney's comments on "labor-hating fakers" is from "Fred Mooney Sets Out Warm Reply to Communist Leader," *UMWJ* 34, no. 23 (Dec. 1, 1923): 15.

93. Dubofsky and Van Tine, *John L. Lewis*, 1986 abr. ed., 88.

94. "The Other Ox Gored," *UMWJ* 32, no. 2 (Jan. 15, 1921): 6.

95. Cornwell's advocacy of an industrial court bill peppers his correspondence, i.e. John W. Simpson to Cornwell, July 20, 1919; Cornwell to Simpson, July 22, 1919, JJC box 107, folder 3; and Cornwell to Nelson J. Rall, Feb. 7, 1920, JJC box 108, folder 5.

96. For Morgan's general views on radicalism and isolationism, see Morgan papers, box 19, folder 1.

97. Morgan to George V. Witten, Mar. 15, 1921. *Morgan* box 3, folder 1.

98. McClaren's bill is referred to in a letter to Morgan from James J. Divine, Mar. 8, 1923. *Morgan* box 19, folder 1. UMWA analysis of the proposed West Virginia bill is from "Industrial Court Bill Introduced in West Virginia Legislature Vicious," *UMWJ* 34, no. 8 (Apr. 15, 1923): 13.

99. Matthew Woll, of the AFL, "Labor Kept the Nation Steady," *Nation's Business* 8, no. 6 (June 1920): 17.

100. See Weinstein, *The Corporate Ideal in the Liberal State*, ix-xv, 3-15, for analysis of the radical individualism of such "old school" industrialists.

101. State of West Virginia, *Official Returns of the General Election* of Nov. 2, 1920 (Charleston: issued by Houston G. Young, Secretary of State), 3. Koontz and Montgomery combined for 266,092 votes to Morgan's 242,327, with Montgomery getting 81,330, or 16 percent. Socialist candidate Matthew Holt received 2,695 votes.

102. W.C. Ruediger, "Unionism among Teachers," *School and Society* 8, no. 203 (Nov. 16, 1918), 589.

103. Alfred H. Forman, "'Unionism' among Teachers—A Reply," *School and Society* 8, no. 206 (Dec. 7, 1918): 682.

104. "American Federation of Labor Convention Adopts an Educational Program Containing 25 Planks," *UMWJ* 30, no. 14 (July 15, 1919), 10. "Miners Teach Teachers," *UMWJ* 35, no. 16 (Aug. 15, 1924): 11.

105. "Unionizing Teachers," from the *School Board Journal*, cited in *School and Society* 9, no. 234 (June 21, 1919): 747.

106. Barbe's abstract comments on individualism from an editorial in *WVSJ* 47, no. 10 (Jan. 1919): 630. His more direct anti-union sentiments are from "Teachers and Labor Unions," *WVSJ* 49, no. 6 (Oct. 1920), 145.

107. William S. John, Secretary of the Morgantown Board of Education, in Minute Book VI of the Board, Nov. 9, 1920, 152.

108. Walter Barnes, "We Must Fight," *WVSJ* 52, no. 6 (Nov. 1923): 182-83.

109. Albion Taylor notes the legacy of the open-shop movement in *Labor Policies of the NAM*, 82. Montgomery's analysis of the American Plan is in *Fall of the House of Labor*, 5-7.

110. Lunt, *Law and Order vs. the Miners*, 166-67.

111. Montgomery, *Fall of the House of Labor*, 6-8.

112. See Singer, "Nanty-Glo," *Labor History* (Winter 1988): 56-65. Dubofsky and Van Tine, *John L. Lewis*, 1986 abr. ed., 70-71, 103-5, 131-47. Williams, *West Virginia*, 168-69, 180-81.

113. "The Commission's Report," *UMWJ* 34, no. 14 (July 15, 1923), 6.

114. Dubofsky and Van Tine, *John L. Lewis*, 1986 abr. ed., 83-85.

115. "Political Policy," *UMWJ* 35, no. 24 (Dec. 15, 1924): 8.

7. Voluntary Associations and Americanization in the 1920s

1. Corbin, *Life, Work, and Rebellion*, 176. Higham, *Strangers in the Land*, 267.

2. West Virginia Woman's Christian Temperance Union, *Addresses and Proceedings*, Wheeling, Oct. 7-9, 1919, 14.

3. Higham, *Strangers in the Land*, 269-71. See his chap. 10, "The Tribal Twenties," 264-99.

4. Ibid., 270. The Morgantown Board of Education used the pervasive expression "unity of thought and purpose," Minute book VI, Apr. 25, 1918, 1.

5. Noam Chomsky and Edward Herman analyze the process of business influence on the culture in *Manufacturing Consent: The Political Economy of the Mass Media* (New York: Pantheon, 1988). Bernays, as reported earlier, popularized the expression "engineering of consent (Bernays, *Public Relations*), 71. Bernays also comments on harnessing the public in *Public Opinion*, 76, 78.

6. C. Wright Mills, "Mass Media and Public Opinion," in *Power, Politics, and People: The Collected Essays of C. Wright Mills*, ed. Irving Louis Horowitz (New York: Oxford University Press, 1963), 577-98, especially 580-85.

7. Graebner, *Engineering of Consent*, 5, and, quoting Bernays on the "competition of ideas," 60

8. Quote by Dr. Charles S. Medbury at the Golden Prairie Biennial of the General Federation of Women's Clubs, June 16-23, 1920, Des Moines, Iowa. Reported by Mrs. Harold J. Brennan, president of the Women's Club of Wheeling (*Yearbook, 1920-1921* of the West Virginia Federation of Women's Clubs [Charleston: Tribune Printing, 1921], 91).

9. De Toqueville, *Democracy in America*, 1945 ed., 1, no. 253.

10. *St. Mary's Oracle*, Oct. 2, 1919.

11. E.T. England, "Law and Order" (speech to a conference of U.S. district attorneys and prosecuting attorneys, Charleston, W.Va., Mar. 31, 1922), 3. PAM 744, WVRHC.

12. Shawkey, *Institute Song Book: All of West Virginia 100% American*, 1919, 80.

13. U.S. War Office, *Education for Citizenship* (Washington: GPO, 1921), 7-19.

14. John J. Mahoney, *Training Teachers for Americanization: A Course of Study for Normal Schools and Teachers' Institutes* (Dept. of Interior, Bureau of Education Bulletin no. 12 [Washington: GPO, 1920], 8, 13-14, 29).

15. "Rule Prohibiting Dancing," Morgantown Independent Board of Education Minute Book VII, May 2, 1921, 170-72.

16. Raymond F. Crist, U.S. Director of Citizenship, Dept. of Labor, to Governor E.F. Morgan, Mar. 7, 1921, Morgan, box 19, folder 1. Crist told Morgan that since 1916 over half the states had legislatively mandated Americanization programs. Hartmann addresses the national government's encouragement of Americanization programs in *The Movement to Americanize the Immigrant*, 235-49.

17. George M. Ford, *Biennial Report of the State Superintendent of Free Schools for the Two Years Ending June 30, 1922* (Charleston: Department of Free Schools, 1922), 9-10.

18. Ibid., 9.

19. "Americanization Schools in Wheeling," *WVSJ* 49, no. 9 (January 1921): 202. Mrs. E.G. Rohrbough, "Report of Department of Americanization," WVFWC *Yearbook, 1920-1921*, 67.

20. Cited DAR activities are drawn from "American's Creed," Elizabeth Ludington Hagans Chapter, box 4, minute book II, May 5, 1920, 72. English night schools, Hagans chapter, box 4, minute book II, Dec. 20, 1922, n.p. Patriotic essay contests, Hagans chapter box 4, book III, Nov. 20, 1923, n.p. "National Industries . . . Freedom," from Hagans chapter 1922 *Yearbook*, PAM 1277 WVRHC. Radicalism, West Virginia DAR, *Proceedings* of the 21st Conference, 1926, 16.

21. WVFWC *Yearbook, 1921-1922*, 104, 103.

22. Mrs. S.C. Christian, national chair of Americanization for the Federated Women's Clubs, "Our Foreign Brother," *West Virginia Clubwoman* 2, no. 7 (June 5, 1923): 3.

23. WVFWC *Yearbook, 1921-1922*, 100.

24. Higham, *Strangers in the Land*, 10.

25. De Toqueville, *Democracy in America*, 1:253.

26. David E. Whisnant analyzes the scientific racial purity idea in the context of progressive reformism in a traditional culture in *All that Is Native and Fine: The Politics of Culture in an American Region* (Chapel Hill: University of North Carolina Press, 1983), 237-40. Higham singles out the influence of Grant's *The Passing of the Great Race* (see chapter 2, above) in *Strangers in the Land*, 155-57.

27. Higham notes Grant's hierarchy of consciousness in *Strangers in the Land*, 157. Tullos's study of white culture is *Habits of Industry: White Culture and the Transformation of the Carolina Piedmont* (Chapel Hill: University of North Carolina Press, 1989), 170 for quote.

28. Phil M. Conley, "The Man from West Virginia," *WVR* 1, no. 1 (Oct. 1923), 19. Hays Brown, "Pure-Blooded Americans," *WVR* 1, no. 5 (Feb. 1924), 33.

29. R.F. Adams, compiler, *Huntington, West Virginia: A City of Optimists* (Huntington: Huntington Chamber of Commerce, 1924), 11. PAM 2517, WVRHC.

30. Mrs. S.P. Christian, "Report of Division of Americanization," WVFWC *Yearbook, 1923-1924* (Charleston: Mutual Printing Co., 1924), 111.

31. Harry Woodyard, *American Citizen* 1, no. 6 (Apr. 15, 1921): 2. JJC box 107, folder 1.

32. Mrs. W.S. Jarrett, "Report of the Division of Americanization," WVFWC *Yearbook, 1922-1923* (Wheeling: West Virginia Printing Co., 1923), 102.

33. Mrs. A.L. Lehman, "Report of Division of Americanization," WVFWC *Yearbook, 1921-1922*, 104.

34. Mrs. Cyrus Hall, "Outline of Work in Citizenship Training for 1924," *West Virginia Clubwoman* 3, no. 2 (Jan. 5, 1924): 4.

35. Keatley to Cornwell, Nov. 12, 1920, *JJC* box 107, folder 1. Conley is mentioned frequently in *CCC*, e.g. 2, no. 9 (October 1919): 11, 15, and 3, no. 5 (June 1920), 1, 44, 47.

36. Keatley to William B. Schiller, Dec. 7, 1920, JJC box 107, folder 1.

37. *CCC* 4, no. 1 (Feb. 1921), 40.

38. Conley's salary was a topic of discussion in Keatley's letters to Cornwell, Nov. 12, 1920, and Schiller, Dec. 7, 1920, JJC box 107, folder 1. A report by State Treasurer W.S. Johnson in an ACA typescript compendium of press releases listed the governor's salary as $10,000; state superintendent of schools, $7,000; state tax commissioner, $6,000; members of the state Board of Control and the chief of the Department of Mines, $5,000. Phil Conley et al., *The Truth about West Virginia* (Charleston: American Constitutional Association, 1922-23), press release no. 19, 4. PAM 8340, WVRHC.

39. Conley to Cornwell, Feb. 19, 1921, JJC box 107, folder 1.

40. Keatley to Cornwell, Nov. 12, 1920, JJC box 107, folder 1.

41. Conley's comments to Keatley about the propaganda and law and order benefits of the newsletter were recounted to Governor Cornwell in Keatley's letter of Nov. 12, 1920, *JJC* box 107, folder 1. The remark about developing a national consciousness is from Conley's statements in the ACA's 1924 pamphlet, *American Ideals*, foreword, Morgan box 19, folder 3. Keatley reported on the *AC*'s access to plants around the state in his letter to Schiller, Dec. 7, 1920, JJC box 107, folder 1.

42. The 1922 *WV Hand Book*, edited by John T. Harris, referred to the distribution of the *AC* to high schools, 694. Conley told Cornwell of the wide distribution of the "America First" placards in a letter dated Feb. 19, 1921, JJC box 107, folder 1.

43. The Mar. 1, 1921 *AC* (1, no. 3) featured a few words on the "snappy sentences" in the placards, 4. Conley outlined his speaking engagements in his Feb. 19, 1921, letter to Governor Cornwell, and to the ACA Executive Committee on Mar. 31, 1921, *JJC* box 107, folder 1.

44. The *AC* 1, no. 3 (Mar. 1, 1921): 4, announced the commitment of the ACA to provide speakers for all occasions. Other summaries of the ACA's speakers bureau are found in the 1922 *WV Hand Book*, 694, and in Conley's *The Truth about West Virginia*, news release no. 1, p. 2.

45. The Mar. 4 *Charleston Daily Mail* reported the intention of the ACA to become a national body. The organization's constitution, reprinted in the 1922 WV Hand Book, gave form to these plans, 696. Conley touted the National American Council's recognition of the ACA in his letter to the ACA Executive committee, Mar. 31, 1921, JJC box 107, folder 1.

46. I.C. White was quoted in "Where We Stand," *AC* 1, no. 3 (Mar. 1, 1921): 2. White became a director of the ACA shortly after its founding, one of "sixteen influential men" so selected, 1922 *WV Hand Book*, 694.

47. Constitution of the ACA, 1922 *WV Hand Book*, 695.

48. Conley's military service and work with Marion County schools was summarized in his *Charleston Daily Mail* obituary, August 2, 1979. Keatley advised Schiller that Conley had been Consolidations's director of welfare work in his letter of Dec. 7, 1920, JJC box 107, folder 1. Conley's achievements as superintendent of schools were often praised in *CCC*, as in 2, no. 11 (December 1919-January 1920),

43, and 4, no. 1 (February 1921), 40.

49. Conley informed Cornwell of his appointment as Americanization director on Feb. 19, 1921, JJC box 107, folder 1. He is listed as supervisor of citizenship and thrift in Superintendent Ford's *West Virginia Teachers' Hand Book, Containing Suggestions, Rulings, Information, and Material for Use of the Teachers of West Virginia* (Charleston: State Superintendent of Schools, 1921), 2. Conley referred to the ACA's move to the Department of Education facility in his Mar. 31, 1921, letter to the Executive Committee, JJC box 107, folder 1.

50. Conley to Cornwell, Mar. 9, 1922, JJC box 107, folder 1.

51. Armstrong's comments are in his column on "Americanism," *WVSJ* 49, no. 5 (Aug.-Sept. 1920), 118. Conley often spoke of the "medium of the children," as in letter to Executive Committee on Mar. 31, 1921, and to Cornwell Jan. 31, 1922, JJC box 107, folder 1.

52. Every West Virginia public school teacher was required to attend a county institute for a least five days of the school year in which he or she taught, unless excused by his or her county superintendent. See House Bill 217, chap. 79 (*Acts of the Legislature of West Virginia*, Regular Session, 1917), 332-33. Conley discussed plans for ACA work at the teacher institutes in *AC* 1, no. 3 (Mar. 1, 1921), 1, and to Cornwell Feb. 19, 1921, JJC box 107, folder 1. He mentioned the potential to reach eleven thousand teachers in a letter to the ACA Executive Committee, July 14, 1921, *JJC* box 107, folder 1.

53. "Institute Schedule 1921," *WVSJ* 50, no. 4 (July-Aug. 1921), 87-89. The ACA contributed a supplement to the *WVSJ* 50, no. 5 (Sept. 1921), listing "American Ideals" between pages 116-17.

54. Ibid., insert between 116-17. *AC* 1, no. 7 (May 1, 1921), 3. The Mineral county resolution is noted in "Institute Resolutions," *WVSJ* 50, no. 6 (Oct. 1921), 124.

55. The topics included "The Making of the American Constitution," "Democratic Ideals Embodied in the Declaration of Independence," "The Story of the American Flag," and "Americanism: What it Means," Conley to Cornwell, Feb. 19, 1921. Conley's report on participation in *AC* 1, no. 6 (Apr. 15, 1921): 2, and quotes from Mabel West's winning essay from *AC* 1, no. 7 (May 1, 1921), 3, JJC box 107, folder 1.

56. Article IV of the ACA Constitution emphasized the organization's nonpartisanship, 1922 *WV Hand Book*, 696. Tullos refers to the assumed interrelationship of habits of industry and the public interest in *Habits of Industry*, 290. The Bluefield Chamber's essay contest is documented in Carroll Woods's *Annual Report* on the Chamber for the fiscal year ending July 1, 1920, 14.

57. F.B. Kaye, "Americanism as an Educational Menace," *The Nation* 115, no. 2974 (July 5, 1922): 11-12.

58. De Touqueville's quote is from the 1945 Vintage edition of *Democracy in America*, 1:253. Kaye's extended quote is from his *Nation* article, "Americanism as an Educational Menace," 11-12.

59. This example of the Legion's self-aggrandizement is from the *Proceedings of the Sixth National Convention of the American Legion*. St. Paul, Minn., Sept. 15-19, 1924 (Washington: GPO, 1925), 98. *The Nation* criticized essay contests in "Legion Essay Contest," 116, no. 3023 (June 13, 1923): 682-83.

60. Conley to ACA Executive Committee, Mar. 31, 1921, *JJC* box 107, folder 1.

61. Shawkey, "The Legion of Americanism," *WVSJ* 49, no. 11 (March 1921), 261, and in his *West Virginia in History*, 2, no. 122-23.

62. Barbe, "A Powerful Ally," *WVSJ* 50, no. 4 (April 1921): 14. Owsley's address to the AFL is featured in "Legion's Heart Beats for Labor," *UMWJ* 32, no. 13 (July 1, 1921): 5. See also Owsley's address in the AFL 41st Convention (Denver, June 15-25, 1921) *Proceedings*, published by the AFL, 1921, 277-79.

63. William Pencak, *For God and Country: The American Legion, 1919-1941* (Boston: Northeastern University Press, 1989), 49-53.

64. Founding of the West Virginia Legion recounted in 1924 *WV Hand Book*, 625. Pencak writes of the publicity drive in *For God and Country*, 49.

65. Pencak, *For God and Country*, 64. Lee cultivated the press with bulletins describing what "really" happened at Ludlow, when Colorado National Guardsmen killed thirteen women and children as part of Colorado Fuel and Iron's campaign to break a miners' strike. The Rockefeller family, which owned CFI, paid wages and expenses for the Guard, who were called in to put down the bitter strike after Baldwin-Felts detectives hired by the Rockefellers had failed. William Graebner outlines Lee's post-Ludlow media strategy in *The Engineering of Consent*, 60-62. A helpful summary of the Ludlow Strike and massacre is in Howard Zinn, *A People's History of the United States* (1980; New York: HarperCollins, 1990), 346-49. Also see Sidney Lens, *The Labor Wars: From the Molly Maguires to the Sitdowns* (1973; New York: Anchor/Doubleday, 1974), 171-72; and Thomas R. Brooks, *Toil and Trouble: A History of American Labor* (New York: Dell, 1965), 128-31. Brooks writes that after the strike was crushed, Lee advised John D. Rockefeller to initiate the Colorado Industrial Representative Plan, or Rockefeller Plan, of labor-management cooperation, which served as the model for company unionism and corporate welfarism.

66. Pencak documents the Legion's Congressional charter and receipt of guns from the War Department in *For God and Country*, 65. Among the Legion publications printed by the Government Printing Office were the proceedings of its conventions, e.g., the 1924 *Proceedings* of the Legion's Minnesota convention.

67. Pencak, *For God and Country*, 66, 73. L.G. Roberts, mayor of Wellsburg, to Cornwell, Nov. 1, 1919, JJC box 108, folder 3.

68. Legionnaires were used as strikebreakers in Kansas during the national coal strike of 1919 and reportedly in West Virginia at some point in the early 1920s. Pencak notes, however, that some Legion posts adamantly refused to break strikes and attempted to maintain neutrality when used to keep order in strike periods. Others, though, "swept away by the hysteria of the Red Scare," often instigated or contributed to the very violence they were supposed to contain (Pencak, *for God and Country*, 211-17). The Legion reserved its most bitter hatred for the IWW. An "overwhelming body of evidence," says Pencak, surfaced in 1936 to prove that the Legion attacked the IWW meeting hall in Centralia, Illinois, during an Armistice Day parade in 1919. Four Legionnaires died in the ensuing battle, which the Legion and the local and regional press described as an unprovoked ambush by Wobblies on Legion paraders. Actually, the assault against the IWW hall was premeditated by Legionnaires and local vigilantes in Centralia, who had resolved that the only way to handle Wobblies was to "clean 'em up and burn 'em out" (151).

69. This analysis of the Legion is from Pencak, *For God and Country*, 212-14, 8, 18. The Legion pledged to promote "one hundred percent Americanism," as recounted in 1924 *WV Hand Book*, 625.

70. Pencak writes on the willingness of Legionnaires to use extralegal methods and on the conservative function of law in *For God and Country*, 18. "Liberty Is not License," or some variation on that slogan, saturates the literature of the period. This particular reference is from Edwin Keatley, "Reverence for Law," in the 1924 *WV*

Hand Book, 705.

71. Terry Radke to David Addlestone, Apr. 26, 1984, Addlestone's personal correspondence. At the time, Addlestone, an advocate for veterans' rights, was legal director of the Vietnam Veterans of America.

72. Pencak, *For God and Country*, 51, quoting from the "Declaration of Principles and Constitution of the Private Soldiers and Sailors of the United States of America," Mar. 1919, and a letter from the organization's Ted Booth to Albert DeSilver, Dec. 30, 1919. Pencak studied the records of the Soldiers and Sailors, which are housed in the files of the American Civil Liberties Union.

73. Lawson McMillan was pilloried in Phil Conley, "The Truth About West Virginia," press release no. 9, Aug. 9, 1922, 1-2, PAM 8340, WVRHC. Harry Curran Wilbur to E.F. Morgan, Apr. 23, 1923. *Morgan* box 19, folder 4.

74. Pencak, *For God and Country*, 49-51.

75. Pencak comments on the extensive access of the Legion to schools in ibid., 22. The 1924 *WV Hand Book* described the Legion as "non-partisan and non-political," 625.

76. American Legion *Proceedings* 1924, 125-26, 141-42.

77. Ambler's observation is in his *History of Education*, 419. The *Daily Mail* mocked "Education Week" in the Nov. 19, 1924 edition. The AFL charges are in "The Menace to Public Education," *Labor Age* 12, no. 9 (Nov. 1923), 12.

78. "American Education Week," *WVSJ* 53, no. 3 (Nov. 1924), 70.

79. The Legion claimed 330,000 participants in the 1924 *Proceedings*, 13. Announcement of the 1924 "Legion Essay Contest" is in *WVSJ* 52, no. 12 (May 1924): 394.

80. Barbe, "A Powerful Ally," *WVSJ*, Apr. 1921, 14.

81. Frederick W. Taylor envisioned the social application of his theories in, e.g., *The Principles of Scientific Management*, 8-10. Montgomery speaks of the social application and of government of "facts and law" in *Fall of the House of Labor*, 230, 240-42.

82. Graebner, *The Engineering of Consent*, 63-64, quoting Lippmann in *Public Opinion*, 31, 383-87, 248-49.

83. Lustig uses the expression "objective data" in his discussion of the political content of facts and their manipulation for particular groups, in *Corporate Liberalism*, 189.

84. Joseph Marsh, "Organized Facts," in his "Here and There" column, *WVSJ* 53, no. 1 (Sept. 1924), 11.

85. Barbe, "Powerful Ally," *WVSJ* (April 1921), 14.

86. Gerstle, *Working-class Americanism*, 8-11.

87. On the communal conservatism of the Legion, see Pencak, *For God and Country*, 18-19.

88. The phrase "through the medium of the children" or variations was used repeatedly by industrial Americanizers. Here, it is in a letter from Conley to Cornwell, Jan. 31, 1922, JJC box 107, folder 1. Woodrow Wilson's illuminating piston analogy is from Lustig, *Corporate Liberalism*, 29-30.

89. This ACLU definition of freedom is from Pencak, *For God and Country*, 15. The "class hatred" charge was directed by Governor E.F. Morgan to Harry F. Ward, chairman of the ACLU, in a letter of Mar. 24, 1923, *Morgan* box 19, folder 2.

90. Lunt, *Law and Order vs. the Miners*, 153-54.

91. The ACA warnings about Baldwin and the ACLU are from "West Virginia Invaded," an undated circular issued as the free speech battle ensued, Morgan box 19, folder 1. Morgan received several reports from the state police, such as that from

V.W. Midkiff on Mar. 26, 1923, *Morgan* box 19, folder 2. Melvyn Dubofsky documents the bitter free speech struggles by the Wobblies, with Baldwin's participation, in *We Shall Be All*, 173-97.

92. Conley informed Governor Morgan of the distribution of literature to thinking citizens on Apr. 3, 1923, Morgan box 19, folder 3. The ACA's misleading claim of disinterest in union organizing, and "Lenine" charge, is from the "West Virginia Invaded" broadside, Morgan box 19, folder 1.

93. Harry F. Ward leveled charges of intimidation by Sheriff Chafin in a letters to Morgan dated Mar. 21 and Mar. 29, 1923, Morgan box 19, folder 2. The governor responded, as "servant of all the people," to Ward on Apr. 2, 1923, *Morgan* box 19, folder 3. A typical letter of praise for Morgan's stance against the ACLU is that from W.H. Cunningham of Cunningham, Miller & Enslow, coal shippers from Huntington, on Mar. 26, 1923, *Morgan* box 19, folder 2.

94. "A Supporter" to Morgan, Mar. 26, 1923, Morgan box 19, folder 2. "Governor Morgan Declines with Thanks," *Industrial Progress*, Apr. 1923. Spiller Hicks to Morgan, Apr. 4, 1923, *Morgan* box 19, folder 3.

95. W.H. Cunningham to Morgan, quoting Mar. 19, 1923, *Wheeling Intelligencer*, Mar. 26, 1923, Morgan box 19, folder 2.

96. "Revolutionary Interests Have Huge Fund with Which to Finance Their Activities in America," *UMWJ* 34, no. 9 (May 1, 1923), 8-9.

97. Association of District 2 with Bolshevik Russia in "Reds Are Boring," ibid., 8. Greenwich Village coal diggers comment from "This Explains Where the So-Called 'Plan' Came From," ibid., 10.

98. The *WVR*'s claim to neutrality is in "Among Ourselves," *WVR* 1, no. 1 (Oct. 1923), 4. References to liberal thinkers etc. and to the subversive menace of Baldwin, Nearing, et al., is from "Radicals," an editorial in *WVR* 1, no. 6 (March 1924), 17.

99. Pencak, *For God and Country*, 157. "The American Legion," *The Nation* 117, no. 3043 (Oct. 31, 1923), 476.

100. Pencak, *For God and Country*, 22.

8. The Sanctification of Industrial Americanization

1. Franklin K. Lane, "The New Americanism," NEA *Proceedings* 1918, 105-8. Phil Conley, "American Ideals," address to the West Virginia Education Association, 1921 *Annual Proceedings*, 51, 54.

2. Herbert Hoover is cited in Graebner, *Engineering of Consent*, 65. Bernays wrote of the mass distribution of ideas in "Manipulating Public Opinion: The Why and the How," *American Journal of Sociology* 33, no. 6 (May 1928): 971. His musings on "intelligent manipulation" are cited in Schlesinger and Kinzer, *Bitter Fruit*, 80, from Bernays's tract *Propaganda*.

3. Pencak, *For God and Country*, 279.

4. Conley, "American Ideals," 1924, introduction, *Morgan* box 19, folder 3.

5. Keatley to Andrew Price, June 12, 1922, Price family papers (hereafter Price), WVRHC, box 5, folder 12.

6. WVFWC *Yearbook, 1922-1923*, 98.

7. E.F. Morgan, "Messages to the People of West Virginia, to be read in Sunday Schools Sunday, July 2, 1922." Distributed by the ACA, Price, box 5, folder 12.

8. *Wheeling Intelligencer*, June 30, 1921 (mayor's proclamation), and July 4, 1921 (minister's statement on law).

9. Sunday School Association president J.D. Steele, and Edwin Keatley of the ACA, were cited in Morgan's "Messages" of July 2, 1922, Price, box 5, folder 12.

10. Shawkey, *Biennial Report* 1916-18, 37.

11. An ACA Press Release, June 6, 1922, claimed one thousand meetings in 1921. Keatley's claim of three thousand 1922 observations in Keatley to Andrew Price, July 13, 1922, Price box 5, folder 12.

12. Conley, *American Ideals*, 1924, introduction, Morgan box 19, folder 3.

13. Representative news accounts in *Huntington Advertiser*, July 2, 1921, *Huntington Herald-Dispatch*, July 3, 1921, *Huntington Advertiser*, July 1, 1922. The ACA press release of June 6, 1922 listed Minnesota, Oregon, Wyoming, Mississippi, Indiana, Idaho, Virginia, Arkansas, and Michigan as planning America First celebrations, with governors in Massachusetts, Maryland, Rhode Island, and Missouri considering such observations, *Price* box 5, folder 12.

14. John Hennen, "Benign Betrayal: Capitalist Intervention in Pocahontas County, West Virginia, 1890-1910," *WVH* 50 (1991): 47-62, especially 54-55. Price is identified as Pocahontas County chairman of the Four-Minute Men in the 1918 *WV Hand Book*, 919.

15. Keatley to Price, May 8 and June 6, 1922, Price box 5, folder 12.

16. "Suggested plan for organizing each County in West Virginia for the observation of America First Day, Sunday, July 2, 1922," Price box 5, folder 12.

17. "To the pastors and Sunday School Superintendents of Pocahontas County," with Price's America First Day oration, n.d., Price box 5, folder 12.

18. Keatley to Price, May 30, 1922, Keatley to Price, a form letter sent to all county chairmen, June 12, 1922, Price box 5, folder 12.

19. On Sunday school involvement, *Pocahontas Times*, June 1, 1922. Hillsboro announcement, June 29, 1922.

20. The Christian pledge is featured on an ACA flyer with "American Ideals" and "Flag Pageant" recommendations, in Price box 5, folder 12. The *Pocahontas Times* reported the universality of patriotic sentiment in the June 29, 1922, edition.

21. *Pocahontas Times*, June 29, 1922.

22. Lustig, *Corporate Liberalism*, 209, 222.

23. Lustig refers to Italian "directed democracy" in *Corporate Liberalism*, 194. Pencak notes common ground between the American Legion and the Italian Fascists in *For God and Country*, 19-22.

24. Pencak, *For God and Country*, 22. See also Dawley, *Struggles for Justice*, 170, and Wiebe, *Businessmen and Reform*, 179-82, 221, and Wiebe, *Search for Order*, 295-98.

25. Lustig, *Corporate Liberalism*, 193-94, expresses this process as "controlling the conditions in which psyches developed and symbols emerged."

26. E.D. Knight quoted in *CA* (June 10, 1920), 1218. Lustig, *Corporate Liberalism*, 194, cites a Selective Service document on "Channeling" and "pressurized guidance," July 1, 1965. Noam Chomsky and Edward Herman summarize the process of indirect persuasion by powerful institutions in government, business, and media: "Most biased choices in the media arise from the preselection of right-thinking people, internalized preconceptions, and the adaptation of personnel to the constraints of ownership, organization, market, and political power. Censorship is largely self-censorship, by reporters and commentators who adjust to the realities of source and media organizational requirements, and by people at higher levels within media organizations who are chosen to implement, and have usually internalized, the constraints imposed by proprietary and other market and governmental centers of power." They point out that their institutional critiques "are commonly dismissed by

establishment commentators as 'conspiracy theories,'" but "our treatment is much closer to a 'free market' analysis, with the results largely an outcome of the workings of market forces" (Chomsky and Herman, *Manufacturing Consent*), xii.

27. William Walton, "The New Education," *WVSJ* 50, no. 2 (July-Aug. 1921), 90.

28. Conley, "Your West Virginia," *WVR* 2, no. 2 (Nov. 1924): 51.

29. Governor E.F. Morgan, "The State and the New Education," *WVEA* 1921 *Annual Proceedings*, 49-51.

30. "Unpatriotic School Teachers," *AC* 1, no. 8 (June 1, 1921): 4. JJC box 107, folder 1.

31. The teaching of patriotism and teacher's oath bills, SB 225 and HB 515, are found in *Acts of the Legislature* 1923 and reprinted in a booklet prepared by the state Board of Education, *Teaching Patriotism and Citizenship in The Schools of West Virginia* (Charleston: State Department of Education, 1923-24), 1, 4-5. Also see 1924 *WV Hand Book*, 368-69. The national movement to regulate loyalty among teachers is summarized in Bessie Louise Pierce, *Civic Attitudes in American School Textbooks* (Chicago: University of Chicago Press, 1930), 237.

32. Todd, *Wartime Relations*, 47.

33. State Board of Education, *Teaching Patriotism and Citizenship*, 1.

34. Bessie L. Pierce refers to the provisions of the West Virginia loyalty oath in *Public Opinion and the Teaching of History in the United States* (New York: Alfred A. Knopf, 1926), 90. Comments on the broad observance of the teacher's oath are from state Board of Education, *Teaching Patriotism and Citizenship*, 4.

35. George M. Ford, state superintendent of schools, *West Virginia Teachers' Hand Book, Containing Suggestions, Rulings, Information, and Material for use of the Teachers of West Virginia* (Charleston: State Department of Education, 1921), 16.

36. George M. Ford, "The First Call to a New Duty," in *Teaching Patriotism and Citizenship*, 5.

37. Ford stressed cooperation with local organizations in "New Duty," *Teaching Patriotism and Citizenship*, 5. Marsh commented on the demand for deliberate organization for patriotic purposes in 1919, in "State Americanism Campaign," *WVSJ* 48, no. 5 (Sept. 1919), 98. His assessment of the "surcharging" of West Virginia's youth is in "Patriotism," *WVSJ* 53, no. 1 (Sept. 1924): 11.

38. Joseph Marsh, "Business Sense," *WVSJ* 53, no. 1 (September 1924): 11.

39. Gerstle, *Working-class Americanism*, 10.

40. E.F. Morgan, inaugural address, Mar. 4, 1921. *State Papers and Public Addresses, Governor Ephraim Franklin Morgan* (Charleston: Jarrett, 1925).

41. The reference to "organized facts" is from Marsh, "Organized Facts," *WVSJ* 53, no. 1 (Sept. 1924), 11.

42. ACA flyer, "Let not the old land marks be forgot; let not the old traditions fail," n.d., JJC box 107, folder 1.

43. Figures on U.S. productivity in "Think it Over, Mr. Pessimist," *WVSJ* 50, no. 2 (May 1921): 32. Marsh's statements on new facts from "Organized Facts," *WVSJ* 53, no. 1 (Sept. 1924), 11.

44. The reference to manual arts is from "Editorial Notes," *WVSJ* 47, no. 10 (Jan. 1919): 631. Comments on Smith-Hughes in "Towards National Control," ibid., 618. For a summary of the state's vocational training in the early 1920s, see Joseph F. Marsh, "Vocational Education," in George M. Ford, *Biennial Report of the State Superintendent of Free Schools, 1922-1924* (Charleston: Department of Schools, 1924), 99-100. The passages on fundamental economic laws, industrial growth, and inquiries into Standard Oil and "Labor Combinations," from the West Virginia Board of Education's

Course of Study for the Junior and Senior High Schools of West Virginia, 1919 (Charleston: Department of Schools, 1919), 4, 56.

45. "Days that Are Gone," *UMWJ* 34, no. 1 (Jan. 1, 1923): 6.

46. "Immigration Bill," *UMWJ* 34, no. 9 (May 1, 1923): 7.

47. "He Wants Cheap Labor" (referring to Elbert Gary), *UMWJ* 34, no. 9 (May 1, 1923): 7.

48. "Labor Shortage," *UMWJ* 35, no. 12 (June 15, 1924): 14.

49. The thrust of this paragraph is extracted from Gerstle, *Working-class Americanism*, 14-15 and 7. Gerstle in turn relied on Warren Susman, "Culture and Commitment," in *Culture as History: The Transformation of American Society in the Twentieth Century* (New York, 1984), 150-210.

50. Joseph F. Marsh, "Report of State Board of Education: Two Years Ending June 30, 1924," in West Virginia Public Service Commission Tenth Annual Report, *Public Documents of West Virginia, 1923-1924*, (Charleston: Public Service Commission, 1924), 2, no. 41-43.

51. State Board of Education, *Course of Study for the Junior and Senior High Schools of West Virginia, 1919*, 47, 46, 45.

52. State Department of Education. *A Manual Containing an Abridged Course of Study for the Elementary Schools of the State of West Virginia, 1921* (Charleston: State Department of Education, 1921), 17, 22.

53. George M. Ford, *Organization, Administration, and Course of Study for Junior and Senior High Schools, 1927* (Charleston: Department of Education, 1927), 172-73, 182.

54. Summary of remarks by Rev. J.L. Hardy, *West Virginia Clubwoman* 11, no. 4 (Mar. 5, 1923): 5.

55. Marsh, "Our University—Present and Future," *WVR* 1, no. 2 (Nov. 1923), 14.

56. *WVSJ* 43, no. 9 (Dec. 1914): 313. Elsewhere in the same issue, "Editorial Notes" claimed that it "is contrary to our modern notion of the worth and dignity of men that it should be possible for a little group of autocrats and military egotists to speak the word and cause millions of armed men to begin to march to the battlefield" (301).

Conclusion

1. Wiebe, *Businessmen and Reform*, 217. Also see Wiebe, *Search for Order*.

2. Collins to Cornwell, Apr. 1, 1919, JJC box 94, folder 7.

3. Kenneth Lockridge, *A New England Town: The First Hundred Years* (1970; New York: W.W. Norton & Company, 1985), 5-16.

4. Phil Conley, "American Ideals," WVEA *Proceedings* 1921, 51.

5. Francis Jennings, *The Invasion of America: Indians, Colonialism, and the Cant of Conquest* (New York: W.W. Norton & Company, 1976), 82.

6. Nellie Sullivan, "Why Laws Are Needed," *CCC* March 1918, 49.

7. Robert Heilbroner, "The Triumph of Capitalism," *New Yorker*, Jan. 23, 1989, 98-109.

8. Cornwell divided people into the lawful and the lawless, or in his words the good and the bad, in his letter to C.C. Lusk of the Ramage UMWA local, Mar. 13, 1919, JJC box 94, folder 6.

9. Ibid., 98, 109.

10. Lawrence Goodwyn, *Democratic Promise: The Populist Moment in America* (New York: Oxford University Press, 1976), vii-viii.

11. Fink, *Workingmen's Democracy*, 6. Goodwyn, *Democratic Promise*, 542. Dubofsky, *We Shall Be All*, 86.

12. Fink, *Workingmen's Democracy*, 22. Goodwyn, *Democratic Promise*, 534.

13. Goodwyn, *Democratic Promise*, 516.

14. E.F. Morgan, "Memorial to World War Heroes," July 17, 1921, *State Papers and Addresses*, 110.

15. Gaventa, *Power and Powerlessness*, quoted from 82.

16. Jennings, *Invasion of America*, 185.

17. Taylor, *Principles of Scientific Management*, 7.

Bibliography

Primary Sources

Personal and Institutional Papers

Waitman Barbe Papers. West Virginia and Regional History Collection (WVRHC), Morgantown, W.Va.

James Morton Callahan Papers. WVRHC.

Oliver P. Chitwood Papers. WVRHC.

Justus Collins Papers. WVRHC.

John J. Cornwell Papers. WVRHC and West Virginia State Archives, Charleston.

C.G. Dickenson Papers. WVRHC.

Howard M. Gore Papers. WVRHC.

Ephraim Morgan Papers. WVRHC.

Morgantown Independent School District. Minutes, 1917-25, WVRHC.

Robert L. Pemberton Papers. WVRHC.

Livia Simpson Poffenbarger Papers. West Virginia State Archives.

Price Family Papers. WVRHC.

Hugh Isaac Shott Papers. WVRHC.

C.E. Smith Papers. WVRHC.

Smokeless Coal Operators. Miscellaneous Documents. WVRHC.

George S. Wallace Papers. WVRHC.

Elizabeth Ludington Hagans Chapter of the Daughters of the American Revolution. Minutes and Papers, 1917-24, WVRHC.

West Virginia Board of Education. Minutes and Papers, 1919-23, West Virginia State Archives.

West Virginia Executive Council of Defense. Minutes and Papers, 1917-19. West Virginia State Archives.

Minutes and Papers. West Virginia State Federation of Labor, 1918-22, WVRHC.

West Virginia University Archives. WVRHC.

West Virginia University History Department Archives. WVRHC.

Addresses and Proceedings

American Federation of Labor. Addresses and Proceedings, 1918-26. Washington: Law Reporter Company.

American Legion. Proceedings, 1921-24. Washington. Government Printing Office.

National Association of Manufacturers. Proceedings, 1919. New York. NAM.

National Education Association. Addresses and Proceedings, 1917-24. Washington: NEA.

National Security League. Proceedings of the Congress on Constructive Patriotism, 1917. New York: NSL.

West Virginia Education Association. Annual Proceedings, 1915, 1917, 1919-24. Various printers, published by the WVEA, Charleston.

West Virginia Federation of Women's Clubs. Yearbooks, 1919-24. Wheeling, Charleston, published by the WVFWC.

West Virginia Mining Institute. Addresses and Proceedings, 1910, 1917-24. Charleston: West Virginia Mining Association.

West Virginia Woman's Christian Temperance Union. Addresses and Proceedings, 1919; 1925-26. Wheeling, published by WVWCTU.

Government Documents and Publications

American Constitutional Association. *American Ideals*. Charleston, 1924. WVRHC. The ACA was not a state agency but enjoyed quasi-official status in the school system, was granted use of state supplies, and had a directorate consisting largely of state officials. (found in various collections of personal papers)

————. *Life in a West Virginia Coal Town*. Charleston, 1923. (found in WV State Archives)

————. Pamphlets and flyers, 1921-25.

Bituminous Coal Operators' Special Committee. *Proposed Findings as to Certain Aspects of the Bituminous Coal Mining Industry*. Submitted to the United States Coal Commission, 1923. WVRHC.

Commager, Henry Steele, ed. *Documents of American History*, 8th ed. New York: Appleton-Century-Crofts, 1968.

Crist, Raymond F. *Federal Citizenship Textbook*. Bureau of Naturalization. Washington: GPO, 1921.

Ford, Muldoon. *Course of Study for the Elementary Schools, 1923*. Charleston, 1923.

Harris, John T., ed. *West Virginia Hand Book and Manual* (later, the *Blue Book*). Charleston, 1918-24.

Hart, Hastings H. *A Suggested Program for the Executive State Council of Defense of West Virginia*. Charleston, 1917.

Irwin, E.J. *An Americanization Program*. Bureau of Education Bulletin no. 30. Washington: GPO, 1923.

Lane, Franklin, and Newton Baker. *The Nation in Arms*. War Information Series, no. 2. Washington: Committee on Public Information (CPI), 1917.

Mahoney, John J. *Americanization in the United States*. Bureau of Education Bulletin no. 31. Washington: GPO, 1923.

————. *Training Teachers for Americanization*. Bureau of Education Bulletin no. 12. Washington: GPO, 1920.

Morgan, Ephraim F. *State Papers and Public Addresses, 1921-1925*. Charleston: 1925.

Sullivan, Jesse. *Report of the Secretary on the Operation of the Compulsory Work Law for the Year Ending June 19, 1918*. Charleston: State Council of Defense, 1918.

United States Congress. *Proceedings and Debates of the Third Session of the Sixty-Fifth Congress of the United States*. Washington: GPO, 1918-19.

United States Department of Commerce, Bureau of the Census. *Fourteenth Census of the United States: State Compendium of West Virginia*. Washington: GPO, 1925.

United States Department of War. *Report of the Conference on Moral and Religious Work in the Army*. Washington: GPO, 1923.

————. *Education for Citizenship*. Washington: GPO, 1921.

West Virginia. *Acts of the Legislature*. Charleston: 1917-24.

West Virginia Board of Education. *Teaching Patriotism in the Schools of West Virginia*. Charleston: 1923-24.

West Virginia Department of Agriculture. *West Virginia War Bulletin*. Charleston, 1918.
West Virginia Department of Education. *West Virginia Teachers Hand Book*. Charleston, 1921.
————. *Institute Program*. Charleston, 1919-22.
West Virginia Department of Free Schools. *Biennial Report of the State Superintendent*. Charleston, 1918-24.
West Virginia Department of Mines. *Annual Reports*. Charleston, 1915-21.
Wilson, Woodrow. *President Wilson's State Papers and Addresses*. New York: Review of Reviews, 1917.

Contemporary Published Sources
Adams, R.F., ed. *Huntington, West Virginia: A City of Optimists* Huntington: Huntington Chamber of Commerce, 1924.
Bogardus, Emory S. *Essentials of Americanization*. Los Angeles: University of Southern California Press, 1919.
Callahan, James Morton. *An Introduction to American Expansion Policy*. Morgantown: West Virginia University Department of History and Political Science, 1908.
————. *Cuba and International Relations: A Historical Study in American Diplomacy*. Baltimore: Johns Hopkins University Press, 1899.
————. *History of West Virginia, Old and New*. Chicago and New York: American Historical Society, 1923.
Chitwood, Oliver P. *The Immediate Causes of the Great War*. New York: Thomas Y. Crowell, 1917; 2d ed., 1918.
Clarkson, Grosvenor B. *Industrial America in the World War: The Strategy Behind the Line, 1917-1918*. Boston: Houghton-Mifflin, 1923.
Creel, George. *How We Advertised America*. New York: Harper and Brothers, 1920.
Department of Labor Research. *The American Labor Year Book*. New York: Rand School of Social Science, 1917-24.
Hansen, Olaf, ed. *The Radical Will: Randolph Bourne, Selected Writings, 1911-1918*. New York: Urizen Books, 1977.
Hart, Albert Bushnell. *America at War*. New York: George H. Doran for the National Security League, 1918.
Kirk, John W. *Progressive West Virginians, 1923*. Wheeling: Wheeling Intelligencer, 1923.
MacCorkle, William Alexander. *Recollections of Fifty Years of West Virginia*. New York: G.P. Putnam's Sons, 1928.
Taylor, Frederick Winslow. *Scientific Management: Comprising Shop Management, the Principles of Scientific, and Testimony before the Special House Committee*. Westport, Conn.: Greenwood Press, 1972. Reprint of 1907, 1911 originals.
War Work of Marshall County, West Virginia: The Fighting Forces and the Inner Lines. Moundsville, W.Va.: 1919.

Contemporary Journals and Periodicals
American Historical Review, 1917-24.
American Journal of Sociology, 1919-24; 1928.
Coal Age, 1917-24.
Collegiate Socialist, 1918-22.
Consolidation Coal Company Mutual Magazine, 1918-25.
Historical Outlook, 1918-24 (continuation of *History Teacher's Magazine*).
History Teacher's Magazine, 1917-1918.
Labor Age, 1921-24.

The Nation, 1917-24.
Nation's Business, 1921-24.
New Republic, 1917-19.
Our Own People, 1917-21.
School and Society, 1916-21.
Socialist Review, 1921-23.
United Mine Workers of America Journal, 1917-25.
West Virginia Clubwoman, 1917-24.
West Virginia Mining News, 1920-21.
West Virginia Review, 1923-25.
West Virginia School Journal, 1916-25.

Newspapers
American Citizen, 1921. Charleston.
Charleston Daily Mail, 1917-24.
Charleston Gazette, 1917-24.
Clarksburg Daily Telegram, 1917-19.
Daily Athenaeum, 1917-21. Morgantown.
Fairmont Times, 1917-24.
Hampshire Review, 1917-21.
Huntington Advertiser, 1919-23.
Huntington Herald-Dispatch, 1917-24.
Logan Banner, 1920-21.
McDowell Recorder, 1918-19.
Morgantown News, 1917-24.
Morgantown Post-Chronicle, 1917-24.
New York Times, 1920-22.
Pocahontas Times, 1917-23.
St. Mary's Oracle, 1917-21.
West Virginia Federationist, 1920-21. Charleston.
Wheeling Intelligencer, 1917-24.
Wheeling Majority, 1917-18.

Secondary Sources

Altschuler, Glenn C. *Race, Ethnicity, and Class in American Social Thought, 1865-1919.* Arlington Heights, Ill.: Harlan Davidson, 1982.
Ambler, Charles H. *A History of Education in West Virginia, from Early Colonial Times to 1949.* Huntington, W.Va.: Standard, 1951.
Avrich, Paul. *Sacco and Vanzetti: The Anarchist Background.* Princeton: Princeton University Press, 1991.
Banks, Alan. "The Emergence of a Capitalistic Labor Market in Eastern Kentucky." *Appalachian Journal* 7 (Spring 1980): 188-99.
———. "Labor and the Development of Industrial Capitalism in Eastern Kentucky, 1870-1930." Ph.D. diss., McMaster University, 1980.
Barkey, Frederick A. "The Socialist Party in West Virginia from 1898 to 1920: A Study in Working Class Radicalism." Ph.D. diss., University of Pittsburgh, 1971.
Bernays, Edward L. *Biography of an Idea: Memoirs of Public Relations Counsel Edward L. Bernays.* New York: Simon and Schuster, 1965.

————. *Public Relations*. Norman: University of Oklahoma Press, 1952.

Billings, Dwight B. "Religion as Opposition: A Gramscian Analysis." *American Journal of Sociology* 96, no. 1 (July 1990): 1-31.

Billington, Ray Allen, ed. *The Frontier in American History*. Huntington, N.Y.: Robert E. Krieger, 1976.

Blakey, George T. *Historians on the Home Front: American Propagandists for the Great War*. Lexington: University Press of Kentucky, 1970.

Bledstein, Burton J. *The Culture of Professionalism: The Middle Class and the Development of Higher Education in America*. New York: W.W. Norton, 1976.

Boris, Eileen, and Nelson Lichtenstein, eds. *Major Problems in the History of American Workers*. Lexington, Mass., and Toronto: D.C. Heath, 1991.

Brandes, Stuart D. *American Welfare Capitalism, 1880-1940*. Chicago and London: University of Chicago Press, 1976.

Breen, William J. "The Mobilization of Skilled Labor in World War I: 'Voluntarism,' the U.S. Public Service Reserve, and the Department of Labor, 1917-1918." *Labor History* 32, no. 2 (Spring 1991): 253-72.

————. *Uncle Sam at Home: Civilian Mobilization, Wartime Federalism, and the Council of National Defense, 1917-1919*. Westport, Conn.: Greenwood Press, 1984.

Brody, David. *Labor in Crisis: The Steel Strike of 1919*. Philadelphia and New York: J.B. Lipincott, 1965.

————. *Steelworkers in America: The Nonunion Era*. Cambridge: Harvard University Press, 1960.

————. *Workers in Industrial America*. New York: Oxford University Press, 1980.

Brooks, Thomas R. *Toil and Trouble: A History of American Labor* New York: Dell, 1965.

Buckalew, Marshall. "The Life of Morris Purdy Shawkey." M.A. thesis, West Virginia University, 1941.

Buhle, Mari Jo. *Women and American Socialism, 1870-1920*. Urbana: University of Illinois Press, 1983.

Burns, E. Bradford. *Latin America: A Concise Interpretive History*. 2d ed. Englewood Cliffs, N.J.: Prentice-Hall, 1977.

Chafe, William H., and Harvard Sitkoff, eds. *A History of Our Time: Readings on Postwar America*. New York and Oxford: Oxford University Press, 1987.

Chomsky, Noam, and Edward Herman. *Manufacturing Consent: The Political Economy of the Mass Media*. New York: Pantheòn, 1988.

Coben, Stanley, ed. *Reform, War, and Reaction, 1912-1932*. Columbia: University of South Carolina Press, 1972.

Conley, Phil. *History of the West Virginia Coal Industry*. Charleston: Education Foundation, 1960.

Corbin, David Alan. *Life, Work, and Rebellion in the Coal Fields: The Southern West Virginia Miners, 1880-1922*. Urbana: University of Illinois Press, 1981.

Cornebise, Alfred E. *War as Advertised: The Four Minute Men and America's Crusade, 1917-1918*. Philadelphia: American Philosophical Society, 1984.

Cubby, Edwin Albert. "The Transformation of the Tug and Guyandot Valleys: Economic Development and Social Change in West Virginia, 1888-1921." Ph.D. diss., Syracuse University, 1962.

Curti, Merle. *The Social Ideas of American Educators*. New York: Charles Scribner's Sons, 1935.

Dawley, Alan. *Struggles for Justice: Social Responsibility and the Liberal State*. Cambridge and London: Belknap Press of Harvard University Press, 1991.

DeWeerd, Harvey A. *President Wilson Fights His War: World War I and the American Intervention*. New York and London: Macmillan, 1968.

Dickerson, Dennis C. *Out of the Crucible: Black Steelworkers in Western Pennsylvania, 1875-1980*. Albany: State University of New York Press, 1986.

Dubofsky, Melvyn. *Industrialism and the American Worker, 1865-1920*. Arlington Heights, Ill.: Harlan Davidson, 1975.

———. *Labor and the State in Modern America*. Chapel Hill: University of North Carolina Press, 1994.

———. *We Shall Be All: A History of the Industrial Workers of the World*. New York: Quadrangle/New York Times, 1969.

Dubofsky, Melvyn, and Warren Van Tine. *John L. Lewis: A Biography*. New York: Quadrangle/New York Times, 1977.

———, eds. *Labor Leaders in America*. Urbana: University of Illinois Press, 1987.

Eller, Ronald D. *Miners, Millhands, and Mountaineers: The Modernization of the Appalachian South, 1880-1930*. Knoxville: University of Tennessee Press, 1982.

Fass, Paula. *The Damned and the Beautiful: American Youth in the 1920s*. Oxford and New York: Oxford University Press, 1977.

———. *Outside In: Minorities and the Transformation of American Education*. Oxford and New York: Oxford University Press, 1989.

Femia, Joseph V. *Gramsci's Political Thought*. New York: Oxford, 1981.

Fink, Leon. *Workingmen's Democracy: The Knights of Labor and American Politics*. Urbana: University of Illinois Press, 1985.

Fishback, Price. "Segregation in Job Hierarchies: West Virginia Coal Mining, 1906-1932." *Journal of Economic History* 44 (September 1984): 755-74.

Fisher, Lucy Lee. "John J. Cornwell, Governor of West Virginia, 1917-1921." *West Virginia History* 24 (April 1963): 258-88; and 24 (July 1963): 370-89.

Fisher, Stephen L., ed. *Fighting Back in Appalachia: Traditions of Resistance and Change*. Philadelphia: Temple University Press, 1993.

Fones-Wolf, Elizabeth A. *Selling Free Enterprise: The Business Assault on Labor and Liberalism, 1945-1960*. Urbana: University of Illinois Press, 1994.

Fussell, Paul. *The Great War and Modern Memory*. New York and London: Oxford University Press, 1975.

Gaventa, John. "The Poverty of Abundance Revisited." *Appalachian Journal* 15 (Fall 1987): 24-33.

———. *Power and Powerlessness: Quiescence and Rebellion in an Appalachian Valley*. Urbana: University of Illinois Press, 1980.

Gaventa, John, Barbara E. Smith, and Alex Winningham, eds. *Communities in Economic Crisis: Appalachia and the South*. Philadelphia: Temple University Press, 1990.

Gerstle, Gary. *Working Class Americanism: The Politics of Labor in a Textile City*. Cambridge: Cambridge University Press, 1989.

Goodwyn, Lawrence. *Democratic Promise: The Populist Moment in America*. Oxford and New York: Oxford University Press, 1975.

Graebner, William. *The Engineering of Consent: Democracy and Authority in Twentieth-Century America*. Madison: University of Wisconsin Press, 1987.

Graham, Otis L., Jr. *The Great Campaigns: Reform and War in America, 1900-1928*. Englewood Cliffs, N.J.: Prentice-Hall, Inc., 1971.

Gramsci, Antonio. *Selections from the Prison Notebooks*, Translated and edited by Q. Hoare and G.N. Smith. New York: International Publishers, 1971.

Grubbs, Frank L., Jr. *The Struggle for Labor Loyalty: Gompers, the A.F. of L., and the Pacifists, 1917-1920*. Durham: Duke University Press, 1975.

Gruber, Carol S. *Mars and Minerva: World War I and the Uses of Higher Learning in America*. Baton Rouge: Louisiana State University Press, 1975.

Haber, Samuel. *Efficiency and Uplift: Scientific Management in the Progressive Era, 1890-1920*. Chicago: University of Chicago Press, 1964.

Halperin, Rhoda. *The Livelihood of Kin: Making Ends Meet the "Kentucky Way."* Austin: University of Texas Press, 1990.

Hartmann, Edward George. *The Movement to Americanize the Immigrant*. New York: ANS Press, 1967.

Hawley, Ellis. *The Great War and the Search for Modern Order: A History of the American People and Their Institutions*. 2d ed. New York: St. Martin's Press, 1979.

Haydu, Jeffrey. "Employers, Unions, and American Exceptionalism: Pre-World War I Open Shops and the Machine Trades in Comparative Perspective." *International Review of Social History* 33 (1988): 25-41.

Hennen, John. "Benign Betrayal: Capitalist Intervention in Pocahontas County, West Virginia, 1890-1910." *West Virginia History* 50 (1991), 47-62.

Higham, John. *Strangers in the Land: Patterns of American Nativism, 1860-1925*. New York; Atheneum, 1975; originally published by the Trustees of Rutgers University, 1955.

Hofstadter, Richard. *The Progressive Historians*. New York: Alfred A. Knopf, 1968.

Horowitz, Irving Louis, ed. *Power, Politics, and People: The Collected Essays of C. Wright Mills*. New York: Oxford University Press, 1963.

Horton, Myles, with Herbert Kohl and Judith Kohl. *The Long Haul: The Autobiography of Myles Horton*. New York: Anchor/Doubleday, 1990.

Jennings, Francis. *The Invasion of America: Indians, Colonialism, and the Cant of Conquest*. New York: W.W. Norton & Company, 1976.

Jensen, Joan M. *The Price of Vigilance*. Chicago, San Francisco, and New York: Rand McNally & Company, 1968.

Jones, Jacqueline. *The Dispossessed: America's Underclass from the Civil War to the Present*. New York: Basic Books, 1992.

Karier, Clarence J., ed. *Shaping the American Educational State, 1900 to the Present*. New York: Free Press, 1975.

Kaufman, Bruce E. *The Origins and Evolution of the Field of Industrial Relations in the United States*. Ithaca: Cornell Studies in Industrial and Labor Relations no. 25, 1993.

Kennedy, David. *Over Here: The First World War and American Society*. Oxford and New York: Oxford University Press, 1980.

Kolko, Gabriel. *The Triumph of Conservatism: A Reinterpretation of American History, 1900-1916*. New York: Free Press, 1963.

Klarén, Peter F., and Thomas J. Bossert, eds. *Promise of Development: Theories of Change in Latin America*. Boulder and London: Westview Press, 1986.

Kurtz, Stephen S., and James H. Hutson, eds., *Essays on the American Revolution*. New York: W.W. Norton, 1973.

Larson, Simeon. *Labor and Foreign Policy: Gompers, the AFL, and the First World War, 1914-1918*. Rutherford, N.J.: Farliegh Dickinson University Press, 1975.

Lasswell, Harold D. *Propaganda Technique in World War I*. Cambridge: The MIT Press, 1971. Originally published as *Propaganda Techniques in the World War*. London: Kegan Paul, Trench, Trubner and Co., 1927.

Leab, Daniel J., ed. *The Labor History Reader*. Urbana: University of Illinois Press, 1985.

Lears, T.J. Jackson. "The Concept of Cultural Hegemony: Problems and Possibilities." *American Historical Review* 90, no. 3 (June 1985): 567-93.

Leland, Waldo G., and Newton D. Mereness, eds. *Introduction to the American Official Sources for the Economic and Social History of the World War.* New Haven: Yale University Press, 1926.

Lens, Sidney. *The Labor Wars: From the Molly Maquires to the Sitdowns.* New York: Anchor/Doubleday, 1974.

Lewis, Helen M., and Myles Horton. "The Role of Transnational Corporations and the Migration of Industries in Latin America and Appalachia." Sommerville Wilson, ed., *Proceedings of the 1980 Appalachian Studies Conference.* Boone, N.C.: Appalachian Consortium Press, 1981.

Lewis, Ronald L. "Appalachian Restructuring in Historical Perspective: Coal, Culture, and Social Change in West Virginia." Morgantown, W.V.: Regional Research Institute Research Paper 9102, 1992.

———. *Black Coal Miners in America: Race, Class, and Community Conflict, 1780-1980.* Lexington: University Press of Kentucky, 1987.

———. "From Peasant to Proletarian: The Migration of Southern Blacks to the Central Appalachian Coalfields." *Journal of Southern History* 55 (1989), 77-102.

Lewis, Ronald L., and John Hennen, eds. *West Virginia: Documents in the History of a Rural-Industrial State.* Dubuque, Iowa: Kendall-Hunt, 1991.

Lippmann, Walter. *Public Opinion.* New York: Free Press, 1922.

Lockridge, Kenneth. *A New England Town: The First Hundred Years.* New York: W.W. Norton & Company, 1985.

Lukes, Steven. *Power: A Radical View.* New York: Macmillan, 1974.

Lunt, Richard D. *Law and Order vs. the Miners: West Virginia, 1907-1933.* Hamden, Conn.: Archon Books, 1979. Reissued by Appalachian Editions, Charleston, 1991.

Lustig, R. Jeffrey. *Corporate Liberalism: The Origins of Modern American Political Theory, 1890-1920.* Berkeley, Los Angeles, and London: University of California Press, 1982.

McCullough, David. *Truman.* New York: Simon and Schuster, 1992.

McCormick, Charles H. "The Death of Constable Riggs: Ethnic Conflict in Marion County in the World War I Era." *West Virginia History* 52 (1993): 33-58.

Mock, James R., and Cedric Larson. *Words that Won the War: The Story of the Committee on Public Information, 1917-1919.* Princeton: Princeton University Press, 1939.

Montgomery, David. *The Fall of the House of Labor: The Workplace, the State, and American Labor Activism, 1865-1925.* Cambridge: Cambridge University Press, 1987.

———. *Workers Control in America.* New York: Cambridge University Press, 1979.

Nelson, Bruce. *Workers on the Waterfront: Longshoremen, Seamen, and Unionism in the 1930s.* Urbana: University of Illinois Press, 1990.

Nelson, Daniel. *Frederick W. Taylor and the Rise of Scientific Management.* Madison: University of Wisconsin Press, 1980.

———. *Managers and Workers: Origins of the New Factory System in the United States, 1880-1920.* Madison: University of Wisconsin Press, 1975.

Noble, David. *Forces of Production: A Social History of Industrial Automation.* New York: Alfred A. Knopf, 1984.

Novick, Peter. *That Noble Dream: The "Objectivity Question" and the American Historical Profession.* Cambridge: Cambridge University Press, 1988.

Oestereicher, Richard J. *Solidarity and Fragmentation: Working People and Class Consciousness in Detroit, 1875-1900.* Urbana: University of Illinois Press, 1986.

Parker, Mike, and Jane Slaughter, eds. *Working Smart: A Union Guide to Participation Programs and Engineering.* Detroit: Labor Notes, 1994.

Pencak, William. *For God and Country: The American Legion, 1919-1941*. Boston: Northeastern University Press, 1989.

Pierce, Bessie L. *Public Opinion and the Teaching of History*. New York: Alfred A. Knopf, 1926.

Pipes, Richard. *The Russian Revolution*. New York: Vintage Books of Random House, 1991.

Reese, William J. *Power and the Promise of School Reform: Grass Roots Movements during the Progressive Era*. Boston: Routledge and Kegan Paul, 1986.

Reid, Herbert. "Appalachian Studies: Class, Culture, and Politics—II." *Appalachian Journal* 10, no. 1 (Winter/Spring 1982): 141-48.

Roediger, David. *Towards the Abolition of Whiteness*. London: Verso, 1994.

———. *The Wages of Whiteness*. London: Verso, 1991.

Rosenzweig, Roy. *Eight Hours for What We Will: Workers and Leisure in an Industrial City, 1870-1920*. Cambridge: Cambridge University Press, 1983.

Roszak, Theodore. *The Cult of Information: A Neo-Luddite Treatise on High-Tech, Artificial Intelligence, and the True Art of Thinking*. Berkeley: University of California Press, 1994.

Salstrom, Paul. *Appalachia's Path Toward Welfare Dependency, 1840-1940*. Lexington: University Press of Kentucky, 1994.

———. "Historical and Theoretical Perspectives on Appalachia's Economic Dependency. *Journal of the Appalachian Studies Association* 3 (1991): 68-81.

Salvatore, Nick. *Eugene V. Debs: Citizen and Socialist*. Urbana: University of Illinois Press, 1982.

Schaffer, Ronald. *America in the Great War: The Rise of the Welfare State*. New York and Oxford: Oxford University Press, 1991.

Schatz, Ronald. *The Electrical Workers: A History of Labor at G.E. and Westinghouse, 1923-1960*. Urbana: University of Illinois Press, 1983.

Schlechtweg, Harold P. "Environmentalism's 'Evil Twin': The Ideological Challenge of the Wise Use Movement." Paper presented at the Conference of Communication and Our Environment 1995, Chattanooga, Tenn., March 30-April 2, 1995. Author's possession.

Schlesinger, Stephen, and Stephen Kinzer. *Bitter Fruit: The Untold Story of the American Coup in Guatemala*. Garden City, N.Y.: Doubleday & Company, 1982.

Schmitt, Bernadotte E., and Harold C. Vedeler. *The World in the Crucible, 1914-1919*. New York: Harper & Row, 1984.

Serrin, William. *Homestead: The Glory and Tragedy of an American Steeltown*. New York: Times Books/Random House, 1992.

Shannon, David A., ed. *Progressivism and Postwar Disillusionment: 1898-1928*. New York: McGraw-Hill, 1966.

Shapiro, Henry D. *Appalachia on Our Mind: The Southern Mountains and Mountaineers in the American Consciousness, 1870-1920*. Chapel Hill: University of North Carolina Press, 1978.

Shawkey, Morris P. *West Virginia in History, Life, Literature and Industry*. Chicago: Lewis Publishing Co., 1928.

Shifflet, Crandall A. *Coal Towns: Life, Work, and Culture in Company Towns of Southern Appalachia, 1880-1960*. Knoxville: University of Tennessee Press, 1991.

Shore, Elliott, Ken Fones-Wolf, and James P. Dankey, eds. *The German-American Radical Press: The Sharing of a Left Political Culture, 1850-1940*. Urbana: University of Illinois Press, 1992.

Singer, Alan J. "Class-Conscious Coal Miners: Nanty-Glo Versus the Open Shop in the Post-World War I Era." *Labor History* 29, no. 1 (Winter 1988): 56-65.

Sklar, Martin J. *The Corporate Reconstruction of American Capitalism, 1890-1916: The Market, Law, and Politics.* Cambridge: Cambridge University Press, 1986.

———. *The United States as a Developing Country: Studies in U.S. History in the Progressive Era and the 1920s.* Cambridge: Cambridge University Press, 1992.

Smethurst, Richard J. *A Social Basis for Prewar Japanese Militarism: The Army and the Rural Community.* Berkeley: University of California Press, 1974.

Sullivan, Charles Kenneth. "Coal Men and Coal Towns: Development of the Smokeless Coalfields of Southern West Virginia, 1873-1923." Ph.D. diss., University of Pittsburgh, 1979.

Taft, Phillip. *The A.F. of L. from the Death of Gompers to the Merger.* New York: Harper & Brothers, 1959.

———. *The A.F. of L. in the Time of Gompers.* New York: Harper & Brothers, 1957.

———. *Organized Labor in American History.* New York: Harper & Row, 1964.

Tobin, Harold J., and Percy Bidwell. *Mobilizing Civilian America.* New York: Council on Foreign Relations, 1940.

Todd, Lewis Paul. *Wartime Relations of the Federal Government and the Public Schools, 1917-1918.* New York: Teachers College of Columbia University, 1945.

Tomlins, Christopher L. *The State and the Unions: Labor Relations, Law, and the Organized Labor Movement in America, 1880-1960.* New York: Cambridge University Press, 1986.

Toqueville, Alexis de. *Democracy in America.* New York: Vintage [Random House], 1970 printing of 1945 Alfred A. Knopf text.

Trotter, Joe William. *Coal, Class, and Color: Blacks in Southern West Virginia, 1915-1932.* Urbana: University of Illinois Press, 1990.

Tullos, Allen. *Habits of Industry: White Culture and the Transformation of the Carolina Piedmont.* Chapel Hill: University of North Carolina Press, 1989.

Tuttle, William M., Jr. *Race Riot: Chicago in the Red Summer of 1919.* New York: Atheneum, 1970.

Vaughan, Stephen. *Holding Fast the Inner Lines: Democracy, Nationalism, and the Committee on Public Information.* Chapel Hill: University of North Carolina Press, 1980.

Wallace, James M. "A New Means for Liberals: Liberal Responses to Adult and Worker Education in the 1920s." *Labor Studies Journal* 11, no. 1 (Spring 1986): 26-41.

Waller, Altina. *Feud: Hatfields, McCoys, and Social Change in Appalachia, 1860-1900.* Chapel Hill: University of North Carolina Press, 1988.

Walls, David. "Whose Bicentennial? Appalachia '76." *Appalachian Journal* 4 (Autumn 1976): 39-42.

Walls, David, and Dwight B. Billings. "The Sociology of Southern Appalachia." *Appalachian Journal* 5, no. 1 (Autumn 1977): 131-44.

Ward, Robert D. "The Origin and Activities of the National Security League, 1914-1919." *Mississippi Valley Historical Review* 47 (June 1960): 51-65.

Weinstein, James. *The Corporate Ideal in the Liberal State, 1900-1918.* Boston: Beacon Press, 1968.

Weiss, Bernard J. *American Education and the European Immigrant, 1880-1940.* Urbana: University of Illinois Press, 1982.

West Virginia Editors Association. *West Virginia Today: For Newspaper and Library Reference.* New Orleans: James O. Jones, 1941.

Whisnant, David. *All that Is Native and Fine: The Politics of Culture in an American Region*. Chapel Hill: University of North Carolina Press, 1983.

Wiebe, Robert H. *Businessmen and Reform: A Study of the Progressive Movement*. Cambridge: Harvard University Press, 1962.

————. *The Search for Order, 1877-1920*. New York: Hill and Wang, 1967.

Wilentz, Sean. "Against Exceptionalism: Class Consciousness and the American Labor Movement, 1790-1920." *International Labor and Working Class History* 26 (Fall 1984): 1-24.

Williams, John A. Introduction to *Thunder in the Mountains: The West Virginia Mine War, 1920-1921*, by Lon Savage. Pittsburgh: University of Pittsburgh Press, 1990.

————. *West Virginia: A History*. New York: Norton, 1976, 1984.

————. *West Virginia and the Captains of Industry*. Morgantown: West Virginia University, 1976.

Yates, Michael. *Power on the Job: The Legal Rights of Working People*. Boston: South End Press, 1994.

Zahavi, Gerald. *Workers, Managers, and Welfare Capitalism: The Shoemakers and Tanners of Endicott Johnson, 1890-1950*. Urbana: University of Illinois Press, 1988.

Zieger, Robert. *American Workers, American Unions*. Baltimore: Johns Hopkins University Press, 1994.

Zinn, Howard. *A People's History of the United States*. New York: HarperCollins, 1990.

Zunz, Olivier. *The Changing Face of Inequality: Urbanization, Industrial Development, and Immigrants in Detroit, 1880-1920*. Chicago and London: University of Chicago Press, 1982.

————. *Making America Corporate, 1870-1920*. Chicago: University of Chicago Press, 1990.

Index